FREEPORT MEMORIAL LIBRARY

Presented by

Delta Sigma Theta Sorority, Inc
Nassau Alumnae Chapter

2012

JIMI HENDRIX

JIMI HENDRIX

A BROTHER'S STORY

LEON HENDRIX

with Adam Mitchell

THOMAS DUNNE BOOKS

St. Martin's Press

New York

THOMAS DUNNE BOOKS.
An imprint of St. Martin's Press.

JIMI HENDRIX: A BROTHER'S STORY. Copyright © 2012 by Leon Hendrix
with Adam Mitchell. All rights reserved. Printed in the United States
of America. For information, address St. Martin's Press, 175 Fifth
Avenue, New York, N.Y. 10010.

www.thomasdunnebooks.com
www.stmartins.com

Design by Kathryn Parise

ISBN 978-0-312-66881-5 (hardcover)
eISBN 978-1-250-01237-1 (e-book)

First Edition: May 2012

10 9 8 7 6 5 4 3 2 1

For our mama—Lucille Jeter Hendrix

CONTENTS

Contents

JIMI
HENDRIX

INTRODUCTION

On an early September morning in 1970, I stood looking out through the bars of my six-by-six cell at Washington's Monroe Reformatory. In the row of arched windows high up on the opposite concrete wall, the first rays of the sun came into view, lighting up the clear blue sky. The beautiful color outside made the pea-green paint on the bars and walls inside my cell look even more depressing. As I got my things ready to report to work in the kitchen, I heard some inmates stirring down below on the first tier of cells. Faint talk was coming from a radio, and more whispering.

Suddenly, someone yelled through the morning quiet, "Don't say that, man!"

"I am telling you, Jimi Hendrix is dead!" another voice said. "They just reported it on the radio."

"Shut up!" the other guy shouted back. "You know his little brother is right up there, man."

At first, I tried not to pay any attention to the two men going back and forth. Every once in a while a rumor circulated that my brother had died, and I figured whatever they were carrying on about was nothing more than made-up nonsense the press was putting out to sell newspapers. For years they'd reported Jimi did all kinds of things he didn't and painted him as a person he wasn't. Typically, there was no truth to the rumors.

But then, a distorted message boomed out over the C-block from the prison public-address system: *"Inmate Leon Hendrix—156724. Report to the chaplain's office."*

After the announcement, my heart sank because in the joint that message usually meant only one of two things. Prison officials didn't call any inmate down to the office unless it was his day to be released or there was a death in the family. I knew I wasn't going to be released; another six months remained on my sentence.

A quiet fell over most of the cellblock as the door to my cell abruptly popped open. The other inmates looked on as I passed on my long walk down to the office. Eerily, Jimi's song "If 6 Was 9" came on over a radio in one of the cells as I made my way. When I finally arrived at the office, the chaplain was standing behind his desk and holding a telephone receiver down by his side.

"There is some bad news," he said, his expression as serious as I had ever seen during the almost nine months I'd been locked up. "Your dad is on the phone and wants to speak with you."

After taking the receiver from him, I carefully brought it up to my ear. The familiar sound of my dad's gravelly voice was on the line. Usually, I was happy to hear from him, but today was different.

"What's going on, Dad?" I slowly asked.

"I hate to tell you this, but Jimi's gone, son. They told me he died last night," my dad said quietly through his tears. "But don't worry. It's going to be all right."

"Okay. I understand." It was the only thing I could bring myself to say at that moment. After hanging up with my dad, I backpedaled out of the office, shell-shocked. When my emotions started stirring in my stomach, I knew I had to make it back to my cell before causing any type of scene. The prison guards didn't react well to scenes.

I hadn't seen Jimi in over a year, just before the army's Military Police snatched me off the streets in Seattle and turned me over to the city police. Now it was certain I would never see him again—not in this life anyway. One of the only things keeping me going since I had been locked up was the idea of reuniting with him after I was through with my sentence. Jimi and I were supposed to go back on the road together and set out on a new journey, but that was never going to happen now.

After returning to my cell, I sat on the corner of my bed mostly in silence for the rest of the day, running through the years my brother and I spent together. The jail guards typically put inmates on a mandatory seventy-two-hour lockdown in their cell after receiving bad news from the outside so they wouldn't cause any disruption to the other prisoners. So, in my cell I sat. Recalling the good times with Jimi brought a smile to my face, and looking back on the hard times broke my heart. No matter how much I tried, it was impossible to hold back the tears. Since entering Monroe Reformatory, I'd always been convinced that I would have no problem serving out my sentence. But now I felt as if there were no hope at all. And in jail, hope was all I had.

Later in the day, I rose from the bed and walked forward to the bars of my cell. Pressing my face against the grid of cold steel, I again looked across at the arched windows high up on the opposite concrete wall. By then, it was dusk and the light outside was fading. As the final rays of daylight passed over the glass of the last window,

JIMI HENDRIX

I couldn't take my eyes off the gradually darkening sky. I stood numb and empty inside, wondering where I was going to find the strength to endure the pain on my own. Before long, the sun was gone.

RAINIER VISTA PROJECTS

One of my earliest memories is of my older brother and me running around in the field next to where we lived at the Rainier Vista housing projects in Seattle, Washington. Our dad, Al Hendrix, and our mama, Lucille, held daily parties at our home and typically instructed us to go out and play whenever the place got too crowded and we started getting in the way. I couldn't have been more than two years old at the time, while my brother was six or seven. As we ran around, we were still able to hear the commotion inside—the tinkling sound of ice being dropped into cocktail glasses and the howling laughter echoing from the living room. When I stopped and looked in through the front picture window every once in a while, our parents seemed as happy as could be. But most of the time that couldn't have been further from the truth. Both Dad and Mama were big drinkers, who loved to be the life of the party. Later in the day, when the booze wore off, life was a completely different reality. That's when the shouting and cussing started.

At that time, their relationship was rocky to say the least, but things didn't start out that way. Early on, the two of them had plenty of good times. Mama was just a kid when she met Dad. She hadn't yet turned seventeen years old back when he asked her along to a dance at the Washington Club. Being six years older, Dad wasn't sure it was going to work out between them, but time told a different story. Both of them loved to dance and party, so they quickly grew close. Before long, they were inseparable. Dad found work in the Seattle downtown area busing tables at a restaurant on Pike Street called Ben Paris, then ground it out as a day laborer at an iron foundry until he eventually left and moved on to Honeysuckle's Pool Hall. Overall, their life together was good.

Then the Japanese attacked Pearl Harbor and everything changed. The U.S. government sent Dad his draft notice around the same time that Mama found out she was pregnant with her first child. They had to make the best of this tough situation. Dad knew he was going to be leaving soon, so he and Mama got married in a quickie cere-mony on March 31, 1942. They were officially husband and wife for less than a week before Dad checked into the armory at Fort Lewis and was later sent on to basic training at Fort Sill in Oklahoma.

Dad was stationed at Camp Rucker in Alabama when he received the telegram from Mama's sister, our aunt Delores, telling him that his child had been born. He was now the proud father of a beautiful baby son, whom Mama named John Allen Hendrix. After Dad shipped out overseas in early January of 1943, Aunt Delores did her best to send him photos of his boy every so often so he could see how big he was growing, but it was hard for Dad to focus on any-thing but the war. He was always on the move and was stationed in the Fiji Islands, Guadalcanal, and then New Guinea.

Back home in Seattle, times were tough for Mama. She left her parents' house to move in with a friend and was soon struggling to make ends meet and take care of her little boy. Mama was only a young kid herself and fell into a routine of going out and partying. She bounced around from one living arrangement to the next until the burden got to be too much. Unable to take care of her little boy, Mama was forced to do something drastic. After a brief time with Grandma Clarice and Grandpa Jeter, Dad's baby boy ended up in the care of a woman named Mrs. Walls for another short time, until she unexpectedly passed away. Fortunately, her sister, Mrs. Champ, came and took responsibility for little Johnny. When Mrs. Champ brought him back to where she lived in Berkeley, California, she sent Dad a letter letting him know of the situation. No matter what was going through his mind, he was halfway around the world and couldn't do much about what was going on back home in Seattle. Now his boy was living in California, and our mama, well, Dad wasn't exactly sure where she was spending her time.

When Dad finally got back from the war in September of 1945 and returned to Seattle, his first order of business was to make his way to Berkeley to get his boy. My brother wasn't at all happy to be taken from the home he was used to living in for close to the first three years of his life. Suddenly, a stranger whom he'd never seen before, except maybe in a blurry war photo, showed up at the door one day and told him he was his father and was taking him to a far-away place. No young boy was going to react well to that type of news. And that wasn't even the worst part. As soon as the two of them returned to Seattle, Dad marched my brother down to the King County office and legally changed his name from John Allen Hendrix to James Marshall Hendrix. Not only had my brother been taken away from the people he had come to know as family, but he was also being told his name wasn't going to be Johnny Allen anymore, it was going to be *Jimmy*.

Dad wasn't back in Seattle's Central District area long before Mama showed up where he was living with my brother at Aunt Delores's house in the projects of Yesler Terrace. I'm sure Dad didn't know what to think about everything that had happened while he was gone in the military all those years. But he still loved her. No matter what she did or how many times she disappeared to do her thing, I don't believe Dad ever stopped loving her. So, they reconciled and decided to give it another go. The back-and-forth pattern was repeated often throughout our childhood.

When I came along, Leon Morris Hendrix, on January 13, 1948, Dad and Mama's fighting was put on hold for a while because Dad was overjoyed to have another baby boy in the family. Because of the war, he'd missed my brother's early years and was now being presented with a second chance to be a father to an infant son. Not long after I was born, the four of us moved into a two-bedroom place at 3022 Genesee Street in the Rainier Vista projects, a former military housing facility. During the war, the military had put up barracks all over the city of Seattle for all of the army and navy personnel because the government thought that Japan was going to invade the country. When the war ended, the facilities became low-income housing for mostly black and Jewish families.

Just shy of a year after I came into the picture, Mama gave birth to another boy, whom she and Dad named Joseph Allen Hendrix. I was too young to remember much of Joe, but I do know that the added mouth to feed put even more strain on our parents' relationship. Also, Joe was born with serious health problems, including a cleft palate, one leg shorter than the other, and a clubfoot. These issues were going to cost plenty of money to treat and Mama and Dad couldn't afford it. For help, Dad turned to his mama, our grandma Nora Hendrix, and eventually decided that the best thing was to send the three of us to live with her in Canada for the summer of 1949. The short break was enough time for Dad and Mama to get things temporarily sorted out. Unfortunately, everything was just as complicated when the three of us returned to the Rainier Vista projects at the end of the summer. The financial situation hadn't changed much. Dad and Mama still couldn't afford to get Joe the medical attention he needed.

In the fall of 1950, not long after my brother was setting off to attend second grade at Horace Mann Elementary, Mama had a baby girl that she named Kathy Ira. Not only was Kathy born four months premature, but Mama and Dad also learned she was blind. Our parents now had four children to care for, two of which had special needs. After trying to hold it together for the next year, there was no choice but to place Kathy in foster care.

In October of 1951, shortly after Kathy was made a ward of the state, Mama gave birth to another daughter she named Pamela. Still scraping by to try to take care of Jimmy, Joe, and me, Mama and Dad were forced to give her to foster care as well.

By then, my brother had begun his third-grade year at Rainier Vista Elementary School and our family was still living in our small two-bedroom apartment. Since he hadn't yet received the proper medical care, Joe still struggled with his health problems. If there was any possibility of him being able to get around without a limp, he needed an operation on his leg. It was a surgery Mama and Dad didn't have the money to pay for.

Our place in the projects remained the site of an ongoing party where people came and went at all hours. Whenever my brother and I sneaked back inside from playing in the fields, we made our way around the room stealing the last drops of beer out of the discarded bottles on the floor and the coffee table. Many people thought it was funny to see me swigging away on a bottle in the middle of the party. I might have believed we were being sneaky and pulling a fast one, but I later found out that Dad and Mama purposely left three or four sips in the bottom of a beer bottle for us. I was especially hyperactive for my age, and they found the little bit of alcohol kept me calm. After a couple hits of beer, I became a quiet, obedient, and, eventually, tired little boy.

Many people don't understand that while growing up, my brother was always called Buster, and rarely Jimmy. He only got used to being called Jimmy much later when he was older and more comfortable with himself and his surroundings. During his childhood, Jimmy was the name our dad gave him after he got out of the army. Whenever Dad insisted on using it, my brother threw a fit. They constantly went back and forth about it.

"That's not my name," my brother cried out. "My name's Johnny!"

"I am telling you for the last time, boy, your name is James Marshall Hendrix!" Dad shouted back. "Jimmy is your name!"

My brother eventually realized Dad wasn't ever going to let him use the name Johnny as long as he was around. So, my brother needed to find an alternative that didn't drive Dad crazy every time he heard it. Not long after we saw the first *Flash Gordon* serial, my brother got the idea for the name Buster from the leading man, Larry "Buster" Crabbe.

On Saturdays, Dad sometimes gave us some change to walk down to the Rainier Vista field house to see one of the serial movies they were showing. It wasn't easy because my brother typically needed to beg Dad for the money to buy the tickets. Even if he intended to eventually fork over the change, he usually made us wait for it for a while. Whenever Dad answered "No," we knew it was a definite refusal, but whenever he told us "Maybe," we knew were almost as good as there. But then came the waiting. Sometimes he'd keep us guessing as long as an hour until finally reaching into his pocket and giving us the change.

For a nickel, we'd be able to get in, and for another nickel we'd each buy a small bag of popcorn. Our favorites were the Flash Gordon serials because they featured spaceships and rockets that magically flew through space. Maybe "magically" is taking it a little far. The strings that held the toy rocket up were completely visible, and they used lit matches for rocket boosters as the spaceships sped across the tiny black-and-white frames on the screen. My brother and I saw fifteen minutes each week and couldn't wait to come back the next Saturday to see the next episode. It probably took two months of going to the activity center before we saw the whole story play out. The serials were a great escape and allowed us to dream of far-off worlds millions of miles away from our hard life growing up in the projects.

From that point on, my brother insisted our whole family call him Buster. Some other members of the family attributed the name to other things, but in my brother's mind he was going to be called after his hero, Buster Crabbe. If one of our family members didn't address him by the proper name, my brother wouldn't even respond. Dad got tired of having the same old argument with him and decided to go along with the program. He didn't have much of a choice. Since my brother didn't want to be Jimmy at the time and wasn't allowed to be Johnny, he was going to be Buster.

He ran around as the character night and day for a while and even made a cape out of an old rag. "I'm Buster, savior of the universe!" he started yelling whenever we were out playing in the field. He truly thought he had superpowers . . . for a while anyway. One afternoon, I stood looking up at him as he climbed onto the roof of our single-story project house, which must have been around ten feet high, and jumped off, flapping his arms. He quickly realized he didn't have any superpowers and fell to the ground with one of the loudest thuds I've ever heard. I was happy to see him spring back up to his feet, but his arm was bleeding.

When Dad, inside the house, heard him crying, he came storming out of the front door. "Are you crazy, boy?" he yelled. "What are you doing jumping off the roof?"

"But, I'm Buster Crabbe," my brother told him through his tears.

To me, at that young age, my brother was a sort of superhero. Daily, he protected and watched over me. When I was hungry, he helped me find something to eat. Whenever our parents fought, he wrapped his arm around my shoulder and comforted me.

Being left alone in the house after Dad set off to work first thing in the morning, Mama usually started partying with her friends, who stopped by throughout the day. It was all fine and good until Dad's quitting time later in the evening. After hitting a bar or two on his way back from work, Dad usually wasn't happy to return home to find unfamiliar people hanging out in his house. If he was in a bad mood and had no interest in joining the party, he'd boot everyone out and go off on our Mama. It soon became a constant. The long days of our Dad's and Mama's drinking only lead to loud arguments later at night. By evening, all the laughter routinely turned into shouting. Sometimes the arguments seemed to go on forever. Dad wasn't violent with our mama and never put his hands on her, but she possessed a fiery temper when she was drinking. Mama didn't hesitate to bust him upside the head with a beer bottle or anything else that was around when she was angry. My brother and I learned to keep quiet when our parents argued. Being a little over five years younger, I always followed my brother's lead. As soon as Buster and I realized they were going to get into it with each other, we closed the door to the back bedroom and waited it out. When things turned especially nasty, we stepped inside the closet and shut the door. In the darkness, we listened to the muffled shouting, hoping for it to end.

"It's going to be okay, Leon," my brother told me, draping an arm over my shoulder and drawing me in closer.

He knew speaking up only made everything worse. Sometimes we'd hide in the closet for up to an hour, until Dad and Mama eventually got tired and passed out.

Neither of us ever knew what to expect. Our parents got along well with each other for short periods, but it never lasted. Three weeks of good would be canceled out by one week of bad, and things continued to get worse. Our dad was always begging Mama to stay with us, but she couldn't take the turmoil in the house any longer. Although they loved each other passionately, they couldn't live under the same roof, and our mama had to move out. By the late fall of 1951, Dad told her he was filing for divorce, taking custody of us, and there wasn't anything she could do. Mama wouldn't be able to support us on her own, so she had to listen to him. Besides, she was having enough struggles with her own demons by then. Not only did the marriage unravel, but the burden of trying to look after three boys was also too much for Dad to handle. In order to ensure Joe could get the medical attention he needed, he and Mama realized they were also going to have to give him to foster care. In the summer of 1952, Joe suddenly wasn't around any longer. He was in his crib one day and gone the next. It would be many years before our paths would cross again.

Despite another heartbreaking experience of having to give up one of their children to foster care and their divorce, Mama and Dad couldn't stay separated for long. Even though she moved out, my brother and I woke up every so often to hear her cooking breakfast in the kitchen. As soon as we caught the sweet smell of pancakes and sausages, we knew Mama was home. They may always have insisted they were done with each other, but they were never done for good. There was no way they could live together, but they couldn't completely stay away from each other either. Whenever Mama showed back up at the house, things were good for about *a minute*. She was gone again almost as fast as she arrived.

What I didn't discover until years later was that Mama gave birth to another son not more than a few weeks after my fifth birthday, at the beginning of 1953. Like three of her children before him, the baby, whom she named Alfred, was born with disabilities and was given to foster care. At that time, it was hard for my brother and I to know what was going on with her. We didn't see Mama for long stretches of time until out of the blue she'd appear at our front door and plead with our dad to see us. It was a few months before she moved into an apartment by the Rainier Brewery with her mother, our grandma Clarice Jeter, and finally we began to spend more time with her. Since Dad didn't have a car, he walked Buster and me the thirteen blocks from our place in the Rainier Vista projects to visit Mama after work, while he was on his way to Edison Tech on Twenty-third and Yesler, where he was attending weekly classes to become an electrician. Because Mama's place was directly over the Rainier Brewery, the strong, sweet smell of hops and barley filled the entire building. The odor was impossible to get away from. To this day, every time I smell hops I think of her.

Any time spent at our mama's was like heaven. To us, she was a saint and could do no wrong in our eyes. I still remember how wonderful her perfume smelled and how beautifully she used to dress up. She took great care of us and cooked some amazing meals. Her favorite for breakfast was brains and eggs, and for dinner it was neck bones, sausage, and sauerkraut. It probably sounds much worse than it tasted, but we didn't have much of a choice back then. If you went to the butcher shop without a lot of money to spend, you got whatever pieces of the cow were left over at the end of the day. The brains sure stank up the place while they were cooking in the pan, but they didn't taste all that bad. Mama's real specialty was sauerkraut, which she made carefully from scratch. After shredding the cabbage and soaking it in a pot of vinegar all night long, she drained it in the morning and boiled it with Polish sausage. The dish was always my brother's favorite.

When Dad got out of class at Edison Tech later at night, he swung back through Mama's place, hoisted me up onto his shoulders, and took Buster by the hand so we could make our way back home. My brother didn't like that I got special treatment and was carried all the way to our house.

"Leon's not sleeping, Dad," he complained. "Just look. He can walk. He's faking it!"

I always made sure to open my eyes and give Buster a quick wink from on top of Dad's shoulder.

Our aunt Delores, God love her, recognized how hard things were on Dad and took it upon herself to help out. Even though she and her husband, Uncle Bob, had eight children of their own by then, she regularly offered to watch Buster and me. I don't know what we would have done without her reaching out to try to ease the strain on our dad.

After years of never having a car, Dad eventually got a beautiful sky-blue '53 Pontiac convertible with a white canvas drop top through a VA (Veterans Affairs) loan from the government. The car was the hottest convertible in the neighborhood. During the summer, Dad drove my brother and me up to Vancouver to spend time with family and dropped us off at his half brother's, Uncle Frank and Aunt Pearl's, where we ended up staying for a couple months. When Dad came back up to Canada at the end of the summer and brought Buster and me back down to Seattle, he soon realized he had a major problem: he wasn't sure what to do with us. Dad was working long hours during the day, and no one was around to take care of us. Fortunately, his sister, our aunt Pat, heard that he was struggling and offered to let us stay with her and her husband, Joe, at their house on Drake Street in Vancouver. Dad had no choice but to pack our things, put us in the car, and race back up Highway 99 to Canada.

Up in Vancouver, Aunt Pat took good care of my brother and me. She put Buster in Dawson Grade School, where Dad also went when he was a kid, and I started prekindergarten classes. Dad made sure to make the trip to see us every other weekend or so to see how we were doing, but we didn't live in Vancouver for long. When Aunt Pat's husband died unexpectedly, she packed up her things and brought us back to Seattle to move in with Dad on Genesee Street. Aunt Pat stayed in one room, while Dad, Buster, and I shared a bed in the other. It was nice to have Aunt Pat around during the day to watch me while my brother started going to school at Rainier Vista Elementary. We were even more thrilled to have her living with us because she also brought her television set. Now Buster and I didn't have to only listen to the Top 40 countdown, we could watch it.

Bless her heart, Aunt Pat lived with us until she met her second husband, who was also named Pat, and they bought a house together down by Lake Washington. Once again, Dad was left in a tight spot without anyone to help take care of us. By the middle of 1953, he was pumping gas for Seattle City Light for a shift during the day and still going to school at night to be an electrician.

Even though money was tight, Dad scraped enough cash to-gether to hire a part-time cleaning lady and babysitter named Edna Murray to watch us. He also didn't waste much time making her his new girlfriend and inviting her to live with us. Neither Buster nor I were too thrilled because we thought Edna was a mean old bat. Although, looking back, it probably wasn't all her fault. We were a lot for anyone to handle. Because there wasn't anything in the house to eat, Edna's specialty became fixing ketchup sandwiches for us. If you've never eaten a ketchup sandwich for dinner, let me be the first to admit that it tastes as bad as it sounds. Maybe worse. But still, when we were hungry, my brother and I ate anything.

When Dad finally made it home, Buster told him what we had had for dinner.

"You boys didn't eat no ketchup sandwiches," he snapped.

"Yes, we did," I told him. "There's nothing in the fridge."

When Dad opened up the refrigerator to see nothing but a half-empty bottle of old ketchup, he couldn't argue with me much further. He didn't want to hear any of our moaning and groaning when he finally arrived home, drunk and exhausted, at the end of his day. Even when he did make it back home at a decent hour after his shift, the last thing Dad wanted to be confronted with was his two needy boys. He usually had one request whenever he shuffled through the front door: "Go to bed."

We may have been poor and underprivileged, but Buster and I didn't know it. We didn't have access to boxes of toys to play with, or a television anymore to sit in front of all night, so we used what we had—our imaginations. My brother and I found whatever we could to keep ourselves entertained. One of our favorite things to do was to lie on our backs out in the yard and stare up into the night sky. Buster often told stories about the constellations and how they each got their name. His mind was full of all kinds of ideas about the universe and space.

"Mars and Venus used to be lovers way back," he told me. "And right now, we are spinning around in the universe on just one planet. Who knows how many of them are out there? I mean, *way* out there. There are faraway places and galaxies nobody even knows about."

Looking up at the tiny, shining dots in the sky, I also wondered how many other civilizations could exist. There was no way of telling, but we were convinced they were out there somewhere. Even back then, lying on the grass, my brother was coming up with the early stages of topics he would write about later in life. Off the top of his head he spouted lines about ice ages, burning planets, and the creation of the universe. To this day, I have no idea where he came up with all of these theories and information. But when my brother told me a story, it seemed to be real. Even being that young, I could easily see something different about how Buster related to the world. I never saw my brother read a book, and his grades were never good in school, but he seemed to possess an inherent knowledge about everything. I always felt he knew something everyone else didn't, so I never had any reason to feel in danger when we were together. I don't know what would have happened if he hadn't been there to take care of me and guide me through life early on in his own special way.

Aside from watching the science-fiction serial *Flash Gordon*, Buster also read some comic books when he could get his hands on them. Superheroes such as Superman and Batman were a few of his favorites, as well as other characters such as Mickey Mouse and Donald Duck. Above all, he was fascinated by outer space and far-off worlds.

"I wonder what it would be like to travel on a ship past all the other planets and stars. I bet space just goes on forever," I remember him saying. "There's no way that Earth is the only planet with people on it."

That way of thinking freaked out all the parents in our neighborhood, but that was the kind of mind he had. And it was passed on to me as well. People thought both of us were crazy. After being exposed to the Flash Gordon serials, my brother and I thought we were going to regularly start seeing spaceships in our everyday lives. I can't say I was all that surprised when we were out in a field one afternoon and he suddenly pointed up to the sky, where a giant disk was hovering off in the distance.

"Look at that," he said softly. "Do you see it?"

"Wow!" I shouted, pointing up at the object in the sky.

"Be quiet. Don't make any noise."

Remaining completely still, I stared at the hovering ship. Lights started pulsating around its edges.

"What is it?" I asked.

"I don't know, but I'm gonna find out."

As soon as my brother took his first careful step toward it, the disk shot up into the atmosphere and disappeared. I searched the sky trying to locate it again.

"Where did it go?" I asked.

Buster continued to carefully scan the sky, but there was no sign of whatever we had just seen.

"Don't worry," he said, turning toward me. "I'm sure they'll be back."

2

VAGABOND GYPSY BOYS

B y the spring of 1953, things were starting to look up for Dad
after he secured a higher-paying job with the City of Seattle,
working as a laborer for the engineering department. Together with
a crew of a few other guys, he drove around the streets day after day,
stopping to trim tree limbs away from power lines and clear brush
from sidewalks. The money he pulled in each week, along with another VA loan, allowed him to come up with a down payment for a
small two-bedroom house on Twenty-sixth and Washington Street,
at 2603 South Washington. Together, we packed up all of our belongings, which didn't amount to much, and made the move out of
Rainier Vista.

The house on Washington was a big upgrade from living in the
projects. For the first time we had a real home with hardwood floors,
a small kitchen, a full fenced-in backyard, a garage, and a basement.
The house also had an oil heater, which Dad relied on Buster and me
to fill every once in a while. Together, we pulled an old wagon with
a five-gallon drum down to Richland's filling station a block away to

get the drum filled. At nineteen cents a gallon, it wasn't cheap at that time.

Not only did Buster and I have our own room and bed in the new house to share, but also our own front yard to throw a football in or to play baseball in day and night. We didn't have much for sporting equipment, but we made the best of it. Our old and withered baseball gloves were literally coming apart at the seams. The laces were broken and the tears in the leather were covered in layers of tape. We were too ashamed to go to the park to play baseball with the other kids, being afraid we'd get laughed at, so we typically invited our close friends over to join us in the yard.

Unfortunately, not long after we settled in, things began to change. Despite working hard to try to provide a better life for my brother and me, our dad was still going heavy on the booze. Any hard-earned money he made working himself to exhaustion every day was eventually blown on gambling and alcohol at night. Some evenings, he never made it back to the house and stayed out partying at the bars, trying to drink away his sorrows. He was unhappy about not getting things worked out with our mama and struggling to try to take care of us by himself. Once Dad was good and drunk, he didn't have to look hard for action. Gambling was everywhere in those days. There was more than enough betting at pool halls, throwing dice in back alleys, and sitting in on card games. As Dad gradually went down in the hole, he spent the rest of the night trying to win his money back, which everyone knows rarely, if ever, happens.

When Dad did make it back to the house at the end of the night with some winnings, he sometimes treated us to a movie over at the Atlas Theater the next day. We typically stopped on the way to get candy before continuing to the theater. Buster always bought a Clark bar while I grabbed a Sugar Daddy. One of the first movies we saw at the Atlas was *Prince Valiant*, shortly after it came out in 1954.

The next day, when I came home from school, I heard what sounded like whimpering from outside our gate in the front of the house. When I checked it out, a dog was staring at me and panting from out on the sidewalk. I called for Buster right away and let the stray dog into our yard. Since he didn't have a collar or any identification, we both were set on keeping him. Luckily, Dad was in a good mood that night and didn't have a problem with it.

We decided to name him Prince and brought him along with us whenever we went out to play, no matter how far away from home we traveled. He was one smart dog and sometimes walked miles to find the two of us. If he was ever separated from us, Prince made the rounds to all of our regular hangouts as well as family and friends' homes looking for us until we were back together.

By that time, Mama moved from near the Rainier Brewery into another apartment at Thirteenth and Yesler. She was doing well for herself and holding down a job as a waitress at the Far West Café, which was located only a block from her new apartment. The café was basically a hangout for the off-duty taxi drivers of the Far West cab company. Sometimes when Dad set off to work, he dropped Buster and me down at the café and sat us in a booth in the corner. We'd watch Mama zip back and forth across the room, taking food orders and delivering drinks to customers until it was quitting time. If we were lucky, the cook sent out a nice meal of biscuits and chicken for us for dinner. Since I was too little to reach the table, Mama sat me on a thick phone book so I could enjoy the delicious food.

My brother and I were forbidden by our dad from making the trip over to Mama's apartment on our own, but we didn't let that stop us from sneaking out. Once Dad set off for work, we perfected an escape route so nobody in the neighborhood saw us leave the house. We were already down through the basement, out the back door, and down the sidewalk before we drew any attention to ourselves. Dad didn't get home until 12:30 or 1:00 A.M., so there was plenty of time to spend over at Mama's before we needed to hightail it back home before he suspected anything.

It was funny because sometimes when my brother and I acted up, Dad threatened to send us off to our mama's place as if it were some type of punishment. We thought of it as being just the opposite. Buster and I couldn't wait to go visit her. We tried our best to get in trouble so Dad had no choice but to have a meltdown and drop us at her apartment. My brother even broke a lamp once to get Dad riled up enough to pack us each a little sack with our toothbrush, and maybe a clean shirt if we had one, and send us to Mama's.

"Dad-gummit!" he shouted. "That's it, boys. I'm sending you over to your mama's!"

The real punishment was being forced to remain alone in a house with no food with the lights turned off. At home with Dad, it seemed as if the three of us were suffering all of the time. Mama's apartment, on the other hand, was a reward. Everything we did together had an excitement. Not to mention she regularly made breakfast, lunch, and dinner. Neither of us could ask for anything better than that.

My brother and I considered it a miracle when Mama came back to spend Christmas with the three of us in 1954. She and Dad were seeing each other again, and Buster and I couldn't have been happier about it. Back in the Rainier Vista projects, the holidays hadn't been that joyful. Buster and I went to sleep under our tiny tree on Christmas Eve hoping to wake up to a stack of presents, but that never happened. The only highlight I can remember was Grandma Clarice's giving us her change purse to split between us. But Christmas at the new house at Washington and Twenty-sixth was different. On Christmas Eve, Buster and I stayed up all night listening to our parents wrapping gifts in the other room. No way could we fall asleep with so much excitement in the air. We couldn't wait for the next morning to come. It was one of the few times it felt as if Dad, Mama, Buster, and I were actually a happy and loving family.

When the sun finally rose the next morning, we sprang out of our bed and raced to the Christmas tree. With ear-to-ear smiles, Buster and I ripped through the wrapping paper as fast as we could. We both yelled and screamed as I uncovered a toy steam shovel, a minia-ture Greyhound bus, and a red wagon, while Buster got a brand-new, glossy red Schwinn bicycle, which was like the Cadillac of bikes. My brother didn't waste any time in giving it a test ride. After we brought the bike outside, Buster hoisted me up onto the front handlebars and we tore away from the house at top speed. He wanted to show all of his friends his amazing new gift. Up until that Christmas, neither of us really ever got presents, so we wanted to make sure everyone saw what our parents had given us. We were overjoyed. Neither of us knew how to react because it was a new experience. Together, we disappeared for the rest of the afternoon on the bike, racing down the neighborhood streets and stopping to show it off to the rest of the kids in the projects. We completely forgot to tell our parents where we were heading, and when we rolled back to the house a few hours later, Dad was drunk and pretty angry.

"You boys missed Christmas dinner that your mama cooked! She worked hard all damned day!" Dad yelled.

That Christmas was about as good as it ever got for the four of us. It was the only joyful holiday we shared as a family. I wish there would have been more. After the warmth of the holidays faded, every-thing unraveled yet again. My brother and I were more than used to the tragic cycle of events and the never-ending roller-coaster ride, but that didn't make it any easier to cope with. Within a few months, the alcohol came back into the picture and the fighting got worse. By then, Dad's once immaculate convertible had been transformed into a beat-up jalopy. He routinely had it jacked up or up on blocks in front of the house. The car was covered with dents and scratches. Its canvas roof was sliced open and one of the headlights was knocked out. Every time we went out driving together, it seemed Dad and Mama got into a fight and he ended up wrecking the thing. With its being a convertible, Buster and I didn't have much room at all to sit in the small backseat.

The last accident we had in the Pontiac was the worst of them all. Things turned nasty one night as the four of us made our way back home after dinner at the Tai Kung Café. As usual, our parents drank heavily during the meal and were at each other's throats by the time we made our way out to the parking lot and climbed into the convertible. The arguing escalated as Dad swerved all over the road attempting to get us back home in one piece.

"We've got two boys in the back, Al!" Mama yelled. "What are you doing?"

"Stop your yelling!" Dad shot back.

In the backseat, Buster tried his best to wrap his arms around me tightly as we began being thrown around from side to side with each jerk of the steering wheel. Mama finally reached over with her left leg and tried to step on the brake pedal. When she did, Dad took his eyes off the road long enough to lose control of the car and swerve dead-on into a tree on the side of the road. The impact sent Buster and me toppling head over heels into the front seat. When we finally came to a stop, both of us began crying uncontrollably. My entire body ached.

Mama opened the door, pulled us from the front seat, and gathered us up in her arms.

"You drunk bastard! Are you crazy?" she yelled. "You almost killed all of us!"

"If you'd stopped yelling at me and let me drive, nothing would have happened," Dad told her.

"No, it's your fault." Mama had finally reached her breaking point. "Oh my God. We can't do this anymore, Al. This is too much."

With that, Mama was gone. Again. But this time proved to be different. She wasn't coming back, and neither Buster nor I saw our parents together after that evening.

As I was younger, all of the fighting and violence didn't have as much of an effect on me as on Buster. He took the full force of the turmoil between our parents. He absorbed the negativity day after day and, having nobody to turn to for help, learned to lock his feelings deep inside. He never let his anger over the situation come out whenever we were around our parents.

After years of going back and forth, it was probably for the best for our parents to finally break it off once and for all, but Dad still always took the separations hard, no matter how many times they went through the routine. He struggled to find a way to deal with the pain and guilt he felt for not being able to make it work between them. Every night before bed, Dad got down on his knees with Buster and me, and we prayed for all our relatives and ourselves. He always started off with "Now I lay me down to sleep, I pray the Lord my soul to keep. If I should die before I wake, I pray the Lord my soul to take." We then finished by saying an Our Father. At that age I didn't completely understand what God was, but I definitely believed in him. After Buster and I finished, Dad usually kept praying for another fifteen minutes or so as we looked on from the bed. Every once in a while, Dad forgot to open his eyes and fell asleep in mid-prayer. Since we were afraid to wake him, we typically turned the lights off and went to sleep. Eventually, he'd snap awake and take his place in the bed with us.

Even at our young age, Buster and I could see that Dad was trying to work out some of his problems and get his mind straight. He was under great pressure with Mama out of the house. He alone had to care for us two young boys, keep a roof over our heads, and the pay the bills. He carried this heavy load day in and day out. Whenever alcohol was thrown into the mix, that task was impossible.

As I entered the first grade at Leschi Elementary School, Buster was making his way into the sixth. Every day after class ended, he came by my classroom to pick me up, and together we set out on our own. Since we were finished with school at 3:00 P.M. and Dad had to be at his job at City Light at the same time, there was no point in rushing back to the house because nobody was going to be there waiting for us. Even though the school was only five blocks or so from our house, day after day we took hours to make it home. Hell, our dad didn't get off his shift until midnight. There was all night to run around if we wanted.

Together, we were two vagabond gypsy boys, young wanderers searching for adventure and excitement. We ran around in nearby Leschi Park, set out into the woods to play cowboys and Indians, or made our way down to the docks and kicked around the train yard. In the downtown area, we found exactly what we were always looking for from all the way back watching the Flash Gordon serials. Many people have no idea that another world exists beneath the sidewalks and streets of Seattle. Subterranean passageways are under the city covered by First Avenue. Originally, the streets of Seattle were built at sea level, so they often flooded after a heavy rain. Potholes in the roads were huge, and people sometimes fell into them and drowned. Then most of the city's central business district, something like sixty blocks, burned to the ground in 1889. After the crazy blaze, the city decided to rebuild the streets above the floodplain. Basically a city was built over a hidden city on the waterfront.

Buster found the passageway down by the ocean. A crack that looked to be about eight inches or so was between two dilapidated buildings. After he slid through, he looked back out of the opening with one eye. "Come on, Leon," he said from the other side. "Squeeze in and step through it."

I was scared to death to even try to push through the opening. "Come on, Buster. My head is way bigger than yours," I whined. "There's no way I'm going to make it."

"You have to see check this place out," he insisted. "There's all kinds of stuff down here."

Thoughts of getting wedged in the opening and crushed by falling debris flashed through my mind, but I gritted my teeth and stepped in anyway. It was a tight fit, but I slid to the other side with only a few scrapes. Once I caught sight of the surroundings, it was hard to believe what I was seeing. We'd literally slipped through a portal into a forgotten world. There was an old, boarded-up barbershop, a general store, and a hotel. All of the sidewalks were made out of withered planks. Up above, the city had built glass blocks into the new sidewalks it installed, so sun streamed through and illuminated our way. After Buster told all of his friends about the waterfront underground, we regularly played down there together. Occasionally, we'd find Indian-head pennies and other old artifacts along the dirt roads. Although the cops made routine patrols of the area, they found it nearly impossible to chase after us because they didn't know where we were entering and exiting from. It was easy to disappear anytime we heard them coming.

It was an ongoing adventure for the two of us. When Buster and I went outside, we went to *play*. As long as we made it back before our dad got home at midnight, we were cool. When we came home dirty, we stayed dirty because most of the time Dad didn't want to waste the water to wash us. We couldn't afford it. When he did get around to letting us take a bath, he used the same dirty water we'd used to scrub our clothes afterward, so it didn't make much difference. I'd look out back and see our worn shirts and pants flapping in the breeze on the clothesline, as dirty as ever. Not many kids wanted to play with us because we were the most ragged children on the block. We sometimes wore mismatched shoes, and when a lace broke, we just tied it back together and kept using it.

My brother channeled much of his bottled-up emotion into drawings and started spending a great deal of time lying on the living-room floor with his sketch pad and colored pencils. The first piece of art of my brother's I ever saw was a pencil drawing of our mama sitting underneath a palm tree. The shadows of the palm were diagonal across her face and she looked so calm and relaxed. Many of Buster's early sketches included our mama. It wasn't tough to see that she was always on his mind. In a way, through Buster's art, she was with us all of the time. The cartoons sketched in his notebook of battle scenes, futuristic race cars, and action sequences of football players fascinated me. I couldn't believe how incredibly vivid and realistic they were. While drawing his battle scenes, he added sound effects to each completed explosion and dialogue between soldiers as he tried his best to capture his fantastic vision on the page. And he still carried on telling stories of the constellations, outer space, and flying saucers.

Listening to my brother's stories also opened my mind to otherworldly possibilities, and one afternoon in the spring of 1955 I had another encounter with the far-off reaches of the universe. It started when what looked like two birds came together and collided over the backyard. There was a loud thud and it appeared as if a bunch of blue feathers drifted to the ground. After one of the birds careened down and landed not far from me, I ran over to take a closer look. But when I got there, there was no bird to be found. Instead, a round, gray piece of metal was sitting on the grass with wires sticking out of the back of it. The ball was some kind of futuristic mechanical device. Thinking it was some sort of expensive toy, I reached down and grabbed it. Not more than a second after I picked it up with my hand, an eye opened on its front and looked right at me. I couldn't drop that thing fast enough. I took off in the other direction and ran into the house screaming my head off.

"Buster! Buster!" I yelled.

"What's wrong?" he asked. "What were you doing out there?"

"A UFO fell out of the sky!"

Buster didn't look surprised at all. It was as if he had been expecting otherworldly entities to make contact.

"So, where is it now?" he asked, casually walking back across the field.

"It's right near the fence," I said, following behind and pointing to where I'd dropped it.

But by then, nothing was to be found, and whatever it had been was long gone. I can still see it in my mind as if it were yesterday. It's usually pointless to tell anyone about such encounters because people immediately think I am putting them on. No matter what I explain, they never believe these types of things, but it's useless worrying about it anymore. Some fantastic things have occurred in my life, and there is no harm in being honest about my experiences. Besides, people already think I'm crazy, just as many parents in the neighborhood back in the day thought my brother and I were crazy for telling stories about aliens and UFOs. More than a few times as the two of us walked down the sidewalk, we spotted mothers dragging their kids inside the house to prevent them from coming out to play. Our family members, our aunties and uncles in the area, who took care of us from time to time, never thought much about our talk about other worlds, spaceships, and the far reaches of the universe. They'd heard the stories before and were used to them. But our talk rubbed other parents in the neighborhood the wrong way, and simply put, we freaked them out.

"I don't want you messin' with those Hendrix boys!" we'd hear them say. "They ain't right in the head."

In the summer of 1955, Dad put Buster and me in the car, and together we drove the four hours up Highway 99 to his mama's, our grandma Nora's, house in Vancouver. Grandma's name was actually Zenora, but everyone always called her Nora. She was beautiful, part Cherokee Indian, and had a great sense of humor. It seemed as if everything was fun when Grandma Nora was around. She'd lived in Seattle earlier in her life with our grandpa, but eventually moved to Vancouver for work in the 1930s. Unfortunately, Grandpa died before my brother and I were born, so we never got to meet him.

When Grandma Nora heard that Dad and Mama had broken up for the last time after he crashed the convertible, she wasn't happy. Grandma and Mama always got along well and loved each other.

"It's your fault, Allie," Grandma Nora told Dad. Her nickname for Dad was always Allie. "It's *you*, not her. You know better than anyone that these boys need a mama. But now you went and messed everything up for good."

Dad didn't argue with her because deep down he knew Grandma Nora was probably telling the truth. Without another word, he shuffled to his car with his tail between his legs and drove back to Seattle, leaving us boys with Grandma for the summer.

Grandma Nora lived down by Vancouver's dockyards on Hastings Street, not far from Dad's half brother, Uncle Frank, and his wife, Aunt Pearl, so Buster and I split time staying between each house. Dad was the youngest of the siblings. Along with Frank, Dad had another brother named Leon, who died suddenly when they were only teenagers. My brother and I used to love getting up at 7:00 A.M. each morning when the horse-drawn milk wagon came down the street. Whenever we heard its bell ringing, Buster and I jumped out of bed and ran down to meet it. My brother always made sure to have an apple ready to feed the horse. Usually around the same time of morning, the iceman was also making his delivery. We looked on as he slid a big block of ice out of the tailgate and grabbed it with a giant set of tongs. After he hoisted it onto his shoulder, we followed him up the front walkway into the house. The ice lasted only about two days, but it sure kept everything nice and cold in the icebox.

Buster and I were just happy to be eating breakfast regularly in Vancouver. Grandma Nora and Aunt Pearl made sure we were well taken care of. Compared to our life back in Seattle, we were in heaven up in Canada staying with our relatives. My favorite treat was when Aunt Pearl scooped the fresh cream that formed in a thick layer in the top of the milk bottle and gave it to me. Buster, as well as Uncle Frank and Aunt Pearl's son, our cousin Bobby, could not have cared less about it. The only thing they were interested in was the milk. In the morning, Aunt Pearl warmed up some applesauce and corn bread, then poured that pure cream over the top. To me, there was no better way to start the day.

As usual, Buster and I were gone from the moment we woke up in the morning until the sun went down at night. Together with Bobby, we walked west on Hastings Street up into Stanley Park near the ocean and played around the train tracks that ran along most of the waterfront. Since Buster and Bobby were older, I found it hard to keep up with them sometimes, especially around the tracks. To me, it looked as if there must have been around a hundred sets side by side, when there were probably only six. The trains were coming and going, constantly rattling their way along. Just as one passed, another would glide along the track in the opposite direction. Buster and Bobby found no trouble running across to reach the ocean on the other side, but I was too afraid.

"Come on, Leon! You can make it!" my brother shouted at me one day from the other side. Still, I wasn't going for it. Instead, I was forced to walk a half mile down to the trestle and cross over that way. It seemed to take forever before I made it back to where Buster and Bobby were already playing on the shoreline. Sometimes, it took me so long that they left me behind and went on their way. I'd end up having to search up and down the shoreline just to find them.

Then one day, I finally got tired of routinely being left behind and decided it was time to face my fears. As usual, Buster and Bobby were already standing on the other side of the tracks, waving me over.

"You can do it, Leon!" Buster shouted. "Come on!"

I knew it was time. In my mind, I was finally ready to make the long dash all the way across. But as I sprang into motion, something went wrong. There was *no* motion. Something was holding me back. Panicked, I glanced down to find my shoelace was caught up in the first track.

"What are you doing?" Bobby yelled to me.

"Hurry up, Leon," Buster added.

Then a strong vibration surged up my leg. There was no mistaking what that meant—a train was coming around the bend. The engineer blasted the air horn, as if I *didn't know* the train was headed in my direction. The thunderous sound of it shook my bones. As the tears began to roll down my cheeks, Buster and I locked eyes. One look let him know that I was in trouble. Without another word, he took off across the tracks, charging toward me. Although I'd never seen him move that fast in his life, the whole scene seemed to play out in slow motion. As he tackled me into the pricker bushes, the train loudly roared past along the track. When we made it back to our feet, Buster was bleeding from his arms and legs. It was a miracle we both survived, but when I looked down, my right shoe was gone. It must have been sucked up into the wheels of the train. Losing one shoe was just as bad as losing both of them, and Grandma

Nora wasn't going to be happy. Where was she going to be able to get a shoe? You can't walk into a store and buy only *one*. She'd need to get me another pair altogether. My brother and I started crying because we knew we were both going to get in trouble when we got back home.

Two girls who were sitting up on the bank saw what had happened and came jogging over to see if we were okay. They took us back to their house a few blocks away and gave Buster some Band-Aids for his cuts and scratches. Their mom even baked a chocolate cake for us. After that day, we stopped by the house whenever we went back down to the tracks because she always had dessert for us to eat. We didn't know her name, so Buster and I called her Betty Crocker. "Let's go to Betty Crocker's house," we'd say every time we were in the area. My brother and I could have eaten her chocolate cake for breakfast, lunch, and dinner.

At the end of the summer, about a week before school was to start, Dad drove up from Seattle to get us. Buster and I got a fresh pair of jeans and new shoes to wear to school every day. Once classes started back up, Dad demanded that Buster and I come straight home after school, lock the front door, draw the blinds on the windows, and keep the lights turned off. The welfare people were gunning for us and he didn't want to give them any opportunity to pull something funny while he wasn't there to protect us. So, in the dark house we stayed . . . for a while anyway.

Since we didn't have a television set, night after night at seven o'clock, we made sure to sit in front of Dad's old-time radio to listen to the Top 40 countdown. Sometimes we'd also listen to a few of the radio shows such as *Gunsmoke* and *The Shadow*. One night, after one of the shows ended, Buster suddenly looked as if something was bothering him. He got up, walked into the kitchen, and jogged back in carrying a handful of tools. I looked on expectantly as he knelt down on the floor and tilted the radio onto its face. He leaned on the screwdriver as he began taking the screws out of the back cover.

"What are you doing?" I asked. "You better not do anything to Dad's radio or we're gonna get a whoopin'." But my brother paid me no attention. He was on a mission and my nagging didn't change his mind.

As he worked, I was surprised to see there wasn't really much to the thing: a receiver, a dial, and a bunch of wires. Buster dissected it for a while before leaning back against the couch with a confused look on his face. After a few silent moments, he gathered the parts strewn over the floor and went about putting the radio back together. However, when he finished, it didn't work. Buster must have lost a wire or a few screws somewhere because the radio was completely dead. There was no sound at all.

When our dad got home, he wasn't happy that his favorite radio was broken. As usual, he was also drunk, so he immediately flew into a rage.

A scowl found its way onto his face. *"Dad-gummit!"* he started out. It was always bad when Dad broke out *dad-gummit* because he rarely said it. Now that he had, the situation wasn't going to turn out well. Buster was already crying as Dad started in on him.

"Why'd you break my radio?" Dad yelled.

Still, there was nothing from Buster. Not even a quick slap across the head made him respond. "What did you think you were doing?" Dad asked.

Buster wiped the tears from his cheeks. "I was looking for the music."

Dad's face contorted again almost as if it were folding in on itself. "You were doin' what?" he shouted. "That's damned ridiculous! What are you talking about?"

"I was looking for the music."

The dismantling of our dad's radio marked the beginning of my brother's journey in search of the sounds—the invisible radio waves and frequencies. If you followed them, where did they lead? Once he set his mind to something, there was usually no stopping him no matter what Dad said or how many whoopin's my brother caught. He wasn't going to be at all satisfied until he one day found the answer to all of his questions.

Dad prided himself on being a strict disciplinarian, and Buster and I got what we called whoopin's as far back as I can remember. I can't think of a time when there wasn't that type of punishment going on in our house. One of us was always getting into some type of trouble and upsetting our dad. It's not like it took much to set him off, especially if he was into a few of his Seagram's or Lucky Lagers. When a whoopin' was coming our way, Buster and I were told to wait in the back bedroom with the door closed while out in the living room Dad took hold of his bottle and drank up the nerve to come back in and beat our behinds. Sometimes we'd be waiting back there, crying and whimpering, for up to an hour. I was only a toddler, so Buster came to my rescue and started taking full blame anytime something happened. When he sensed a punishment coming, he didn't waste any time speaking up.

"I'm sorry, Dad. Leon didn't do anything. It's all my fault," he said.

My brother stuck up for me as long as he could, but over time Dad got wise to the sacrifice Buster was making. So, not to be tricked again, Dad decided that we'd both get a whoopin' whenever either if us caused trouble.

"Come here, Leon," he'd say, sitting down on the bed. Dad typically used his hand and never hit us with a belt or a switch. One after another, Buster and I bent over Dad's lap and he did his thing. After the first couple of smacks on the behind, I couldn't feel anything anyway. Before I knew it, it was all over. I withstood a few swats, then Buster received the rest of what Dad intended on giving. If it was a particularly bad whoopin' for something we had done, he might feel guilty enough to take us for ice cream afterward. To tip the scales, we sometimes made sure to yell and scream for a greater effect. There was nothing wrong with a little embellishment as far as we were concerned. The two of us followed a formula: more yelling equaled more ice cream afterward.

Once school got out in the summer of 1956, we had even more time on our hands. Without classes, we were completely on our own day and night. There wasn't much, if anything at all, to eat for breakfast, so my brother and I began getting up at 4:30 A.M. to catch the bus out into the bean, carrot, cucumber, or strawberry fields to work with some of our friends. Typically, the bus picked us up at 5:30 A.M., so we always made sure we were there in plenty of time. If we were late, the bus left without us, especially if the driver saw we were only a group of kids. Because Buster was thirteen years old and I was only eight, they didn't want to let us on even when we were on time. Although people sometimes complained that we weren't able to work as hard, we didn't care. We only wanted to make some money. All of the boys in the neighborhood were poor, and if we knew one thing, it was that we needed to earn money by any means necessary to put food in our stomachs. Because we were so young, picking in the fields was one of the only jobs available.

It was typically cool in the early mornings, but as the day wore on, the heat and humidity rose in the fields. We could pick two or three bushels during the first half of the day. Then, at noon, we'd kick off work and have some fun. Typically, we made $1.50 a day, which after quitting time we spent on fifteen-cent hamburgers and fries for a dime. For dessert we could get a Hershey's bar as long as your arm for around a nickel.

That summer, Buster's idea of fun was beginning to change; now, girls were in the mix. Every now and then I'd look around in the field and not be able to find him, so I walked up and down the rows hollering his name. When I caught up with him, he was usually tumbling around with a girl.

"Shhh, Leon," he'd tell me.

"What are you two doing out here in the cornfield? Are you hiding from someone?" I'd ask. I was too young to figure out what all the fuss about girls was. It made absolutely no sense to me.

The fields weren't far from the Green River, where Buster and Cousin Bobby usually cooled off after work by splashing around in the water. They'd jump in a few times while I stood on the bank and waited for them to get through. They ribbed me about not joining them, but the current looked way too strong. Back in Vancouver, a passing train at the waterfront tracks had already almost shredded me to pieces. I was in no rush to test my luck in the currents of the river. Like at the train tracks, a trestle led to the opposite bank of the Green River. So, I had to walk down, cross it, and then walk back up to where Buster and Bobby were on the other side if I wanted to play with them. It was fine for a while, but the ribbing started getting to me. Still, the current was no joke. You had to swim upstream, at an angle, if you wanted to get to a point directly opposite you on the other side.

I don't know if they wore me down or I simply got tired of walking the quarter mile or so each way to the trestle every time we went to the river, but I had enough. All it took was Bobby's yelling, "Come on, Leon! Quit being a baby!" from the other side one afternoon for the situation to get on my last nerve. Standing on the bank, I braced and then made a move for the water. Being a little afraid, I couldn't bring myself to jump. I sort of slumped over and fell into the river. Almost immediately, the current whisked me away no matter how hard I paddled against it. Stroke after stroke, I was being pulled farther and farther downstream.

"Kick your feet!" I heard Buster yell from the opposite bank.

I tried, but that wasn't making any difference either. Then something unexpected popped into my peripheral vision. A *dead pig* was floating by, bobbing up and down in the water. It might have been the worst thing I have ever smelled. As soon as its rancid odor hit my nostrils, I started choking and gagging. It was already difficult enough to breathe, and now I had the fumes coming off a dead pig to deal with. One thing was certain: I was in trouble.

And then everything got quiet as my head submerged underwater. The last image I saw was Buster's panicked expression from the opposite shoreline. Just as everything faded into darkness, my head popped back up out of the water as I approached the bridge—*the same damned bridge I should have walked over in the first place.* Then it was back under the surface to choke down a few more mouthfuls of river water. I was sinking fast and everything was again turning dark. Although the first few mouthfuls of water were painful, I began experiencing a type of euphoria. A part of me felt like giving up in that moment, and an eerie sense of calm came over me. Okay, I thought, I guess it's time to say good-bye to the world. At that moment, from below the surface, I looked up to see Buster diving off the bridge straight down toward me. The house key hanging from the string around Buster's neck glistened in the shafts of sunlight above. He pulled me up above the surface and struggled to keep me afloat until we reached the shore, where Bobby helped drag me up the bank.

My brother was more than relieved when I got back on my feet and regained my senses. "My God, Leon, you know what would happen to me if anything happened to you? I would have gotten a whoopin'!" Buster told me. A moment went by, then another thought hit him. "And I would have gotten even a bigger whoopin' if you drowned!" He and Bobby got a good laugh out of that one.

It was the second time that my brother had saved my life. I have no idea how in the world he made it out to where I was in the middle of the river so fast. A few more moments and I would have been a goner. Yet, I wouldn't have needed him to keep saving me if he and Cousin Bobby stopped getting me into so many dangerous situations.

Dad was mostly out of the loop, and if he'd ever caught on to some of the things we were doing, we would have been in deep trouble. He tried to take care of us as best he could, but every time he put the effort forth, it seemed to backfire. The only time I can remember Dad trying to cook Buster and me something for breakfast, he nearly set the house on fire. We woke up to find the house filled with smoke and Dad passed out on the couch. I guess he came home late at the end of his shift and realized we'd be waking up soon. He got as far as putting some eggs on the stove, then lay down on the couch and dozed off.

Late one night I suddenly heard a loud pounding on our front door. Since it was Dad's day off from work, he was home and quickly answered it. He swung the door open to reveal two men in suits, who identified themselves as social workers from the city welfare department. Evidently, they'd received a bunch of reports from concerned neighbors that Dad worked the three-to-midnight shift and left Buster and me home without any supervision. To get them off his back, Dad told the men he would immediately make arrangements for someone to watch us while he was away at work. But once they left, he had a different idea. In his mind, the answer to the problem was simple. After sitting us down on the living-room couch, he told us, "You boys make sure to come straight home from school every single day, draw them blinds on the windows, turn out all the lights, lock that door, and don't open it for anyone. Both of you know that if you answer that door for those men, they'll take you both away and we'll never see each other again."

I'm sure the guys in suits weren't buying the promise Dad had made to them to find another home for us to stay in while he was at work. Before long Buster and I started seeing the dark green car with WELFARE DEPARTMENT stenciled in white on the door routinely cruising the neighborhood. Every time they knocked on the front door, we'd hide in the bedroom closet, doing our best to keep quiet. A few times, I didn't think they were ever going to stop knocking and go away. It was official—they knew nothing had changed and Dad had lied to them. I was scared to death they'd find us and take me away from my dad and brother.

With no other choice, Dad brought in Aunt Pat's daughter, Gracie, whom we called Cousin Gracie, and her husband, Frank, whom we called "Buddy," to live with us. Dad gave them one bedroom and he, Buster, and I shared the double bed in the other bedroom. It was perfect timing because Gracie and Frank were looking for a place to stay, and Dad desperately needed someone to watch over us. Plus, having a woman in the house looked good to the welfare suits. Now, every time they came around knocking, Cousin Gracie was there to greet them at the door.

"Hi, gentlemen," she said to them with a kind smile. "Yes, I'm living here now. I have a good job working down at the YMCA, and I'm watching the boys while Al is at work."

How were the welfare guys going to argue with that?

It did the trick for a while, but when Cousin Gracie and Frank moved out, we were right back to where we started. It was back to full lockdown mode, and Dad repeatedly telling us to hide and hope for the best. Even as young as I was, I recognized our game of cat and mouse with the child-welfare people wasn't going to last forever.

FOSTER CARE

Dad occasionally dropped us over at Mama's place, but that situation was becoming more of a sore subject as time went by. By then, Mama had a boyfriend, so Dad was even more bent out of shape. He didn't want to have anything to do with her from that point on and made sure both Buster and I knew it. Anytime we asked about her, Dad turned sour.

"I don't want to talk about your mama!" he'd snap. "I don't know where the hell she is at. So you boys just leave it alone."

Our situation at home continued to worsen over time. After months of dealing with regular calls at work from school principals, concerned neighbors, and workers from the welfare department, Dad's bosses at City Light had enough of the nonsense and sent him on his way. With few options, Dad got a job at Bethlehem Steel, basically sweeping up around the factory, but at a considerable drop in pay. He returned home every night covered head to toe in black shavings and reeking of burnt metal.

Since Dad never felt comfortable leaving my brother and me

home alone together with the welfare department lurking around the neighborhood, he started stopping by the house to pick us up when he got off work. The only way Dad could go out at night was if he brought us along. Sometimes, he took us to the Atlas Theater and treated us to a movie for twenty-five cents apiece. But most of the time, he couldn't fight the urge to gamble and instead brought my brother and me with him to a downstairs pool hall called the Casino Club. After telling the guy in the kitchen to give us a bowl of rice and gravy, Dad usually began the night by going off to buy "pull-tab tickets" and sit in on a card game. The pull-tabs each had two sides and came out of mechanical dispensers. They cost anywhere from twenty-five cents to two dollars. One side had the winning combinations, the winning cash amount, and the total number of tickets. The other had perforated tabs that you'd pull to see if you won. The only real draw was the odds: a quarter could end up returning five or ten dollars if it was a winning tab. The promise of laying down small money to cash in on big winnings always got Dad's blood pumping. But I can't remember him ever winning.

Dad was always on "a streak" when he was gambling. Even if it started out a winning streak, it usually ended a losing one. It was only a matter of time before he went broke. Unfortunately, he never found the strength to pull himself away from the table when he was up. Of course he was forced to stop when he went broke because there was nothing left to play with. As hour after hour passed, Buster and I usually fell asleep under one of the pool tables until Dad was finally ready to leave for the night.

On the off chance that Dad did walk out of the Casino Club with a few extra bucks in his pocket, he made sure to take us out to the Pike Place Market for ten-cent horse-meat hamburgers. As odd as they sound, those things were a treat for me at that age. I considered hanging out in the pool hall an exciting adventure, but I'm sure

Buster had a much different take on everything. In no way was he thrilled to be hiding in our house after school every day and sleeping under pool tables at night. Although times were always hard for the three of us, I never wasted any effort complaining. Dad was always trying his best to make ends meet, and that is what mattered most to me.

After Dad lost his job at Bethlehem Steel, our electricity and water were turned off seemingly every other month, and he struggled to scrape enough money together to make the mortgage payments. Dad spent plenty of time salvaging whatever he could find and reselling it. He became the King of Recycling in my mind—a true professional. Cans, bottles, sheet metal, copper, plastic . . . you name it and Dad had a way to make a little money from it. He began keeping multiple large plastic barrels in the back of his truck: one for brown glass, one for clear, one for green, and one for cans. Tin was big back then, but aluminum was just getting started, so we got only three cents a pound for the aluminum cans we collected and redeemed every week. Dad regularly pulled over to the side of the road anytime he spotted something worth grabbing.

"Look at them cans over there, boys," he'd say, craning his neck out of the driver's-side window. "And don't forget to snatch them bottles, too!"

This was like a game of treasure hunt to us. My brother and I jumped out of the cab of the truck and rounded up whatever was there.

A friend of Dad's who still worked at City Light was able to give him plenty of help finding copper. He told Dad where the larger electrical jobs were located in Seattle, so we drove with him in his truck to gather up all of the leftover wire. At each job site, the three of us loaded the tangled short ends into the back of the truck until Dad thought we had enough for the day. As soon as we returned home, Buster and I went to work on the wire. After taking our red wagon down to the store and buying a few gallons of diesel fuel, we'd return and burn each section of wire in our home stove until the plastic coating melted away. Both of us took turns using a big set of tongs to hold the wire over the flames as if we were cooking hot dogs at a campfire. When we finished, Dad took the remaining copper and redeemed it for money.

Since salvaging alone wasn't going to do the trick, Dad eventually found another way to earn money by working for our uncle Pat at his landscaping business. On the weekends, Dad started taking us along with him to help out with his yard work. Since he was new to the business, the more difficult jobs Uncle Pat wasn't interested in taking were kicked down to our dad. We'd regularly show up to a place to find acres of tall grass growing over our heads. Although Dad owned a lawn mower, it wasn't going to do a damned thing to grass that long. So, he bought a sickle that must have been fifty years old and taught Buster how to use it. Dad made sure my brother learned everything about gardening as time went on because in his mind the two of us were going to be taking over the family business one day. After every hundred strokes or so, the sickle completely lost its edge, so it was an incredible amount of work. As Buster chopped the grass down, I followed behind cleaning up and tying it into bundles.

On one job, Dad simply dropped us off with all of the equipment and split. As Buster and I worked to the point of complete exhaustion out in the field, Dad didn't return all day. By the time we finished, he still was nowhere to be seen. We were sweaty, dirty, and weak. I was lying on the ground clutching my side, and Buster didn't look much better.

"I'm starving," I told him.

"I know," he said, looking down the road. "Me, too."

I got to my feet and followed behind as he led me from the house we were working at to an IGA market not too far away. Once we shuffled our way inside, my stomach began aching even more. Although we passed aisle after aisle of food, we knew we didn't have money to buy anything. My brother and I were desperate. After checking the aisle for any grocery-store workers on the prowl, Buster discreetly pulled a loaf of white bread down from the shelf. Almost in a single motion, he speedily opened one end of the bag, snatched two slices, and put it back in its original place on the shelf. Then, we went by the refrigerator where they kept the sliced, packaged meat and he took a couple of large disks of baloney. After he slid the meat between the slices of bread, he carefully ripped the sandwich and gave half to me. We ate our food out of sight in the corner of the store. It tore my brother up inside to have to steal from the supermarket, but it felt as if there was no alternative. Buster always provided for me. He was one of the most honest people I have ever met in my life, and being forced to steal food from the market stayed with him for a long time.

When we returned to the house, Dad was loading the equipment into the back of his truck. His eyes lit up when he spotted us walking down the road toward him.

"Where in the hell have you boys been?" he yelled. "I told you to wait here!" One look and I could tell he had been drinking at the bar all day. He charged forward and grabbed me by the arm.

"No, don't whup Leon," Buster pleaded with him. "It was my fault."

But Dad didn't listen. Over time, he'd caught on to my brother's game of taking the blame for both of us. Nothing either of us said that day was going to change his mind, and he gave both of us a whupin' right there in the field.

Although a year had passed since the welfare department's last
visit, Dad and the office again started their game of cat and mouse.
Cousin Gracie did a good job of helping Dad keep them at bay for a
while, but when she decided to move out on her own, we knew it was
going to be trouble. The officers were constantly snooping around,
trying to keep tabs on us. Fortunately, some of the women in the
neighborhood, mostly older Jewish mothers, recognized how bad our
dad was struggling to keep it together and offered their help when
they could. Since Buster and I were afraid to ever open the front
door, they'd talk us into letting them in from the other side. I can
still hear them as if it were yesterday: "Come on, boys. Open up. I've
got some fried chicken for you. I know you are hungry in there."
Over time they also started doing a special and unique knock to let
us know it was safe to open the door. If Dad didn't come home later
at night, they let us stay overnight at their house. If he still hadn't
returned the next day, another family usually stepped forward and
offered us a meal and a place to sleep. Since our neighborhood was a
fairly even mix of Jewish and black families, we were either eating
fried chicken or matzo balls.

Once in while, Dad gave us a cheese sandwich and an apple to go
to school with, but those times were few and far between. At night,
he sometimes got around to making a giant pot of spaghetti and left
it in the refrigerator for us to ration out for three or four days.
With Dad's making meals now and then and the neighborhood
women swinging through, the situation worked out for a while, but
Dad eventually wore out his welcome with the women in the neighborhood.

One night, Buster and I were over at Mrs. Mitchell's house, which
was kitty-corner to ours, when Dad came home drunk as hell. Somewhere around 3:00 A.M., we woke up to find him causing a commotion out on the sidewalk. Dad knew from experience that we usually

ended up at one of the neighbor's houses, so he made his way along the street, stopping at each door.

"Where are my boys?" he asked whoever answered.

As Buster and I peeked out the living-room window at him swaying back and forth, Mrs. Mitchell came over and sat next to us on the couch. The three of us watched as Dad slowly made his way from the Weinsteins' door to the Greenburgs'.

"Be quiet," she whispered, holding a finger up over her lips. "You boys aren't going to have any fun going home right now. Just stay put."

It made sense to us. We'd probably get a whoopin' for being out of the house anyway. Neither my brother nor I knew what to do because we were both scared.

"Who has my boys?" Dad loudly asked again from out on the street.

Outside, lights were being turned on up and down the block. Curtains opened and people took notice. Mrs. Mitchell retied her robe and went out the front door. We looked on as she walked toward Dad in the middle of the street.

"Go to bed, Al," she kindly told him. "We've got the boys. They've had a bath and eaten dinner. They're fine, so why don't you just go to bed."

Dad stood looking at her for a stubborn moment, but was in no condition to push his luck any further. He was tired and out of it. Buster and I watched as he staggered down the sidewalk to our house, clumsily climbed the front step, and disappeared inside.

Shortly after that night, Dad figured it was best for me to stay at Pat and Pat's house down by Lake Washington for a while. At first, I didn't mind being sent over there to spend time. They let me have my own bedroom, and together we watched *The Ed Sullivan Show* and *Lawrence Welk* on Aunt Pat's television. However, after the initial excitement wore off, I was miserable being separated from Dad and Buster. And Pat and Pat weren't all that thrilled to have me living with them either. I was a real handful at that age and I drove them crazy. A month into my stay, they both picked up and moved to California, so I was again back at home for the start of school in 1956.

When I returned to our house, not much had changed. Since everyone on our block was fed up with what was going on in our household, the complaints continued to the welfare department. A week later, a pair of social workers showed up at our house. Buster and I were playing on the front lawn when two dark green Chevys came rolling up to a stop behind us. I thought we were in the middle of some kind of army raid. But these guys weren't soldiers. They were men in suits. Momentarily frozen with fear, I looked over at Buster, who immediately took off toward the front door. I didn't waste any time in running into the house after him and closing the door behind me. Buster dead-bolted the door, and together we ran and hid in the back bedroom closet. Once the hard knocking on the front door stopped, we made our way out to the living room and made sure the coast was clear. It was the closest scrape we'd had with the welfare officers. Day by day, they were getting closer and closer to catching us.

Notice after notice from various Seattle city services was delivered to our house. Finally Dad couldn't ignore them any longer. Together, we drove down to an office and he met with a woman named Mrs. Lamb, who was assigned as our family's caseworker. Dad sat Buster and me in the waiting room and closed the door.

Mrs. Lamb explained that she didn't have a problem with allowing Buster to remain in Dad's custody because he was almost fourteen, but as I was only eight and a half, they were concerned for my safety. When Mrs. Lamb broke the news that they intended to keep me, Dad broke down, and when he let my brother and me know what was going on, we both started crying. Dad was devastated and pleaded with them for another chance, even confessing that he had been meaning to have me stay with another friend of the family for quite a while. After listening to what he had to say, the welfare people granted him one more opportunity to make things right. They gave him twenty-four hours to place me with a family or they would be back out to our house to do it for him.

The next morning, the three of us cried together as Dad helped me gather my things and pack a bag of clothes. It wasn't that difficult because there wasn't much for me to choose from. It was sad that almost everything I owned fit into a little carry bag. I was heartbroken and frightened to death of being separated from my family. For every day of my life, the three of us had been together, and now that wasn't going to be the case anymore. I was going to be by myself and all alone. We piled into the truck and drove over to a house not far from where we lived.

Dad ended up putting me with Urville and Arthur Wheeler, an educated black couple with college degrees and good standing in the community. Four other foster kids were already living with the family when I arrived, so Mrs. Wheeler had her hands full. She greeted the three of us at her front door and flashed me a kind smile. As I stood crying and shaking, she stepped forward, placed a hand on my shoulder, and said, "It's going to be all right, baby."

Dad composed himself long enough to give me a hug. "It's okay, son. This is your new auntie."

"I'll see you soon, Leon," my brother told me, wiping the tears from his eyes.

I was inconsolable as they drove off and down the street. Still, I never blamed my dad for the hard times we all went through when we were little boys. Deep down, he truly loved my brother and me, but the booze always got in the way. When someone is finding it hard to make ends meet, alcohol isn't the best friend to lean on. As Dad fell into that darkness of abuse, he was doing nothing but fighting a losing battle day after day. Now he'd finally surrendered another of his sons because of it.

While living in the projects, I'd heard plenty of horror stories about foster-care families only taking in needy children to earn a check from the government each month, but I found the Wheelers to be incredibly kind and loving. For the first time in my life, I regularly ate warm meals and dressed in new clothes. The entire lifestyle was foreign. Although I first knew her as my new "auntie," I quickly started calling Mrs. Wheeler "Mom." I was missing my own mama so much that I guess was looking to form a similar type of connection with her. Even though the Wheelers treated me as if I were one of their own children and did everything within their power to help me adapt to being away from my family, I still couldn't accept the situation. I would have traded it all in a heartbeat to be returned to where I belonged.

The day my brother and Dad dropped me off at the Wheelers, Buster told me he was going to see me soon, and he wasn't lying. Since the Wheelers' house was only five blocks from our dad's, Buster came by almost every day after school to throw the football around in the front yard or play baseball with me and some of the other boys. The Wheelers were churchgoing folks who regularly welcomed kids who were in need. From the start, they accepted my brother as if he was one of their own. He already knew the other boys who lived in the house through school, especially his good friend Jimmy Williams, so he loved stopping by to check up on me. He also knew he could get a warm dinner when there was nothing for him to eat at home. The Wheelers' house instantly became like my brother's second home. Buster was going through a similar type of experience to mine because he was alone now, too, in an empty house. We were both enduring a confusing time in our lives.

Another bonus was that although I was required to live at the Wheelers' during the week, I was allowed to return home on weekends. So, immediately after school let out on Fridays at 3:00 P.M. until after dinnertime on Sundays, I was back home with Dad and Buster.

Dad stopped by the Wheelers' during the week now and then to bring me a new pair of shoes or a shirt. He bought me a little $15 suit so I had something to wear when the Wheelers took me to church on Sundays. Not that I expected much, but that gift meant a lot to me during that dark time.

One afternoon around a month later, Dad went even further. I was playing in the park with a few of my friends when his truck drove by. Since I figured he was on his way to the lawn mower shop to get his mower fixed, I followed him. After running up and surprising him in the parking lot, he gave me a rub on the top of my head. It was all Buster and I ever got out of our old man—a quick pat or rub on the head. That was his only way of showing either of us any affection. Deep down, he may have loved us more than anything else in the world, but he had difficulty showing emotion.

"How you doing there, Bodacious?" Dad asked, smiling.

Bodacious was a nickname he started calling me over time. He also came up with one for Buster as well: Razzle Dazzle.

I couldn't have been happier to see Dad that day at the lawn mower shop. Anytime I saw him drive by on the way to one of his gardening jobs, I wanted to jump into the truck with him and go back to my real home. Dad must have been doing good business that day because he brought me inside the lawn mower shop and let me pick from a selection of used bicycles hanging up along the wall. I was smiling from ear to ear as the shop owner took down a nice Schwinn and wheeled it to where I was standing. After paying the $15 price, Dad and I went back out to the parking lot. Without another word I jumped on the bike and sped away down the street pedaling as fast as possible. I couldn't wait to make my way around the neighborhood and show all my friends what my dad had bought for me.

Not long after I received the bike, it got a flat tire. When I called Dad to ask him to help me fix it, he told me he didn't have the money. He was always losing whatever he made gambling, so it didn't surprise me in the least. But then a few mornings later, I walked out onto the porch to find my tire repaired. Not only that, but Dad also left a patch kit in case it happened again. That was his way of operating. When he was able to pull himself away from the booze, he was a good and responsible man. He didn't want to make a big deal out of the situation.

At first, Dad came over now and then, but those regular visits didn't last long. The guilt was just too much for him to handle. He had trouble recovering after the welfare people broke the three of us up, and without his boys together he slipped into a free fall. In many ways, I also began falling apart. I acted up in school and regularly found myself getting into trouble. What did everyone think was going to happen after being snatched away from my family? Not many nine-year-olds were going to react well to that. I ran away from the Wheelers' house a few times, but always returned at the end of the day. Overall, it was just an attempt to let out my frustration over the way things had turned out for me. Not until many years later did I realize that all of my acting out was basically an attempt to get attention. I just wanted to be back at home with Buster and Dad.

4

FINDING THE MUSIC

After a few months of living at the Wheelers' house, I realized how awful things were over at my dad's. Earlier in life, it was tough to know any better because I had nothing to compare to the way we were living. But now it was easy for me to see we were the poorest of the poor. And things continued to fall apart for Dad.

By the fall of 1956, Dad could no longer swing the $19-a-month mortgage payments and the bank went ahead and repossessed the house. From Washington and Twenty-sixth, he and Buster moved into a single, second-floor room in Mrs. McKay's boardinghouse on Twenty-ninth Avenue. The place was essentially the size of a large walk-in closet. When I came back to stay with them on the weekends, the three of us were back to sleeping in the same bed. A single bathroom was down the hall, which everyone in the building's four apartments shared, so there wasn't much privacy. Buster and I threw the football to each other in the hall and caused a real commotion. Anyone who wanted to get to the bathroom needed to navigate through, over, or around us.

No matter how many times people explained the concept, I still found it difficult to understand why I wasn't allowed to live with my dad and brother full-time. After I moved in with the Wheelers, I thought it was only going to be temporary. But as time moved on, circumstances weren't getting any better so I could go back to living with my family. We had been through so much together. We had already made it this far through countless horrible situations. I thought there wasn't anything we couldn't overcome. We got strength from being with each other. Apart, we all suffered and struggled to keep it together.

I'm not sure how Dad managed to wake up so early every morning to be on time for his landscaping jobs. It must have been close to impossible some days, but he was one of the most dedicated workers I've ever known. When he knew there was work, nothing was going to get in the way of his making it to a job site, rain or shine. He took us with him on the weekends whenever he needed extra help on his larger jobs. Together, we pruned trees, weeded lawns and gardens, picked up garbage and took it to the dump—basically, any odd job people had they called us for.

Little did I know the long chain of events that would be set in motion the day the three of us woke up one Saturday morning and set out to one of Dad's jobs in Madison Park, a rich, gated community at the northeast corner of Seattle on Lake Washington. The owner of the house, an old woman named Mrs. Maxwell, received a referral from a friend that Dad was a good gardener and odd-jobs man. She wanted us to come over and completely clean out her two-car garage, which was packed with old furniture and random junk—or what Mrs. Maxwell considered junk. We were surprised when we rolled the garage door up and discovered anything but garbage. Most of the items she kept stored were in good shape, and some looked as if they might even be valuable. My dad may have been a lot of things, but he wasn't dishonest when he was on the job. After looking over the contents of the garage, he knocked on the back screen door to the house.

"The job won't be a problem, Mrs. Maxwell," he told her. "We can take everything out and get it to the dump. But I was thinking, is it all right if we kept some of the things in there instead of trashing them?"

"As long as my garage is cleaned out, you can keep anything you want," she answered.

After getting permission, the rest of the day was like Christmas morning for Dad. Being a natural-born hoarder, every item, no matter how damaged or banged up, held some type of value in his mind. No matter what he found, he was convinced he could fix it and sell it for a decent profit. His place already resembled a small salvage yard, and his collection was only going to grow larger by the end of the day.

So, the three of us went to work. We spent most of the morning dragging everything out of the garage and tossing it into the bed of the truck. Although most of the stuff was set to go to the dump, Dad set aside many things. The crown jewel of his treasure hunt was a set of old Civil War rifles buried under a mattress in the corner, which he put in the truck's cab for safekeeping.

Around midafternoon, Dad jumped in his truck, declaring, "I have to go do something for a bit," and he would be right back. But Buster and I were all too familiar with that phrase. It usually meant Dad was taking a break to grab a cold beer. As he pulled out of the driveway, Buster and I kept digging through the garage, looking for that next piece of buried treasure. Before long, Buster walked out holding a beat-up ukulele. When he plucked at it a few times, a smile swept across his face. Being shy, Buster strolled around the backyard holding the ukulele down by his side. Although Mrs. Maxwell had already told Dad it was fine for us to take what we wanted from the collection of junk we were clearing out, Buster was still nervous about actually taking her up on the offer. It took him a while to work up the nerve to knock on the back door to the house to make sure it was truly okay.

"Yes, son?" she answered.

"Um, I was wondering, Mrs. Maxwell, would it be okay if I kept this? It was in with the rest of the stuff in the garage."

"Of course you can keep it."

Noticing that Dad had left to run an "errand," as she put it, Mrs. Maxwell invited us inside for lunch.

When Dad finally returned, he was very interested in the ukulele that Buster had found. "That's a nice instrument, boy. We'll be able to sell it and make some money."

"No way," my brother told Dad. "Mrs. Maxwell said I could have it."

"What are you gonna do with something like that?"

"I want to learn how to play it."

Dad didn't push it any further. The bottom line was that the ukulele was now Buster's, and no way was he going to give it up for sale. Besides, looking at the old, beat-up thing, you wouldn't think it was worth much. After all, it only had one string.

After Buster carried that old ukulele home, he messed around with it for hours and hours. Even though he didn't know much about music, he sat and plucked at the lone, slack string while watching it vibrate in place. It just flapped there like a loose rubber band, so it was tough to make out the low humming sound. Then a thought hit him. When he reached up and turned the tuning peg on top, the note went up in pitch and got louder. At that moment, it was as if something magical happened. The tone suddenly sounded musical and not like a loose wire flapping against the body of the ukulele. If Buster tightened it a little more, it got even higher and vibrated less. He began turning the tuning peg as he strummed to make the pitch go up and down. Even though he was playing single notes, he still followed along to a couple Elvis Presley songs on the radio. Buster did it all by ear and matched up the notes.

Music was in Buster from an early age. Back when we were spending a summer up at Grandma Nora's in Vancouver, I remember him crying to her that his ears hurt. "Grandma, Grandma, there's something in my ears," he would tell her. Grandma Nora usually heated up some baby oil, put a little on a cotton swab, and cleaned out his ears. Buster was hearing sounds, but he was afraid because he didn't know what they were. As he got older, he realized the noises in his head were song melodies.

My brother developed a unique sense of sound and was constantly searching and experimenting with tones. The ukulele was like a key that opened the door to another world. The search for complete expression began, and he was going to follow the path as far as it was going to take him. When the ukulele failed to hold his attention any longer, Buster got creative. He found anything he could to tie from post to post of the old cast-iron bed he, Dad, and I shared—strings, wires, even long rubber bands. As he plucked each one, they vibrated in place and made their own unique tone. Then he realized that if he didn't string them the entire length of the bed and only attached them between the bars at the foot of it, the pitch was ten times higher. This buzzing made the posts hum and vibrate against the bedroom floor. Not only could you hear the notes, you could feel them as they flapped against each other.

Mrs. McKay lived in a room at the opposite end of the hall and often watched Buster and me when our dad wasn't home. Like many of the other kind women we'd grown up around, Mrs. McKay took to us and didn't mind having us over every now and then. Each of us usually got a snack and then sat down on the living-room floor to watch her television. The giant, six-foot-high cabinet had about a four-inch screen in the middle. It wasn't even black-and-white; it was more like green-and-white because of the odd color. Dad was happy to have someone close who could watch over us when he was out.

In June of 1957, at the end of my third-grade year at Leschi, Mr. and Mrs. Wheeler contacted Mrs. Lamb at the welfare office to let her know they were interested in adopting me. She thought it was a decent idea until she spoke with my dad, who couldn't have been more against it. To him, the entire foster-care situation was only a brief detour for me. As soon as he got back on his feet, he intended to file the necessary paperwork to bring me back to stay with him and Buster. So, as the next school year quickly approached, I was moved from the Wheelers to live with a woman I called Mama Jackson. Almost immediately after I moved in, she started complaining to Mrs. Lamb. Mama Jackson had every right to complain because I was causing all sorts of trouble. My fights at the Harrison Grade School were getting to be routine. But for the time being she and I were stuck with each other.

While Dad and Buster were living at Mrs. McKay's and I was over at Mama Jackson's, I don't think any of us saw much of Mama. It was hard on Buster and me because Dad still never mentioned her name. On the rare occasions when he did bring her up, it was usually to get something negative off his chest. I was younger, so most of what he had to say went over my head, but Buster absorbed all of it full force. Despite that he absolutely hated Dad's talking bad about her, I never once saw my brother lash out. He hung on to all of those emotions and kept them bottled up inside.

When Dad did finally mention Mama, it wasn't because he had good news to share. One evening, he led Buster and me over to the foot of the bed and sat us down. "Your mama's not well and is in the hospital right now," he told us. "So, get cleaned up because we're going to go down to see her."

When the three of us went down to the government-run Harborview hospital on Ninth Avenue, we found our mama all the way down the dark, winding corridor, lying in a bed out in the hallway. She didn't even have her own room, and they left her by herself. The floor was overcrowded and patients were everywhere under the flickering fluorescent lights. The place was like a haunted house to me. A nurse came over and helped Mama out of her bed and into a wheelchair. Carefully, she pushed her over to where Dad, Buster, and I were standing along the wall. We hadn't seen her in a while, and she looked like a different person. Her body was draped in a white sheet and she looked tired. She told my brother and me that she was sick, but she would probably be okay once the doctors helped her. "I will see you next week," she insisted, trying her best to smile. Before the nurse wheeled her back toward her bed, Mama hugged and kissed us and told us how much she loved us. Buster and I looked on as her wheelchair slowly glided away down the dim corridor. Before she rounded the corner, Mama reached back and gave Buster and me a wave.

It was the last time we saw her.

About a week later, Dad sat us both down again at home and quietly explained that our mama had passed away. Just having turned ten years old, I didn't completely understand what that meant and figured we'd see her sometime soon anyway. I didn't cry at the time, but my brother was inconsolable. Nothing Dad tried to tell him provided him with any comfort.

On the day of our mama's funeral in early February of 1958, Dad cleaned us up as best as he could and drank heavily throughout the morning. When it came time to finally leave the house around midday, he was in bad shape. Buster and I were scared to death to hop into his truck with him behind the wheel, but we didn't have much of a choice. No matter what, it was important to both of us that we got a last chance to tell Mama good-bye. As we hit the streets, we yelled at Dad every time he started to swerve so we wouldn't go off the road and crash. It only got worse. Together, we drove around for what seemed like forever, turning down wrong streets and stopping to try to get directions to the funeral parlor. Before we knew it, the sun went down and we still hadn't made any progress. Buster was beside himself and cried his eyes out.

"Where's Mama?" he whined. "I want to see her!"

"Dad-gummit, Buster! Stop! I'm trying to find the place!" Dad yelled from behind the wheel.

Not until sometime around 8:00 p.m. did we make our way to Chinatown and finally pull into a Pentecostal church's parking lot. After Dad knocked on the broken-down, old building's front glass door, a man appeared dressed in a sharp black suit. He looked surprised to see us, almost panicked.

"May I help you, sir?" he nervously asked Dad.

"We're here for the Jeter ceremony," Dad told him.

Puzzled, the man remained staring off into the parking lot.

"You know, the Jeter wake," Dad added.

The man looked back at him. "I'm sorry, sir, but that service took place at two this afternoon," the man said gravely.

Dad didn't have much to say after the revelation. Stinking drunk, he brought his two boys to their mama's funeral six hours late. Buster was too angry to even look in his direction, and the three of us drove in silence for the entire ride home.

It typical fashion, Dad had what he considered the perfect answer for any day's problems. "Come here, boys. We're going to give a toast to your mama Lucille," he announced, pulling his bottle of Seagram's Seven from the cupboard. First, Dad led us in dropping down to our knees in the middle of the room and saying a prayer for Mama. When we stood up, he raised the bottle up in the air and looked at the two of us. His eyes were starting to tear up.

"This is to your mama," he remarked, pulling the bottle to his lips.

After a healthy swig, Dad passed the Seagram's to Buster, who reared back and also took a big slug. Then, Buster handed it to me to drink from. Aside from the leftover liquid in the bottom of empty beer bottles when I was only a toddler, the whiskey was my first exposure to alcohol. To this day, I've never forgotten the warm feeling that washed over me when the sweet taste of that Seagram's hit my system. Only one word came to my mind to describe the sensation: relief.

Not long after the night of giving a final toast to our mama, Buster and I started sneaking drinks from Dad's bottles here and there. Almost immediately, Dad was suspicious and figured something was up. He began marking the level on the bottle with a black pen, but that wasn't going to deter us from dipping into his stash. Whenever we finished, Buster simply put another line on the bottle so that it matched up with how much booze was left. By the time Dad noticed the level the next time he went looking for a drink, he didn't have any idea where the line was supposed to be. My brother and I looked on more than a few times as he pulled the bottle up close to inspect it.

"Damn," he'd mutter, shaking his head. After trying to recall if the current marked line was where it should be or not, he'd shrug the whole thing off and pour himself a drink anyway.

My brother's personality changed in many ways after our mama died. He became even more withdrawn and quiet whenever we were out in the neighborhood playing with our friends. I could tell he harbored a great deal of resentment for our dad. Buster placed most of the blame on him that things did not work out with Mama and, in some ways, probably even held him partly responsible for her death at such a young age. She was only thirty-two years old when she died.

Buster's anger never boiled over when Dad was around. He was only able to let out his frustration when we were alone together. "He is *not* our dad," he told me more than a few times. "Don't think that he is. Mama told me all about it. And now she is dead because of him."

My brother sometimes mentioned he had conversations with our mama about the situation while she was still alive. He said that she once came right out and told him that Dad was not our real father. Buster repeated this message to me many times over the years, but I didn't get many other details.

Much later in life when I was a grown man, my aunt Delores alluded to how my brother's real father may have been a man named Johnny Page. He supposedly had a brief thing with our mama at the same time she was going with our dad, and some said that the two of them continued to see each other while Dad was overseas in the army. Unfortunately, that was about as far as our conversations went. Aunt Delores didn't open up about the situation any further.

My brother never elaborated on what our mama ever specifically told him about Dad. Although Buster may have meant "He isn't our dad" in a literal sense, I also believe my brother was simply venting his frustration over how, in his mind, a true father would never treat his sons the way he was treating us at the time. Buster was holding Dad responsible not only for keeping us away from our mama while she was alive, but also for forcing her into an early grave.

Although at that point in my life, I usually believed whatever my brother told me, this time was a little different. As far as I was concerned, Al Hendrix was my father. He had been there since the beginning and was the only father I ever knew.

One day while Buster and I were staying at Mrs. McKay's for the afternoon, he found an old, beat-up Sears, Roebuck Kay acoustic guitar in the back room. Mrs. McKay had a young son who was in a wheelchair, and I guess he used to play it before he got sick. Who knows how long it had been sitting back there in that room? It had three rusted strings and a bent, warped neck. The glue was dried out and the panels of its wood body were literally coming apart at the seams. But for Buster, it was love at first sight. He'd already exhausted the options for his ukulele, and tying wires to the big brass bed wasn't holding his interest anymore either. For the first time in his life, Buster was holding a real guitar.

"Can I have this, Mrs. McKay?" he asked. "Please, please, please."

"I'll tell you what. I will sell that guitar to you for five dollars," she said. "And as soon as your father gives me the money, I'll let you have it."

Buster begged Dad as soon as he got back home to get it for him. But Dad wasn't having it. He was a strict disciplinarian from the Depression era. He thought playing music was a waste of time.

"I'm not buying no guitar for you, Buster," Dad told him. "You gotta learn to *work* with your hands, boy. We're in the fields every day, digging ditches, cutting grass, and taking trees down . . . that's what you need to do to make money. You got no business playing a guitar!"

Buster didn't know what to do because Dad was only giving him a dollar a weekend for helping him, and I was maybe getting fifty cents. It would take forever to save up the $5 Mrs. McKay wanted for the guitar. But maybe there was another way. Buster made sure to tell our aunt Ernestine about the beat-up guitar while we were at her house for Thanksgiving dinner. The more she heard of the story, the more interested she became. She clearly wasn't too happy with Dad for not at least trying to help Buster save up enough money. When she gave Dad a dirty look from across the table, he immediately became defensive.

"The bottom line is that I'm not buyin' no guitar for Buster," Dad explained. "I don't want him going down the wrong road."

His excuse was funny to me. It wasn't as if my brother and I were already busy going down the *right* road. I thought Dad was going to continue on with something even crazier like *I want my sons to learn the values of working hard out in the fields all day, drinking all night, and losing all their money gambling.* Aunt Ernestine couldn't believe what she was hearing. The two of them got into an argument right at the table over whether Dad would give Buster the money for the guitar. When he cussed at her, she became so enraged that she actually slapped him across the face. Buster and I watched in stunned silence. We had never seen someone stand up to Dad like that before. He didn't have much to say after that. It may not have been the proper thing to do, but Aunt Ernestine definitely shut him up. After she regained her composure, she went into her purse and brought something over to the table: a $5 bill.

"Here, Buster. Now, go buy yourself that guitar you want," she said, handing my brother the bill.

Our old man was fuming after that scene. Still, he didn't have much of a choice but to let Buster go down the hall to Mrs. McKay's and finally buy the guitar. Although Dad didn't prevent him, it didn't mean he was at all happy with the situation. However, he'd been overruled by Aunt Ernestine. He did everything he could to hold his tongue and allow Buster to do what he had his mind set on.

A couple of my brother's friends who had also started playing guitar took him down to the music store to get him a full set of catgut strings for seventy-nine cents. I was surprised to find out they weren't

actually made from cats. The name was short for "cattle guts" and
the strings were produced out of animal intestines. At that time they
used gut strings on classical guitars, and most of the flamenco-style
players preferred them. When the guys at the music store strung the
guitar up for Buster, they did it the traditional way, right-handed.

My brother had already been practicing his moves playing air
guitar with our dad's broom, so he couldn't have been more thrilled
to finally have the real thing. One of the very first licks he picked up
on his new acoustic was the theme song to the *Peter Gunn* television
show, probably because it could be played all on one string. To keep
me from bothering him, Buster literally tied a colored pencil around
my wrist with a string and sat me down with blank sheets of paper.
As he played, I colored and sketched for hours on end. Buster had
always been left-handed, so his natural tendency was to hold the
right-handed guitar upside down. Instead of the strings being from
low to high, everything was reversed for a while before he restrung
the guitar so he was able to play it left-handed. Still, our dad didn't
like any of it. He had a lot of superstitions about anything that wasn't
considered "normal." A lot of people did back in those days. To
him, being left-handed was like a sign of the devil. Not that our dad
should have been the one to judge anybody. He was born with six
fingers on each of his hands. Grandma Nora was a nurse, so she
knew how to get rid of the fingers. Back in those days you'd get a
swath of silk and tie it around the unwanted fingers, then every day
you'd tighten it. Eventually, it severed the finger and it fell off. But
my dad's ended up growing back, and he had little claws on the side
of his hands.

After leaving Mrs. McKay's boardinghouse, Buster and Dad lived
with Cousin Gracie and her husband, Buddy, for a short time on
1434 Pike Street at Twenty-ninth Street. As they made their move, I
was also making my way from Mama Jackson's house to stay with

another family, named the Dominics, who lived across the street from Meany Junior High on the outskirts of Seattle. Since their house was a few miles away from Dad's place, it was the farthest I'd ever been from them. Although my brother was off doing his thing with his friends and didn't stop by as much, the football team he played on, the Capitol Hill Fighting Irish, regularly came to Meany to play their games. So, I still got to see him once in a while.

While my brother and Dad were living at our cousin Gracie's, Cousin Bobby also came over to play once in a while. I noticed he was starting to treat Buster and me differently. For some reason, Bobby enjoyed making cruel comments about our mama. It was tough to understand where his anger was coming from, and it deeply upset me.

"Look at Leon. He's not your brother. He's from somebody else," Bobby teased the two of us one afternoon. "Your mama went out and had sex with another man, and then she had Leon."

It was shocking to me that Bobby, whom we were always close with, would talk about our mama in such a way. His harshness was too much to take and I couldn't help but start crying.

"I'm telling Dad!" I yelled.

Nobody talked about our mama and got away with it. I couldn't stand it any longer and ran out. Buster tried to stop me from leaving the room, but when he grabbed for me, I lost my balance and fell headfirst into the doorknob. My eye instantly swelled up to the size of a golf ball.

Later, my brother explained to Dad that I fell while we were messing around and playing. He decided to leave out the comments Bobby had made about our mama.

Dad placed one of his big hands on the side of my head and surveyed my swollen eye. "Well, you've got many, many bumps still coming in life, son. You'd better get used to them."

The incident over at our aunt Gracie's that night pretty much marked the end of my brother's relationship with Bobby. He wasn't going to forgive Bobby for what he'd said. They were distant and rarely spoke to each other from that time on.

In the spring of 1958, Dad and Buster moved from Cousin Gracie's to a house on College Street where Aunt Ernestine and her husband, Cornell, lived. Since their last name was Benson, my brother and I called him "Uncle Ben." Aunt Ernestine was kind enough to let Dad and Buster stay with her while Dad attempted to get his act together . . . again. No matter what happened, he still never learned his lessons about drinking or gambling. It was bad enough that he routinely fell into the darkness of alcoholism, but his gambling could flush his entire week's paycheck away in an evening. And that happened more often than he would have liked. So, he and Buster moved into Aunt Ernestine's back garage in the Beacon Hill area. Again, I was back to sleeping in the same bed with Buster and Dad from Friday to Sunday. By then, it was winter, so we had to huddle together to keep warm. We had one heater to share among the three of us, so we'd take turns hugging the thing.

"Goodness, Al, how can you live this way?" Aunt Ernestine would ask him. "You've got to wash these sheets here!" Her criticism typically fell on deaf ears, and eventually she stripped the bed herself and threw the sheets in the laundry machine.

Since Aunt Ernestine owned a record player and a stack of records, my brother and I listened to plenty of blues over at the house. Suddenly, the Top 40 didn't seem as important when we had Muddy Waters and Robert Johnson songs to look forward to. Buster particularly liked Robert Johnson because he was a raw and passionate guitarist and singer. Johnson didn't play perfect chords on the guitar, and the recording wasn't clean and polished. It was dirty and soulful. Although Buster got hooked on the blues, he still had a pop-music foundation from listening to the Top 40 radio shows for all of those years when we were younger. Now, when he strummed along to songs such as Elvis Presley's "Hound Dog," "Blue Suede Shoes," and "Heartbreak Hotel," they had a unique type of swing to them. The same went for the Buddy Holly and Chuck Berry songs he loved to play. Buster pieced together different elements of the white pop music and the black soul and blues sound. I recognized the songs from the radio, but the way he was playing them was a cross between the genres.

The acoustic guitar did the trick for a while, but as Buster started hanging out with other guys who were starting bands or already playing with groups, it wasn't working out. Everyone else he tried to play with had electric guitars and amplifiers. No way was his beat-up Kay acoustic going to be able to cut it in that kind of company. If he was going to continue with his interest in music, my brother was going to need to get himself a real electric guitar.

JOINING BANDS

When Aunt Ernestine's landlord came over one day in the early spring of 1959 for a routine inspection of the house, he wasn't too thrilled to discover Dad and Buster shacking up in the back room. Without much further discussion, he let Auntie know they needed to move out immediately. Luckily, Dad put together just enough cash from the regular landscaping jobs he was working to move into a dilapidated second-floor studio apartment at 1314 East Terrace on Seattle's First Hill. Together, the three of us lived in some really run-down dwellings over the years, but the new apartment was on a whole other level. The building was crawling with cockroaches, and Terrace Street was a complete slum. I always called it "ghetto beyond ghetto." People wandered around on the streets at all hours of the night, drinking and fighting. Prostitutes stood on the corners and worked out of a house at the end of the block. You didn't want to be caught hanging out on the street at night if you knew what was good for you.

The apartment was almost directly across from the city's juvenile-court building, which I started visiting every now and then. I was often hanging out on the streets and causing trouble. They called me "incorrigible" and at one point wanted to send me off to juvenile hall. Mrs. Lamb tried her best to explain that what she had in mind was moving me to some sort of Catholic boys school. At the beginning of my fifth-grade year, she drove me out to what was then called the Briscoe School in south Seattle. From the moment I set eyes on the place, it was easy to see that it was basically a juvenile prison. But Mrs. Lamb was well aware of the troubles I was having in school and thought a change would be good. However, I took one look at the place and knew it wasn't for me. I wanted no part of the scary brick building, the students dressed in uniforms, and the dormitories. About halfway through the tour, I started crying like a baby and made a run for Mrs. Lamb's car in the parking lot. As far as I was concerned, she couldn't get me out of there fast enough.

Once the Briscoe School was out of the running, the next stop on my foster-care tour was the home of Mrs. Magwood, a kind old lady who lived over on Twenty-fourth and Olive Street in the Central District. I was thrilled to be living with Mrs. Magwood, not only because she was a nice woman, but also because instead of being a few miles away from Dad's house at the Dominics, her home was about eight blocks from his rattrap apartment on East Terrace.

At the end of work every day, Dad brought all of his gardening equipment up into the room so nobody could steal anything from the bed of his truck. The entire apartment was wall-to-wall gasoline fumes and the reek of damp grass. At first, it was tough to deal with the stench, but I somehow got used to it. After a few weekends, it was difficult to even notice the gas fumes. Thankfully, Buster and I didn't spend much time there anyway.

Since my brother got off to a later start with music than many of the other guys in the area, at first he found some trouble breaking into the local musical circles and finding a band that wanted him to join. The first time I ever saw Buster play along with other musicians was when he and I walked over to an old black man's apartment one Saturday afternoon. After the guy set up a microphone and a little portable recorder on a table, they both jammed on a few Muddy Waters songs. When they finished, the three of us sat together and listened to the recording in the old man's living room. I wasn't sure what to make of it, but the old man seemed pretty pleased with the way the finished version came out. It was the first recording my brother ever made, and I could tell by the look on his face that he was as happy as ever.

Buster hooked up with the old black man again when he was invited down to a shack they used to call the Little Red Rooster in Renton, Washington. The tiny joint had a woodstove in the middle of the room to keep everyone warm in the winter. We walked to the place one night out on Empire Way, which is now called Martin Luther, and Buster joined a group of older musicians for a little jam session. His acoustic was fine in the shack because nobody else was playing with electric amps. Most of the older players were drawn to him and recognized his talent from the beginning. While they supplied the jams with soul and character, my brother contributed a raw energy many of the old-timers hadn't seen before. Even though he was soon veering off on tangents when he played lead, they still wanted to include him. That the older musicians took a liking to my brother and inspired him to play more was nice because early on it was difficult for him to speak up. No way on his own was he going to ask the guys if he could play with them again.

One afternoon, Mrs. Magwood told me to go into the backyard and pick some mustard greens from her garden. She asked that I deliver them to a friend of hers, Mrs. Penniman, whose house was two blocks up the street. When I arrived, I spotted a shiny black limousine parked out front. As I passed by the lowered rear window, I stopped in my tracks and found myself face-to-face with none other than her nephew, Richard Penniman, also known as the famous rock star Little Richard. At first, it was tough to recognize him in his white tank top and tight do-rag. But there was no mistaking who he was once I saw his face. I was blown away. Buster and I watched Little Richard on television all the time and were huge fans of his music. We ran around the apartment singing his songs "The Girl Can't Help It" and especially our favorite, "Lucille." Along with Elvis, Little Richard was one of our idols. It turned out Mrs. Penniman was Little Richard's aunt.

I wasted no time jumping on my bike and pedaling the four blocks to my dad's place to tell Buster. He was strumming his acoustic when I exploded through the door and yelled, "Little Richard is over at Auntie's house!" Before he had the chance to second-guess what I was telling him, I pulled him out the front door and led him over to his bike. Together, we made our way back to Mrs. Penniman's, so Buster could meet Little Richard as well. I knew my brother would be thrilled to be face-to-face with a genuine rock-and-roll star. Buster and I remained wide-eyed, watching Little Richard make his way around Mrs. Penniman's kitchen cooking up ham hocks and the mustard greens I'd brought by the house earlier. Just before we left, Little Richard was nice enough to also give us each an autographed photo.

Later that afternoon, Buster and I dressed up in our church clothes, our Sunday best, and went down to the Goodwill Baptist Church at Fourteenth and Spring to see Little Richard address the congregation. We arrived to find the building packed with parishioners and only found room standing at the back. Everyone wanted to catch a glimpse of the famous rock star. The word going around was that

Little Richard was dead set on retiring from rock and roll and becoming a preacher. The entire church hung on his every word as he pranced around the pulpit hooting and hollering about the almighty power of the Lord. He explained that he had recently had a vivid dream in which a diamond-encrusted airplane he was flying in crashed to the ground. When he woke up the following morning, he said he had a feeling that rock and roll wasn't going to be his ultimate destiny. It was clear as day to him that God was telling him he needed to become a preacher.

"Woo woo!" Little Richard shouted toward the end of his sermon, raising his arms over his head. "Amen, my brothers and sisters!"

The congregation erupted, spilling out into the aisles while also holding their hands up to the heavens above. "Amen! Praise God!" they yelled.

Buster and I also attended Little Richard's sermon the next evening, and it was a similar experience. For two nights, he turned the regular church service into a big event. Seeing a genuine rock-and-roll star had a lasting effect on my brother and inspired him to continue on his musical journey. He had already been getting together with other guys in the neighborhood to play, and meeting Little Richard only motivated him more to get out and work on his music. My brother jammed in the neighborhood with anyone who knew or didn't know how to play.

The guys in the bands recognized my brother was good, but he definitely made even more of an impression on them after that evening. Soon, they began inviting him out to other gigs and practice sessions. Since Dad put him in charge of me on the weekends, I tagged along. Sometimes we'd walk miles together to get to a spot where a group was jamming.

By that time, Buster had his mind set on one thing: electricity. He was through trying to strum ridiculously hard to keep up with the amplified instruments in the groups. Once in a while, one of the other guys would lend him equipment to play on for a few minutes, but then it was right back to his old acoustic. From weekends of working with Dad, my brother was able to save up a few bucks, and together we went down to Seattle Music to see what was available. The salesclerk told us an electric pickup was for sale, but my brother would have to wire it up by himself. Buster didn't think there was anything he couldn't do with his guitar, so he went ahead and bought the pickup.

The run-down guitar became his personal science project, although when he brought the electric pickup home, getting the thing to work was a bit harder than he expected. He needed to punch the holes in the guitar's body with an awl because we didn't have a drill. The holes were too large for the screws, so he wrapped tape around the pickup to try to hold it down to the guitar's body, which didn't work all that well. It was loose underneath the strings and flapped around every time he moved it. Extra wires also poked out of the side. If Frankenstein were a guitar, Buster would have been playing it. But the most important thing was that *it worked*. Now he finally had his pickup together, but nothing to plug it into. No way was he going to be able to scrape enough cash together for an amplifier. Those things cost big money, and Buster could barely afford the pickup.

As in many times of desperation while we were growing up, he got creative. Dad had an old record player sitting in the corner of the apartment on which he listened to his rhythm-and-blues records. Somehow, Buster cut in on the signal coming from the needle on the record and switched it so the speakers picked up the signal coming from the pickup on his guitar. Presto—he had a guitar amp. Well, sort of. He needed a little assistance from me to make it work. Since we didn't have a soldering gun, he tried to tape down the wires in the back of the record player. It wasn't even called duct tape back then; it was called general tape. But it wasn't doing the job and the wires kept disconnecting and cutting the signal.

"Come here, Leon," Buster told me, kneeling down next to the record player. "I need you to hold that black wire down on this connection right here." After showing me what to do, he walked over and grabbed his guitar, leaning against the wall. But there was a problem—when I made the connection, an electric shock surged up my arm. Although sound came booming through the speakers at first, it cut out as soon as I let go of the wires.

"This thing is hurting my hand," I complained.

"Come on now, make sure you push on it good," Buster told me.

I was as excited as my brother to try to make the thing work. On the next attempt, I buckled down and put up with the sharp pain. Our eyes met as soon as the first blast of sound came booming out of the stereo. For the first time ever there was an electric guitar in the Hendrix household. When Buster reared back and hit another chord on his guitar, the speakers started crackling and buzzing. Not only did we have an electric guitar going on, but we also had *distortion.* The signal coming from the pickup was too much for the tiny speakers to handle. The sound may have been muddy and muffled, but at least it was amplified. After kneeling next to the record player holding the wire connection for a while, I must have gotten used to the shock because it didn't even bother me anymore. Looking back, I guess you could say I was my brother's first guitar tech.

Unlike the time Buster took apart Dad's beloved radio while trying to "find the music," he didn't have a problem reassembling the stereo so it was in perfect working condition once again. Dad never knew the difference. Over the next few weekends, converting the stereo to a guitar amplifier became a routine after Dad left for the day.

Buster knew that his raggedy acoustic wasn't going to do the job if he intended on getting into a legitimate band. The thing was already half beat to death when he bought it from Mrs. McKay, so there was no use in sinking any more money into it. So it was time to get a true electric. But when Buster asked Dad about helping him get a new guitar down at Seattle Music, he got a familiar answer— "Oh, *hell no!*" Dad wasn't having it. In his mind, getting the acoustic guitar in the first place was bad enough. In no way did he want to do anything else to point Buster in "the wrong direction," as he put it. But as time passed, he became more and more used to Buster and his playing. Dad was smart enough at the end of the day to recognize he didn't have much choice in the deal. My brother was sixteen years old and going to do what he wanted anyway. So, Dad continued to talk a big game about playing guitar being no good and bands being pointless, but he still forced himself to go along with the program in some ways. Although he wouldn't go right down to the music store and help Buster get an electric guitar, he did give him an opportunity to earn money toward one.

Around the beginning of the summer of 1959 Buster eventually saved a little money, and Dad took us down to the Sears store on the south side of Seattle near our mama's old place to see what was available. After we checked out a guitar in the music section of the store, the salesman filled us in on the deal.

"What we can do is have you put a down an initial deposit and then put together a payment plan over the course of—"

"Naw, naw, naw," Dad interrupted, shaking his head. He had already been drinking, and suddenly he wasn't interested in anyone trying to work a deal for him. Nothing was going to make him happy in his current the state of mind. No matter what arrangements or payment plans the salesman came up with, Dad would still have believed the guy was trying to screw him in some way. Dad was always much more agreeable when he wasn't drinking. As soon as he started with his Seagram's Seven, he became edgy and irritable. Getting him to do anything was difficult.

"Sorry, but we can't do it, Buster," Dad said, leading us out of the department store.

The trip to the store was a real letdown for my brother, and neither of us thought Dad, after that day, would ever let Buster continue to follow his passion for music. But after a week or two passed, Dad did reconsider the situation. For all of the times when our dad was at his worst, he did have his shining moments. On some rare occasions, he surprised even us. To me, it was his true personality shining through in the moments when his drinking wasn't clouding his judgment. One night, as the three of us were sharing a big pot of Dad's spaghetti, Buster said that his beloved Kay acoustic had finally fallen apart. The guitar was unplayable and the other guys didn't want to lend him their guitars any longer. That's when one of those magical moments came, catching both my brother and me off guard.

"Well, you know, Buster, I was thinking," Dad suddenly piped up, "why don't the three of us go down to Myer's Music tomorrow and see what they've got down there." Both my brother and I perked up. Dad sure sounded serious, but we could never be sure. He'd say something one second, then do a complete turnaround and tell us to forget it the next. Not to mention, he had already taken my brother through the motions during our trip to Sears, then backed out at the last minute. But this time was different. Dad continued, "And maybe we can take a look for one of those guitars you've been talking about. Besides, I've been wanting to get myself a saxophone."

Somewhere in the back of his mind, Dad probably realized there was no stopping his boy. Buster was beginning to play regular gigs with bands and it took up most of his time. Dad had to get on board with what Buster was doing or get completely out of the way. Nothing he did or said was ever going to change Buster's mind about playing in a band. And although Dad didn't want to acknowledge it, it was close to impossible not to recognize what kind of talent Buster had for the guitar.

The next afternoon, we did as planned and made the trip down to Myer's Music. The new Kay electrics at Sears, Roebuck were around $29.95, but a Supro Ozark model at Meyer's was on sale for $15. Buster's eyes lit up as soon as he caught sight of the light gray, almost-champagne-colored guitar. Dad rented a saxophone, just as he'd said he would. I don't know exactly what possessed him to go for a saxophone, but he told us that he'd wanted to play either the saxophone or the trumpet all of his life but never had the opportunity. Go figure. It was news to Buster and me. There was only one problem: Dad didn't have enough money to pay for both instruments outright. So, he decided to put $5 down on Buster's electric to hold it and told the salesman we'd be back as soon as we had the rest of the money. It was a letdown for Buster not to be walking out of the store with his guitar that day, but he hoped we'd be back for it before long.

When we returned to the music store around a week later, the salesman cleaned up the guitar for Buster and outfitted it with a gleaming set of new strings. From the moment the guy handed the guitar to him, Buster didn't put it down for literally a week. He was already wailing away on the ride home in the front seat of dad's truck. Although the salesman had strung it right-handed for my brother, he quickly changed the string arrangement to lefty when we got back to the apartment. That night, he went to sleep with it resting on his chest, and when he woke up the next morning, he picked up right where he'd left off. It was as if sleeping were only a pause in some long, continuous song he was playing. As for Dad, he couldn't play a lick on his saxophone. My brother obviously got his musical talent from Mama's side of the family. When we set off for the bus stop, he slung it over his shoulder and took it with him to school. He never put that thing down and carried it around the house with him at all times. When inspiration hit him, my brother wanted to be ready with his guitar at hand.

Spirits were always important for Buster and me. For both of us, *inspiration* meant "in the spirit." Divine influences came over us without any notice at all. One second nothing, then *bam*, a spirit came upon us. We had to move, to write, to jump, or to run. These impulses presented us with an immediate direction, a starting point, then drove us to spontaneously create something, push something out of our souls. The last thing Buster wanted was for that spirit to come upon him and not to have his instrument, his beloved champagne Supro Ozark electric, ready to translate the messages it was sending. That's why he carried it with him day and night. He wasn't channeling those strong signals into his drawings of battlefields and sports scenarios any longer. His instrument became the main tool for his inventiveness. He knew he had to be ready when the sensations hit because they aren't something that run on a schedule. The spirits function much like the wind and are gone almost as fast as they come. Even God calls the wind a spirit. It is 100 percent real, but it has no body. It has no substance. Just as my brother would go on to write about how sweet music dripped through his fingertips, he wanted nothing more than to caress and touch music, feel it, and grab it as if it were material. If he focused hard enough and harnessed all of his spiritual energy, he was convinced he could actually make something extraordinary happen. So, whenever he felt the sensation coming on, he knew exactly what to do—grab his guitar, sitting right by his side.

I always felt that music, notes and sounds, were also a part of my DNA. After seeing Buster having so much fun playing around with his guitar, I asked Dad if I could get one, too. He looked at me as if I were crazy.

"Have you lost your mind?" he asked, rolling his eyes at me. "I already got one of you fools playing guitar, and there is no way I'm gonna let another one of you get one of those damned things!"

Many times, Buster and I would be sitting at the bus stop together while my brother strummed his guitar, and his friends would drive by and try to get him to come with them.

"Come on, Buster. Let's go have some fun. We're ditching school," they'd say.

But my brother wouldn't even answer them. He'd just sit there with a determined look on his face as he picked at the strings of the guitar. His mind was always somewhere else when he had his hands on that electric. Kids were looking to break him out of his musical trance. None of them liked being ignored, but nothing they tried was going to change his attitude. For him, the rest of the world wasn't even there.

From around that time forward, I barely saw my brother pick up a pencil to draw, jog out onto a football field, or step onto a baseball diamond. He dropped all of his other interests because he'd finally found the thing he had been looking for his entire life. His guitar was going to allow him to express his deepest emotions and feelings he never talked about. It was going to allow him to release the anger that he kept inside. All of the powerful emotions he couldn't bring himself to speak of in conversations, he would express on his guitar.

After moving on from Washington Junior High School, Buster began tenth grade at Garfield High School at the beginning of September 1959. But now that his focus was on music, he didn't have much interest in school. Before long, he started getting together to play with a few guys in the neighborhood, among them his friend Pernell, who also played guitar, and a saxophone player named Luther Rabb. They called themselves the Velvetones and were a ragtag band whose lineup changed from week to week. The band started gigging regularly at a club called Birdland up on Madison and

Twenty-second Avenue and also played some Friday nights at the Yesler Terrace Field House in the Yesler projects. I was especially thrilled to tag along to the band's practice sessions on the weekends because the boys' mamas cooked me tasty meals such as fried chicken and corn on the cob upstairs while the boys practiced downstairs in the basement.

Dad ranted constantly about my brother's playing every time I was back at the apartment. He'd thought the guitar would be nothing more than a passing hobby for Buster, but that wasn't turning out to be the case. The band's weekly practices and gigs were also getting on his last nerve. Dad often cursed the day he'd taken us down to Myer's Music and bought my brother an electric guitar. Every time he saw my brother strumming along to a record at home, he had something negative to say. It was all in keeping with Dad's split personality on the issue. He helped Buster get the guitar in the first place, but worked himself into a rage every time he saw him actually play it. Dad wanted him to concentrate more on the landscaping work he was doing with him on the weekends and the *Seattle Post-Intelligencer* paper route Buster had picked up. In his mind, they were far more important.

"You need to *work* with your hands, boy!" he snapped at Buster more than a few times.

One day our dad came home early and Buster popped up from the couch to show him what he and the guys were working on all day. He didn't get more than a few notes into his guitar lick when Dad exploded.

"What did I tell you, boy?" Dad said sternly. "I don't want to see no left-handed playing in this house! It's the sign of the devil!"

Dad lunged forward and slapped my brother across the head in front of all of his friends. The rest of the band quickly filtered out of the apartment and went home.

My brother also got a steady girlfriend named Betty Jean Morgan, who also went to Garfield High School. She was the love of his life, and the two of them were together constantly. Sometimes I tagged along with him when he visited her at her house on Twenty-ninth and Yesler, which he would later refer to as the Red House, even though it was brown. While he and Betty Jean spent time together, her mama cooked me the most amazing fried chicken, potatoes, and gravy. And if the delicious meals weren't enough, Betty Jean also had a pretty little sister named Mattie B, whom I became interested in. Before long she and I also started going with each other. My brother and I began spending most of our free time on the weekends over at their place.

Once other musicians in the city saw Buster play out in the clubs, they regularly came at him with offers to join their band. They promised more money and free guitar equipment if he made the change. So, at seventeen years old, my brother moved on to play with a group called the Rocking Kings, which was also made up of high school kids around the area. The group wore a uniform of black slacks, white shirts, and black ties. But most important was their signature red suit coat. Buster pulled together the rest of the costume, but had trouble scraping together the cash for the coat. When Dad offered to pay him $5 for a day's worth of landscaping work on the weekend, my brother didn't have much of a choice. With Dad's unexpected help, my brother went to Wilson's clothing store that Saturday afternoon and returned home with the jacket, just in time for a gig the band was playing that night.

Since my brother still didn't have an amplifier, a few of the guys in the band lent him an extra speaker to play through. It was a single speaker that he wired together so that he was able to plug a guitar cord into it. Buster even took some scraps of wood and constructed a box for it to sit in the way the rest of the guitar players had, so he

---

finally had his amplifier cabinet. It was an important accomplishment because things weren't miked in the clubs back in those days. There weren't any PA systems and mixing boards to even out the sound, so a band had to work ridiculously hard to sound good. If Buster didn't have a decent amplifier, he was left out of the mix no matter how hard he played.

As usual, I was expected to stay in my foster home during the week and attend school daily, but on the weekends I tagged along to the Seattle clubs with Buster. Dad was usually nowhere to be found and held Buster responsible for looking after me. The welfare department knew nothing about our Friday- and Saturday-night activities because if they had, they would immediately have put a stop to them. The other band members knew I was part of the package and didn't seem to have a problem with having me around for the gigs. The band kept busy and played at such venues as the Encore Ballroom, the Washington Theater, Parker's West and South, the Spanish Castle, the Black and Tan, the 410 Supper Club, and of course Birdland, the place bands played when they had finally hit it big in the Seattle music scene. Nightly, they ran through rhythm-and-blues covers of such songs as "Let the Good Times Roll," "Charlie Brown," "Yakety Yak," and "Do You Wanna Dance?"

Not long after joining the band, Buster's guitar was stolen when he left it backstage after a gig at Birdland. When he told me, he was sick over it. Not only had he lost his most prized possession, but he also knew he was going to get a good whupin' when he finally told Dad what happened. I'd never seen him so unhappy. Without his guitar and music, it was as if the world were crashing in around him.

But all was not lost. With the small amount he made from landscaping on the weekends and some money given to him by a few of his bandmates, Buster was able to buy himself a Danelectro Silvertone with a matching amplifier down at Sears, Roebuck for $49.95. Everyone could see my brother was a tremendously gifted guitarist and musician, but he had trouble fitting in. Buster raised eyebrows when he painted his new white guitar red and attached a few eagle feathers to its body. He even took the tiny gold tassels off our dad's bottles of Seagram's Seven Crown whiskey and used them as decorations. Every time I saw him with his guitar, it looked completely different. I could almost hear the other members of the Rocking Kings asking themselves, *How does all this fit into a* soul *act?* Buster was like a hippie before anyone even knew what a hippie was. The rest of the band was constantly trying to reel him in, but there was no use. Buster may have been a background player wearing the same red sport coat and dress slacks as the rest of the band, but it was impossible to keep him in the background.

In the early summer of 1960, Dad and my brother finally moved from the ramshackle Terrace Street apartment to a small house at 2606 East Yesler Way. By then, I'd made my way from Mrs. Magwood's house to live with the Steele family and also moved on from Horace Mann School to enter Washington Junior High School. Dad pleaded with Mrs. Lamb at the end of the year to move me as close to him as possible because he was having trouble keeping his '36 Lincoln truck running. So, she placed me with Aunt Mariah Steele, who lived only a block away. Despite living the closest I'd ever lived to my family, I was still as unhappy as ever and caused trouble at every chance. Mrs. Lamb even sent a psychiatrist over to the Steeles' home shortly after I arrived to examine me.

"What's wrong?" the woman plainly asked.

"*What's wrong?*" I repeated. "Buster and my dad are living right down the street a block away and I am stuck in this place. All I want to do is go home."

"You have to understand that your dad can't take care of both of you boys right now. Unfortunately, this is how it has to be right now and you are going to have to accept it."

But I never came close to accepting it in the past and certainly wasn't going to anytime soon.

Inspired by my brother, I wanted to put something together for Washington Junior High School's annual talent show. So, I raced up the block to Dad's house one afternoon to ask my brother if I could borrow his guitar. He rarely let anyone else play it, and I wasn't sure he would go for the idea, but luckily I caught him when his mind was elsewhere. When I walked into the apartment, his door was closed and he and Betty Jean were messing around in the bedroom. When I lightly knocked on the door, he cracked it open enough so he could look out at me. If Betty Jean weren't there, I'm not so sure my brother would have let me take his guitar. Buster simply wanted to get me out of the apartment as soon as possible.

I finally got my chance to be just like my big brother the next day at the school talent show when I strutted up onto the stage and did my best air guitar as Chubby Checker's "Twist" played in the background. I didn't have a clue of how to play a single lick of the song, but I sure looked pretty cool strumming along. The rest of the kids loved it because few of them had ever seen an electric guitar before. I made sure to return Buster's guitar to him on my way home from school because he needed it for band practice that night. Thanks to my brother, I was the hit of the school talent show. In the back of my mind, I thought there might even be a future in music for me as well.

FROM THE ROCKING KINGS
TO THE ARMY

In the summer of 1960, the Rocking Kings continued to gig around the city and made frequent trips to the military bases to play many of the officers' clubs. The government built fifty or so forts after World War II started because everyone thought Japan was going to invade the country. The band hit every one of the five major locations in the Seattle area, everything from McChord Air Force Base to Fort Lawton.

In addition to the military installations, there was also Washington Hall on Thirteenth and Yesler, not far from where our mama lived. This black rhythm-and-blues joint was rarely packed for the band's gigs, but was a good venue nonetheless. The Encore Ballroom was similar and packed with pimps, prostitutes, and low-level drug dealers. When I was in the clubs, I had to stay backstage and keep out of sight because they were selling alcohol out front. There would be big trouble if I wandered out there because I was only twelve years old.

As time passed, more and more club workers recognized me and didn't have a problem sneaking me in through the back door of their establishments. They'd take me into the kitchen and fix me some real tasty chitlins, which are stewed pig guts, with mashed potatoes and hot sauce. There definitely weren't any hot dogs or hamburgers around. It was more like ham hocks and mustard greens. "Here come those Hendrix brothers," the bouncers would say as soon as we showed up together with the band in tow.

Sometimes after the band went on to perform, I curled up and fell asleep under the stage. I became so used to the blaring rock-and-roll music that my brother needed to wake me up to let me know it was time to leave. I was that oblivious to it all. My brother wasn't always happy having to drag me along with him during his weekend gigs. He was simply trying to play his music and get girls, so I'm sure I was cramping his style most of the time. After the gigs, he would get especially mad if he needed to search for me once the band made their way offstage and finished packing their equipment. I tended to wander off.

Eventually, I tried to dress a little classier and make my way around the clubs as the band played. Well, as classy as I could considering I didn't have much for clothing. I made an attempt to blend in and took a shot at picking up girls, but I was obviously only a kid. Most of the girls who went to the clubs didn't pay me much attention at all. I was going to have to wait a few more years for that time to come.

My brother, on the other hand, got plenty of interest from girls. I used to walk alongside him for miles out in the suburbs so he could go see girls he was into. One time, we must have walked around seven miles out to a girl's house and seven miles back. When we got there, Buster disappeared in through the bedroom window around the side of the house, and I sat on the lawn staring up at the stars in the night sky. When he was done, he popped out of the window and we made our way back home. It must have taken us almost three hours. I hadn't hit puberty yet and couldn't understand why we were going through all this trouble just so he could hang out with girls. And, boy, did they love my brother.

My brother may have been only seventeen years old, but he was more experienced on his electric guitar than many other players. We showed up to some of the Rocking Kings practices and he tore the roof off the place. It was almost as if the rest of the guys were getting in his way. I preferred listening to my brother play by himself. Buster knew every lick of each song by heart. Practice? He'd been doing that for long enough. When he got up in front of people, he *performed*, whether it was for an audience only of fellow band members or a packed house down at the Encore Ballroom.

Once he began insisting on dressing a little different from everyone else and making weird sounds come out of his amplifier, the rest of the band could see there was no need for him to be sitting in on the regular practice sessions. If inspiration hit Buster in the middle of a song, he veered off on an improvised tangent, exploring other ranges of notes and tones. The other guys were only coloring inside the lines as far as he was concerned. Every opportunity for my brother to play music was a chance for him to go outside himself. I could understand where the other guys in the band were coming from; when you got a full blast of Buster's feedback and improvised licks for an entire practice session, it messed with your mind. Even back at that time, Buster had already moved on to some other level and left them far behind.

"Listen, Buster, we don't really need you at practice anymore. The other guys are the ones that need the practice," the group's manager, James Thomas, told him one day. "So, you don't need to show up during the week. Just make the gigs on Friday and Saturday, and then come Sunday, you're fired," he told my brother with a smile.

As my brother gigged with the Rocking Kings throughout the city at different venues, he stopped showing up for his classes at Garfield High School. Dad started getting word from the high school office that Buster was missing classes regularly. So, Dad sat him down and had a few talks with him about it, but nothing Dad said was going to make any difference. I heard rumors also of an incident with a white girl Buster started spending time with. I guess the principal and a few of the teachers didn't like to see them together in the hallways and caught them holding hands once in the back of a classroom. When it came right down to it, Buster was done dealing with the hassle of high school. He didn't see any future for himself in organized education. Neither my brother nor I were ever interested in school. It never seemed to hold our interest because we were always focused on experiencing more than the teachers were offering. Besides, he had his band, and in his mind that was all he needed. My brother continued ditching class, and in late October of 1960, not more than a month before his eighteenth birthday, he officially dropped out of Garfield High School.

Of the Rocking Kings' many gigs I tagged along to, I especially remember the first trip to the legendary dance hall the Spanish Castle Ballroom, in late 1960. The group's manager, James Thomas, drove the band out to the club in Kent, Washington, not far from the corner of Highway 99 and Des Moines Way, in his giant, green 1956 Plymouth Fury with long, exaggerated fins on the back. I was amazed by the design of that old car because it looked like a spaceship from another galaxy. Then again, it was probably the most fitting ride for us. Years later, after my brother wrote his song "Spanish Castle Magic," I often heard people remark that the club wasn't "half a day away" as he said in the lyrics. Everyone knew it only took about an hour to reach Kent from Seattle's Central District. However, what people didn't realize was that the trip *did* take half a day when the car you were riding in broke down. That is what happened while the band was on their way to the Spanish Castle. The car stopped running and we stood around for most of the afternoon waiting for it to be repaired.

After a rough patch of gigs, the Rocking Kings broke up, and their manager, James Thomas, put together a new act called Thomas and the Tomcats, which my brother also joined. Although he still had an opportunity to make money by playing in a band, Buster was getting tired of grinding it out. Not only were the long drives and late nights at clubs taking their toll on him, but Dad wasn't helping matters much either. He was all over my brother at every opportunity.

"I don't know why you're still wasting your time with this devil's business. What you need to do is come out on the job with me and earn an honest day's pay," Dad told him.

But if my brother had the ability to earn some money from playing music, he wanted no part of landscaping. No way was he going to make backbreaking yard work any part of his future. He certainly had no interest in working side by side with Dad every day. The two of them were already constantly at each other's throat, and they'd tear each other apart if they ever spent that much time together. My brother figured there had to be something better waiting out there for him. But there was also plenty of trouble waiting out on the streets if he wasn't careful.

I might have been used to getting into trouble, but my brother's personality couldn't have been more opposite. Although he was weary of people trying to pull him into bad situations, he sometimes found it hard to say no to his friends. At times he certainly made mistakes and followed along with the rest of the crowd. Fortunately, there weren't really violent gangs back then as there are today. It was mostly just groups of friends running around causing trouble and looking for a rush. The other guys put a lot of pressure on Buster to go out with them, and if he wasn't following along, they made fun of him. Instead of putting up a fight, he usually went with the flow.

One night, he and a few of his friends got the bright idea to break into Wilson's clothing store, which was a real mom-and-pop-type shop on Twenty-third and Union Street. They forced their way in after hours, grabbed a stack of shirts and a few pairs of jeans, and bolted out. The next morning, Buster felt so terrible about what he had done that he actually dragged himself back to the store and returned the clothing. The police came by the house but said that Mrs. Wilson, a nice old black woman, wasn't going to press charges, so Buster's good deed worked in his favor. Dad wasn't happy when he found out what had happened.

On May 2, 1961, Buster paid the price for running around with the wrong crowd of friends. I guess he was out joyriding with some buddies when the police pulled them over and discovered the car was stolen. They immediately arrested everyone and took Buster down to the juvenile detention center, which was directly across the street from Dad's old apartment on East Terrace. I got home from school one Friday afternoon to find Dad racing around the house looking for the keys to his truck.

"Your dad-gum brother," he started out, "I'm getting sick of you guys. Every time I come home from work I've got to deal with something because of you two!"

When my brother came home from the police station, he was worried about having to go to court the next week and finding out what sentence the judge was going to hand down. With the thought of possibly being locked up looming over his head, the army started looking like a sensible option. Now and then, Buster talked about wanting to join the military, and he often did drawings of wild battle scenes, tanks, and warplanes when he was younger. He also specifically mentioned his fascination with the special Screaming Eagle patch worn by the soldiers in the 101st Airborne Division.

When it came time for him to be sentenced, Buster agreed that instead of serving the two-year stint they were seeking, he would join the army. So, a week later, my brother officially signed up for the 101st Airborne. He'd been making regular trips down to the service office to talk the whole idea over with the recruiting officer. Dad thought Buster was only going to get into more trouble hanging around with the same old characters in Seattle and figured a stint in the army was the best thing for him.

The night before Buster was due to officially join the army, Buster, Betty Jean, Mattie B., and I went to a street dance in the central area of Seattle on Madison and Twenty-third. The girls dressed up in their short skirts, bobby socks, and saddle shoes, and I put on what I considered my best threads. Buster wore his stage getup because he and Thomas and the Tomcats were playing what was their last show together that night. It was a fantastic evening. After his gig, Buster asked Betty Jean to marry him and she said yes. Buster was on cloud nine. As soon as he finished his time in the army, he planned to return home and the two of them were going to get married.

The next morning, Dad, Buster, and I piled into Dad's truck and drove to the giant government building down on the waterfront. It was sad to see my brother go, but there was nothing for him in Seattle. He knew that it was time to move on and do something else with his life.

"Keep your head up, son," dad told him as we stood out on the sidewalk. "This is the best thing for you right now. Everything will be all right."

When the army took Buster in and moved him out to Fort Ord on Monterey Bay in California, it was one of the few times he'd ever traveled out of state. Other than living in Berkeley with Mrs. Champ when he was just a toddler and our summer trips to Vancouver to visit Grandma Nora, my brother and I had never traveled anywhere. After he was settled, he wrote a postcard telling Dad and me that the training was grueling but he'd made it down to California just fine.

It was tough not having my big brother around, but there was some good news. My case worker, Mrs. Lamb, dropped by the Steeles' house one evening to let me know that I was officially being released from the foster-care system and placed back into Dad's custody full-time. After more than four years of being constantly on the move, I was finally headed home sweet home to live with Dad again.

"I finally got rid of one of them and here comes the other one moving back in!" he hissed the first time I tested his patience. But Dad was only being dramatic. He loved having me living with him again . . . at first. Dad may have thought my brother was bad, but he didn't have a clue of what was coming down the pike with me.

A few months after Dad and I dropped Buster off at the recruiting center, he returned home on a one-week leave before he was due to ship out to Fort Campbell, Kentucky. Since he couldn't come up with the cash for a plane ticket, he was forced to take the bus back to Seattle. That trip alone burned up three of his seven leave days. So, instead of enjoying a full week at home, he only had four. The first time I caught sight of him in his carefully pressed army uniform and shined black shoes, I couldn't have been prouder. His hair was buzzed short, and all of his clothes were clean and neatly pressed. Since he was making $65 a month in the army, he was nice enough to give me a $5 bill and then take me out for a burger. I didn't see much of him for the rest of his leave because I was hanging out with my friends all over the city and he was spending time with Betty Jean. Before I knew it, he was back off to the army.

Dad was doing his best to keep his landscaping business paying the bills, but times were still tough. I had to beg him to get me a new pair of shoes before the new school year started. When he finally gave in and took me down to the Chubby Tubby store, he ended up buying me *brogans* of all things, which I absolutely hated. The shoes were more like an ugly ankle-high boot. They were durable and lasted forever, so I was going to be stuck with them for a long time. When Dad couldn't afford a winter coat for me, Aunt Ernestine came to the rescue and bought one.

Being thirteen years old, I was ready to go out and find a little job for myself after school each day in order to put some money in my pocket. I managed to find an opening at the local youth center doing odd jobs around the area. Most of the projects dealt with cleaning up the community. A couple weeks in, I started to notice another boy constantly staring at me. Apparently, he had already been working at the center for a year because his photo was posted on the wall as being an employee. At first, I was a little suspicious and kept an eye on him as he made his way around the community center. He walked with a limp and there was something wrong with his arm.

"Hey, what's your name?" I asked one afternoon.

"Joseph," he answered.

"Joseph what?"

There was an uncomfortable silence as he looked down nervously. "Joseph Hendri," he finally said.

It immediately clicked in my mind. The little kid standing in front of me was my younger brother. We hadn't seen each other in almost ten years.

"You know, I am your brother," Joe told me.

"I figured that," I said with a smile. "Man, you look just like my dad. Where'd you get "Hendri" from?" I asked.

"Well, I figured you guys got rid of me, so I got rid of the X." It was a response I felt he had been thinking about for a long time.

"Come on, Joe. Don't say, 'you guys.' I didn't have anything to do with it."

I was only a kid myself when Joe was sent away, and I barely escaped being put into the same foster-care system. My heart ached because I saw the pain in his eyes. Joe explained how the family he grew up with told him the Hendrix family had abandoned him. Nothing I said was going to erase what happened. There wasn't much I could offer other than my friendship.

Eventually, I let Dad know I had reconnected with Joe. He tried to pass it off like it was nothing, but I could see emotion welling up in him. He may have been able to hold back the tears that day, but things were different when the two of us were out for a drive a few weeks later and happened to spot Joe making his way along the sidewalk near the park.

"There's your brother right there, Leon," Dad said, pointing across the road.

"I know. Remember? I've been working with him," I said sarcastically.

Without another word, Dad pulled the truck over on the side of the street and popped the driver's-side door open. "I'm gonna go talk to him," he said.

I looked on as Dad jogged across the road and approached Joe. It was the first time they had been face-to-face since the day he put Joe into foster care. Their exchange didn't last long, and when Dad got back to the truck, he couldn't do anything to hold back the tears from streaming down his cheeks. He sat silently behind the wheel for a few moments before wiping his tears away with his hand.

"He don't want anything to do with me," he said quietly.

Joe and I didn't expect anything from each other and got along well while we worked together for the community center. I eventually stopped working in order to spend more time hanging out on the streets with my friends after school.

Not much changed in my schooling after I went back to live with my dad. It was a miracle if I made it to all of my classes at Washington Junior High. Instead of going home at the end of the day, I typically spent the night over at friends' houses. Some very kind families looked after me back then. Even though they sometimes didn't have enough food to feed their own families, I still got an equal portion at dinner each night.

Once Buster left, Dad had me take his place landscaping alongside him on the weekends. As I transitioned into being a teenager, I began noticing certain things about my appearance that didn't resemble any of Dad's features. The differences had never dawned on me when I was younger, but as I matured, they were getting more apparent. One day when I was working with my dad, a question popped up in my head.

"Why is my hair so much straighter than yours?"

"It's probably because you take after your mama," Dad explained. "Both you and your brother take mostly after her."

"But what about—"

Before I got another word out, Dad stopped me. He knew where the conversation was leading. "Listen, I am the only father you ever had." He looked me in the eyes. "And I am the only father your brother's ever had. So just stop talking. None of that matters now, boy."

"Okay, Dad."

"I'm serious, Leon. I don't want to hear another word about it from this second on."

It was true. He took care of us our entire lives and did the best he could. In his mind, there was absolutely no point in second-guessing the past and causing more confusion and problems in our lives.

At night, Dad brought me along with him to the pool halls, where I quickly became one hell of a pool player; actually, make that one hell of a pool *hustler*. Some kids were talented at sports and others were tremendously bright in school. My skill was in hustling. I didn't pick it; the lifestyle almost seemed to choose me. I guess it shouldn't be too surprising to understand. After all, my dad served as the perfect teacher. He showed me everything I needed to know about playing pool, shooting craps in the alley, and playing cards. If there was a way to try to hustle a dollar, he sure knew it. Not that he was exactly good at it, but he still considered it his specialty.

He even recounted times back in the day when he was young when he made decent money from reselling cartons of cigarettes. He explained that he'd buy a carton, take one cigarette from each individual pack, then seal them up so it appeared they had never been opened. Not only would he then resell the carton, but also the extra cigarettes as singles.

Early on, Dad was proud of my pool hustling ability. Many nights, he'd sit off to the side sipping on his Lucky Lager and smiling ear to ear as I ran the game on some poor bastard who didn't know what he'd gotten himself into. It was almost as if we were becoming buddies by going out together so often. He'd also take me to private poker games, where we worked as partners to try to get an advantage.

"All right, son," he told me, "if I give you a signal that I've got a good hand, it means you raise it. Even if you've got a really bad hand, you still raise the bet. You understand?" The signal was a serious look. If I glanced up and his eyes were staring straight back into mine, it was time for me to do my thing. Then, hopefully, the other players at the table folded, and when it got back to Dad's turn, he'd raise and I'd fold the pot to him. To be honest, and few gamblers are about their winning and losing, Dad and I usually lost. But a few times we walked out of a bar with some extra cash. When we did, the two of us grabbed a nice dinner and got drunk together on good booze.

In early 1962, Buster sent a note back home saying he wanted Dad to send him his guitar, which Dad did. I think by that time Buster had hooked up with an army buddy of his named Billy Cox, and they were gigging as a band called the King Kasuals at some of the military bases in the South. My brother's note was short on details, but it sounded as if he was at least making enough money to support himself.

Despite my complete lack of interest, I got good grades in school. The problem was that I started getting kicked out of class regularly for being a pain in the ass. When the new city antisegregation laws went into effect, they started busing me out to Ballard Junior High School, where it seemed as if every student but me was either Swedish or Norwegian. So, there I was, the street kid surrounded by blue-eyed and blond-haired kids who were afraid of me because they'd never met a black person before. Most of them wanted to kick my ass from the moment the bus dropped me off in front of the school. My half year going to school at Ballard was a nightmare. I tried to keep to myself, but other students messed with me daily, and I constantly got into fights. Every time punches were thrown, I was the one dragged down to the principal's office to be punished. No matter the circumstances, the principal always blamed me for causing trouble. He couldn't understand why I was repeatedly getting into fights in his school.

"Listen, Leon," the principal told me one afternoon, "we didn't have many incidents at all before you started attending our school."

I fought off the urge to jump up and yell, "Just look at me! Who do you think is messing with whom in these situations? I'm the only black kid here!"

Every morning, the bus ride was an hour out to Ballard. It wasn't exactly a good way to start my day. If I fell asleep in my seat, the bus driver didn't bother to wake me up and took me all the way to the end of the route. When the bus hit that last stop he'd yell back and tell me to get the hell off his bus. He was a prejudiced old man who could not have cared less what happened to me. After school, it was another hour's ride back to my home.

The only good thing about going to school out at Ballard was that the girls really took notice of me. Sure, it's a common stereotype, but I was the only one who knew any moves at the school dances. The girls usually broke the ice when they saw me off by myself, and they'd gather around as I took them through the steps of the Mashed Potato and the Pony. That attention at least made my time at the school a little more bearable. Still, I wasn't at Ballard long. I became fed up with the crazy white boys trying to kick my ass every day and the unforgiving teachers constantly accusing me of causing trouble.

In late May of 1962, Dad and I received a letter from Buster letting us know that he'd injured himself jumping out of an airplane and was getting medically discharged from the service. He also sent me a Screaming Eagle patch of my very own in the envelope. (Man, I wish I knew today where that patch ended up.) Once he was officially finished with his service, his initial plan was to return home to Seattle within the coming weeks. But that time came and went. In his next letter, he explained he was going to pursue his interests in music for a while. Instead of returning home, he and a few other musicians he'd met in the army had decided to play the Chitlin' Circuit clubs down South. The Chitlin' Circuit was a series of clubs and other venues across the Eastern and Southern states where black acts tended to play. He was still playing in his band with his buddy Billy Cox, and they were making their way all over the Deep South toward the end of 1962. I guess Buster spent some time living in Nashville, Tennessee, because in one of his letters home, he mentioned that they were fast becoming the best rhythm-and-blues band in the city. Once Buster set off to play the Chitlin' Circuit, Dad and I got postcards and letters from time to time letting us know what was going on in his life. My brother was off doing his thing and I was off doing mine.

After I left Ballard, Dad enrolled me in Cleveland High School over on Fifteenth Avenue South in the Beacon Hill area of Seattle, which was a much better fit for me. It was easy to make friends, and together we quickly became our own little club. We called ourselves the Playboys and spent our time after school playing baseball or hanging out. Back then there were gangs all over the city. During my brother's final year of school before he dropped out, a gang called the Cobras attempted to recruit him, but he didn't want any part of them. His music was much more important to him. The overall landscape was much different from what it is today, and nobody was running around crazy carrying guns and knives. The Playboys functioned more as a social club than anything else. Sure, we had some scrapes with other groups here and there, but it was usually over some petty argument. Everyone would convene at a baseball field and a simple fistfight settled any scores. Sometimes by the time we went out to the field, kids had already got bored with the beef, so nothing happened. Everyone simply hung out and smoked some cigarettes together.

From our time hanging out in pool halls such as the Green Felt, my buddies and I became tight with a few street players in the area. We quickly realized that simply by hooking a few people up with a joint or two, we were able to earn some easy money. It wasn't as if we were actively going out and selling, but if we heard somebody wanted some weed or something, we certainly knew where to get it. I started even being able to give Dad a few bucks here and there when he was short on cash, which was basically all of the time. He didn't have a problem with the help and thought the extra money was coming from a part-time job I temporarily picked up over at a local golf course. Even if he was a little suspicious, he wasn't going to ask me where I made the money, and I wasn't going to come right out and tell him.

LIFE WITHOUT BUSTER

My brother and the King Kasuals continued to play the Chitlin' Circuit, and Buster crossed paths with legendary guitar players such as B.B. King and Albert King. But it was still a tough situation. Even though Buster was always on the go, he at least kept in touch with Dad and me and let us know how he was doing. Through his occasional postcards, I sensed he was down on his luck and struggling most of the time. I'm sure it wasn't easy always being on the road and playing for little or no money. I kept hoping he would return home for at least a little while to visit, but his mind was set on other things.

What I didn't know at the time was that he took a break from gigging with the King Kasuals at the end of 1962 and traveled by bus all the way to Vancouver to stay with Grandma Nora for a short time. Although it was only a few hours away, he never made the trip south to visit Dad and me in Seattle. Instead, my brother remained in Canada during the start of 1963 while he picked up gigs playing for a group called Bobby Taylor and the Vancouvers. I later found out that the group's lead guitarist at that time was Tommy Chong, who would years later go on to perform with Cheech Marin in Cheech and Chong. I didn't blame my brother for not returning home to visit. For the most part, there wasn't much waiting for him in Seattle. He was smart enough to know that pursuing his music was the right thing to do no matter where it took him.

When he got bored with the scene in Vancouver, he returned to the Southern Chitlin' Circuit and reunited with the King Kasuals as they backed up a popular soul singer named Solomon Burke. My brother would later write in a postcard home that he also had the opportunity to play with the legendary Otis Redding during one of the short tours, as well as open up for Jackie Wilson and Sam Cooke. To me, it sounded as if he was well on his way to making things happen for himself.

I should also probably have been focusing on achieving goals. But as I moved on from Washington Junior High School and started tenth grade at Cleveland in the fall of 1963, the only thing I was interested in was hanging out with my buddies in downtown Seattle. The weed hookups my friends and I were regularly putting together kept cash in my pocket. It may sound strange to some people, but in my adolescence, hustling truly felt like my calling in life. Everything in my childhood prepared me to go out into the world and *get money* by any means necessary. I finally had the extra money I'd always wanted while growing up, and there was no problem getting girls. On the weekends, I headed into the city and hit up the pool halls and gambled.

My buddies and I also began regularly drinking in high school. It wasn't hard for one of us to find booze. Someone older was always around to go to the store and buy us a bottle of White Court or Thunderbird, which were the cheapest and nastiest bottles of poor man's wine around. We mixed in a packet of Kool-Aid with the stuff to give it some flavor, then passed the bottle around until it was kicked. Along with the booze, you could also buy a decent-size joint for about fifty cents from a store called Bloomers, which was a Jewish deli and convenience store. If you ordered a bagel with cream cheese for five bucks, they'd throw in a little matchbox of weed with it. Add a coffee in there and it wasn't a bad way to start the school day.

It was as if my friends and I were invincible and I didn't have a care in the world. Eventually, the excitement and small financial benefit of selling weed wasn't doing the trick any longer. The Playboys and I decided it was time to step up our efforts. Since we heard decent money could be made selling off stolen property, we figured it was time to try our hands at stealing. We had no interest in robbing people; we wanted to take some merchandise from larger chain stores and move it at a discount to some friends we knew downtown.

I was young and misguided. In my mind, by going after larger chain-type stores, we were beating the system. It was David against Goliath. The idea seemed great until everything suddenly turned bad when we decided to do a job at a Nordstrom department store. We had cased it out for a couple weeks before, and we couldn't wait to get our hands on the racks of expensive mink and chinchilla coats in the women's section. We weren't sure how to actually make it work until we noticed a window all the way up on the fourth floor that was always open during the daytime and wasn't connected to any type of alarm system. So, the four of us walked into Nordstrom and hid out until the store closed. After all of the employees went home, we grabbed every coat we could get our hands on and began tossing them out the open fourth-story window to where we had two guys waiting with a car in the side parking lot down below. They stuffed the merchandise into the trunk of the car as fast as we tossed it down to them. The plan went off without a hitch until we had trouble making our escape. We couldn't simply drop down four stories out the window, so we had to force our way out the front door, which took longer than anticipated. It turned out that it was much too long.

"Everybody down on the ground!" a voice shouted as soon as I took my first step into the parking lot. When I glanced over, a cop stood pointing his gun directly at me. The other officers already had my friends facedown at gunpoint. There wasn't going to be any type of getaway this time. The Seattle cops hauled me down to the station, and since I was only fifteen, I got six months in juvenile hall. Dad showed up at the youth court for the sentencing and, surprisingly, wasn't as angry as I thought he was going to be. He'd already been through some similar times with Buster, so it was nothing new to him. That being said, he still wasn't necessarily happy about the trouble I'd gotten into.

"Boy, when you get out, you're gonna get a whoopin' like you never seen. That'll teach you for running crazy around the city," he said after my sentence was handed down.

They put me in the Youth Center, which was in a way pleasing to Dad. "At least now I'll know where you're at," he told me. The barbed-wire fence around the perimeter of the place made it look pretty ominous at first, but I soon found out it wasn't all that bad. When the facility's administrators got their hands on my school transcripts, they saw that my grades were good and my six-month sentence was reduced to four. As I'd done throughout my life whenever times were tough, I adjusted. After everything Dad, Buster, and I had gone through, I felt there wasn't a hard time invented that I couldn't handle.

The Youth Center was essentially a huge dormitory with a couple of gyms. Most of my time was spent playing basketball or soccer, and I kept to myself. During the day, I attended classes in one of the buildings and finished tenth grade. During my entire time at the Youth Center, I was reprimanded maybe once, for sneaking a cigarette into my room. It was a quick four months and I was out.

"All right, boy, it's time for your whoopin'," Dad told me the day I arrived back at the house.

"No. That's not going to happen," I said, smiling at him. "You aren't putting your hands on me anymore." It was the first time I'd stood up to him in such a way, and I wasn't sure how it was going to pan out. But I meant every word. I wasn't a little boy any longer. We found ourselves locked in a standoff for a few moments.

Before things went any further, Dad hung his head and looked down at the carpet. "Okay. I don't want to whup you no more either."

"Good, Dad."

As I found my way in and out of trouble, my brother dropped us another line from out on the road. In early 1964, Dad and I heard from him by phone after he made a move north to New York City. After filling me in on his plans, he put his new girlfriend, Fayne, on the line. She seemed like a nice girl and explained they were staying at the Hotel Seifer together. A few months later, in March of 1964, Buster called again to say he'd joined the Isley Brothers' band, and he went out on the road with them throughout the East Coast as well as to gigs along the Chitlin' Circuit. The Isley Brothers were one of the biggest R&B groups at that time, and Buster went into the studio to do some recording with them. He even ended up playing on a song called "Testify," which got a decent amount of airplay on the radio.

Later that summer, he called and told me he'd hooked up with Little Richard of all people and was playing guitar in his backup band called the Upsetters. I couldn't believe he was playing in a backup band for one of our childhood idols. In my mind, my brother had finally made the big time, but he made sure to let me know he wasn't there yet. Buster explained that Little Richard was sensitive and temperamental out on the road, and Buster was getting tired of it. Regardless of what he said, to me he still seemed to be well on his way.

In the fall of 1964, I switched over to Franklin High School for eleventh grade. It was a little closer to the house than Cleveland, and all I had to do was walk down Empire Way. One might think that after spending four months in a juvenile detention facility I might have made a true attempt to walk the straight and narrow, but there was no chance of that. I soon slipped right back into my old ways. Not much had changed in my mind. My buddies and I had been careless, made some mistakes, and gotten caught. I figured we were too good to ever allow something like that to happen again.

In early 1965, Buster sent a postcard home to let Dad and I know that he was still touring with Little Richard and playing in the Upsetters. I think he was living in Hollywood, California, but it wasn't for long. When the tour with Little Richard was over, Buster left the group because of the frequent clashes between him and Little Richard over my brother's stage antics and made the move back to New York City. Buster called home not long after he arrived. He sounded tired and road weary. When he asked me how school was going, I couldn't do anything but laugh and tell him everything was fine, but he obviously knew the truth. I'm sure Dad had filled him in on my little stint at the Youth Center.

Although I spent my nights gambling and hustling, my schoolwork at Franklin somehow didn't suffer. I maintained an A average and my artwork attracted a lot of attention from the teachers. They recognized my talent for doing mechanical and architectural drawings as well as engineering blueprints. My drawing teacher, Mr. Curtis, was so impressed with my ability that he submitted some of my work to the Boeing company for a contest they were having throughout the high schools of Seattle. I didn't think much of it until Mr. Curtis invited me into his office one day and congratulated me for winning the Boeing contest for Franklin High School's entire student body. He slid a certificate out of a manila envelope, handed it to me, and said, "It looks like Boeing has a job waiting for you as soon as you graduate."

It was exciting to hear the good news, but I wasn't interested in waiting to claim my prize. It may have been a little impulsive, but I went down to Boeing the next day with my certificate to get a job. My jaw nearly hit the floor when my supervisor told me I would be making *$100 a week*. Hell, at that time it was like instantly becoming a part of the upper-middle class.

The buildings at Boeing were gigantic, with thousands of employees. The supervisor gave me a tour of the facilities, and then led me through a labyrinth of hallways until we approached an endless row of cubicles. I wondered how anybody was able to find anybody else in such a huge place. He directed me to a desk in the back of a long row.

If I didn't know what the expression *burning the candle at both ends* meant, I was about to find out. As soon as I finished school every day at 3:00 P.M., I jogged over to catch the Boeing bus, which took me to work at 3:30 P.M. At the end of my eight-hour shift, I jumped on the bus back home, crashed for a few hours, then went to school in the morning. At first, I absolutely loved the job at Boeing. All I had to do was draw the same nuts and bolts every day, and the detailed process quickly became second nature. But the repetition wore on me as I realized I was literally *drafting the same nut and bolt every day.* The company also required that everyone wear cloth gloves to prevent our skin from making contact with our work and smudging the ink. The gloves wouldn't have been so bad if it weren't hot as hell in the workroom. I found it hard to keep myself from sweating, and if a single bead of perspiration hit my paper, my boss made me start my sketch over. It was enough to drive anyone crazy. There had to be a more efficient way of doing things, and I decided to speak up.

"Hey, man," I said to my shift supervisor one day. "We have that big Xerox machine right over there in the corner. Why aren't we using it to copy all of these nuts and bolts?"

"Mr. Hendrix, we've been making airplanes here at Boeing for a *long* time," he told me, trying to force a smile onto his face. "Trust me. We know what we are doing. The company has a routine and we stick to it."

Well, so much for my bright idea. The guy wasn't in the mood for any feedback, especially from a high school kid like me.

In the spring of 1965, I heard from my brother again during an evening phone call. He was still in New York, but his luck had changed. He sounded as happy as I had heard him in a long time as he told me about the exciting things he was putting together there. After hooking back up with the Isley Brothers, he did a string of dates with them, but ultimately decided to set out on his own. After years of playing in backup bands, wearing uniforms, and taking orders, my brother was ready to call the shots. He wanted to have full control of his musical future.

"I formed my own band, the Blue Flames, and I'm making good money playing each week," he told me over the phone. "I'm going by Maurice James right now. It's like a stage name."

"That's great, Buster. But when are you coming home?" I asked.

"I'm not really sure. Everything is starting to come together for me in the city. And you know what? I also just got enough money together to buy a car. It's almost like that old Plymouth we used to take out to the Spanish Castle. It's a great ride, but the steering is messed up. I have to turn the wheel *twice* around before the wheels on the thing finally start to move."

Although I was disappointed that he wasn't coming back to Seattle to visit anytime soon, it was still nice to hear my brother was doing well in New York City. I don't know how much time I would have had to spend with him anyway. I was simultaneously juggling a budding career at Boeing and my classes at Franklin.

A few weeks of long hours at Boeing and short sleep left me completely exhausted and unable to function. My concentration level was down to zero, and something had to give. After considering my options, I decided to drop out of high school. I could either work at Boeing without a diploma and make money, or stay in school and get a diploma, but not have much money. That job and a weekly paycheck at Boeing were too precious to pass up.

Dad didn't have much of a problem with my decision. He thought I'd already made it the moment I'd been awarded the job. Many of my relatives had tried for years to get positions at the company, and Dad knew it would be crazy for me to not take full advantage of my lucky break. Besides, if it didn't work out, I could always go back to finish at Franklin in the future.

It would have been the perfect situation for many kids my age, but no matter how much money I was making from my legitimate job, the streets were still calling my name. Deep down, there was nothing I'd rather be doing than hanging out with my buddies hustling or gambling. So I figured out a new work routine for myself: I punched in at Boeing, escaped downtown for the evening, and then came back to the company offices at midnight to clock out. The plan worked for a while, but one of the supervisors soon caught on and reprimanded me. Although he started keeping a closer eye on my activities while I was at my cubicle, it didn't stop me from still attempting to do my thing. Before long I found the one spot on the Boeing campus where guys were throwing dice behind a warehouse. That's how it works with gamblers—you can spread us out anywhere and try to separate us, but eventually we're going to find one another and get some action going. When I wasn't throwing dice behind the warehouse, I was dropping nickel after nickel into the pinball machine in the employee lounge.

My brother continued to call home once in a while, but I wasn't around much with my hectic schedule. Dad told me that he was still playing with his band in New York City. When I did finally talk to him after I dropped out of high school, he still sounded happy and excited about things on the horizon. At the time, he explained that his band was making $100 a week.

"You know what? I'm making money, too," I told him over the phone. "I'm getting $5.25 an hour over at Boeing."

"Nice, Leon," he said. "I'm proud of you."

I kept going with my insubordinate routine at Boeing, but I wasn't fooling anyone, especially not my immediate supervisor. A company such as Boeing may have been incredibly big with thousands of employees, but management kept track of everything. In the early spring of 1966, my supervisor summoned me to his office and let me go. It was a bit of a letdown, but it wasn't as if I was the least bit surprised. Still, I considered my time at the company a major achievement for a seventeen-year-old, especially someone like myself who didn't have much motivation to lead a regular workingman's life.

Dad and the rest of my family were blown away when I didn't take my job all that seriously and was eventually let go. At least I earned enough to buy myself a nice Ford Thunderbird.

As the school year came to a close, I knew I had no interest in going back to Franklin in the fall to finish twelfth grade. My buddies and I didn't move on to full-time jobs and starting families—we graduated to downtown. All of my friends and I came from the same type of background and we didn't have much. We sure as hell knew that nobody was ever going to give us anything. The only way to get what we wanted was to go out and hustle or gamble or sell. I was tired of being poor all my life. It didn't matter as much when I was a young kid because I didn't know any better, but as I gained a greater awareness of the world, it started to bother me. Besides, the downtown lifestyle came natural to me. I'd been trying to talk my way out of whoopin's from the time I could stand. It was something I got good at over time. My growing understanding of the art of hustling started telling me something: fast-talking allowed me to get what I wanted without having to put a gun or a knife in anyone's face and rob him. If you shove a pistol in somebody's face, he'll be sure to give you his money, but he will never give you anything else again. But if you use your words, he'll hand over that same amount of money maybe *three* times before he figures out what the hell is going on.

It was the 1960s and everyone was experimenting with new drugs. As soon as I developed tight connections with a few guys downtown, I was able to hook people up with a list of substances in addition to weed. That's how I made money. I knew where to get anything out there. Whether it was crisscross speed, Christmas trees, Black Beauties, or a nice sack of weed, there was no problem scoring.

I was probably popping close to as many pills as I was pushing. I stayed away from the Black Beauty downers because they messed with my game. The pills slowed me down and didn't let me hustle the way I needed to. I was no good sitting around all night blown out on downers. It was important to be out there in the mix making things happen, pulling that money in, and watching my ass. Besides, the speed helped me stay sharp, on the edge, and exactly where I needed to be. Other street guys were constantly looking for an opportunity to rob me, not to mention that the cops hanging out around downtown were trying to jam me up on something. And the ones who weren't looking to arrest me were going to at least try to muscle me and shake me down for cash or drugs.

Although I was technically still living with Dad at his place at Twenty-sixth and Yesler, I was out late most nights and preferred to book a hotel room downtown. That way it was easy to come and go as I pleased at all times. Sometimes I didn't see Dad for weeks on end and only stopped by to give him some spending money. After a great deal of moaning and groaning, he accepted the cash. But not without making sure to let me know he wasn't happy about the situation. He knew exactly where I was getting my money.

But when I did decide to return home to Dad's one night, I came back to find every single light in our apartment out. It seemed odd until I discovered the power had been turned off. Absolutely nothing was out of the ordinary about that. As I shuffled around in the dark, I didn't spot any furniture either. Everything had been cleared out, and nothing was left. It looked as if Dad hadn't lived here for a while.

When I finally got ahold of him, he told me, "I got a new lady friend and a new place, son. I moved up to Howe Street in the Queen Anne district."

He told me his new lady was Ayako Fujita, a Japanese woman he had been going out with for a little while. Since people had trouble pronouncing her name, she just went by "June." She had five children, all of whom were grown and out of the house except for a three-year-old daughter named Janie.

I was glad Dad had found a girlfriend, but I didn't know if everything would be comfortable for me in the house. Mostly, I lived in hotels downtown, but Dad had moved all of my belongings from our place on Yesler into the new apartment on Howe Street. I was in no rush to stay with him and his new girlfriend. Hotels were just fine for me. Besides, my buddies and I were making plenty of money. There was no reason to want to be anywhere else.

Typically after a good score, we relaxed for three or four months and enjoyed throwing our money around town—hitting up the finest restaurants, buying the sharpest threads, and partying. Once our crew started getting short on cash, we'd start staking out our next job.

Eventually, I made my way back to Dad's new place to stay with him. In September of 1966, Dad and I received a call from Buster just before I was getting ready to go out for the night. I'd talked to my brother maybe a few months earlier, and he was making some progress with his music in New York City, but I hadn't heard from him since then. When the operator informed Dad that Buster was calling *collect* from London, England, he flew off the handle.

"Did you say, '*London* calling'?" he asked the operator. "*Dad-gummit!*" he snapped. "Yes, I'll accept the charges." There was a pause as the operator made the international connection. "Come on now, you know how to write, boy! I can't believe you're calling me and putting all of these charges on my bill," Dad quickly scolded my brother over the phone.

I'm sure my brother was wondering why he'd even made the mistake of calling back to the house in the first place. Instead of simply being happy to hear from his boy who was doing everything he could to follow his musical dreams, Dad was enraged over what his next month's phone bill was going to look like. Everything calmed down a bit when Dad handed the phone to me.

To me, traveling to London was like going to another planet, and I'm not even sure I could have found the city on a map right away. Buster mentioned he was changing the spelling of his name to J-I-M-I, and the manager he'd hooked up with back in New York City, Chas Chandler, who had also played bass for the Animals, was going to start billing him as the Jimi Hendrix Experience. To me, the name sounded spacey and weird. The Experience? I didn't get it at all.

"Check this out, Leon," Buster said. After setting the receiver down, he grabbed his guitar and started playing and playing . . . and playing. I even put the phone down and came back a minute later to find him still going. If Dad saw me just listening there on the phone like that he would have flipped out. It was tough to make out what Buster was strumming because the connection was full of static, but it was easy to tell he was going through a creative awakening. The ideas were coming to him in waves.

"I'm calling this one 'Foxy Lady.' . . .

"Here's another thing I'm working on—'The Wind Cries Mary.' . . .

"I've got this song, 'Purple Haze,' that's coming out soon. It's got a cool beat to it, but it's not like dance music or anything. I think we're going to make a record."

I wasn't paying close attention. The only thing running through my mind was *Great. Here we go again.* My brother's incessant playing was nothing new to me, so the guitar lines he was cycling through over the phone weren't holding my interest. I was more preoccupied with where I was going to meet up with my buddies downtown later that night. I only recall the titles of the songs he was running through. When he mentioned he was doing a rendition of a country-and-western song called "Hey Joe," I almost busted out laughing. Country and western? None of it made sense. I thought, *Man, Buster needs to get a real job or something.* It goes to show how much I knew back then.

I was doing my thing downtown during the week, but on the weekends I still landscaped with Dad from time to time. I didn't exactly look forward to it because the hours were long and the work was backbreaking, but at least we made decent money. Dad cut the grass with the mower, then I followed behind with the trimmer to clean up the edges and make sure the lines were straight. After we cleaned up, Dad dropped a bill in the mailbox and we continued to our next job.

Dad and I didn't talk much about Buster's music career. Neither of us knew what the future would hold for him. I didn't think much of any of it at the time. Maybe Buster was going to put out an album and do some touring, but Dad and I weren't sure of anything. My brother was so far away that it didn't make much difference.

Not until the middle of May in 1967, when I was listening to Seattle's WKGR, did I hear what would become in time the signature opening guitar lick blasting over the airwaves. Once the groove kicked in, then vocals came . . . *Hey Joe, where you goin' with that gun in your hand* . . . Even though I vaguely remembered my brother mentioning the song during our conversation on the telephone, I didn't make the connection. It never dawned on me that it was his voice as I absently nodded along to the beat while staring off into passing traffic.

"And that was the Jimi Hendrix Experience with 'Hey Joe,'" the disc jockey commented as the song gradually faded out.

"What?" I said aloud in the car. "*What!*"

When I made it back to the house, I was in a full daze. Although my brother had mentioned the record in passing, it was still tough to know what to make of what had come over the airwaves. Man, Buster was *on the radio*. But then again, did I hear the disc jockey wrong and make a mistake? Maybe I had. My mind started playing tricks on me, and I convinced myself I had imagined the whole thing.

I had little time to think about the song on the radio because, as soon as I arrived home, Dad and June were in the middle of another argument. They had been going at it nonstop for a while, and things were getting so bad that it looked as if they were going to go their separate ways. It was like a flashback to when Dad and Mama used to fight. Who knows what kind of effect it had on June's little daughter, Janie, at the time? I had already been through it myself when I was about her age, so I knew it certainly wasn't a good scene for a young kid. I'm not sure what all the fuss was about. My dad was paying most of the bills and supporting June and her daughter. Despite all the financial support, June was always on the warpath about something. I'm sure it had to do with my dad's drinking, which was an ever-present problem in any of his relationships. Dad even confided in me that we were going to have to start looking for a new place to live because he knew it was only a matter of time before they broke up. Then, suddenly, Dad told me that he and June were going to get married. This jarring change of events didn't make much sense to me. But Dad was telling the truth. They went from being at each other's throats all of the time to being husband and wife.

In October of 1967, Dad and I were home on a lunch break when suddenly the walls of the room started vibrating. The glasses and plates in the cabinet shook, clanking against one another. It took a moment before I realized it was because of the loud music booming from the apartment next door. Something caught hold of me and the melody was vaguely familiar. This time, there was no mistaking the unique groove.

"Dad," I said. "That's Buster!"

"Huh? What are you talking about?" Dad asked, paying me little attention. He was slipping his boots onto his feet and his thoughts were elsewhere. "Come on, let's pack up our stuff and get going back to work."

"No, seriously! That's him. Don't you remember when he called from London and said he was going to be playing as the Jimi Hendrix Experience? That's his music coming from next door."

Dad came to a stop in the living room and stood listening for a moment. A confused look found its way onto his face. "Come on now," he muttered. "You're *joshin'*. That can't be true."

"No! I'm telling you," I insisted, walking out the front door of our apartment.

I went into the hallway and started banging on our neighbor's door. When the guy who lived there answered, clouds of weed smoke swirled throughout the room behind him. He and his girlfriend, Cornflake, were full-blown hippies and usually played their music loud when they were partying.

"Hey, what are you playing on that record player?" I loudly asked him over the music. It was hard to contain my excitement.

He gestured back into the room. "Oh, this? It's Jimi Hendrix."

"Man, that's *my brother* on that record!" I yelled, pointing at the glossy black disc spinning on the player.

Shuffling forward through the doorway, I spotted Cornflake curled up on the couch with a weed pipe in her hand. She stared at me as smoke escaped from her mouth. "Nooooooo waaaaaaaaay," she said numbly. At first, they seriously thought I was putting them on, but after glancing down at the album jacket sitting on the coffee table, everything registered and Cornflake's eyes widened in awe. "Oh my God! You look just like him!" she told me.

Some people might not immediately have seen the resemblance, but Buster and I did look alike in many ways. Although our hair and facial features were different, we were both lean and shared a similar complexion. We were also almost the exact same height and weight.

The couple had picked up a copy of the Jimi Hendrix Experience's *Are You Experienced* and had been listening to it nonstop.

Their minds were completely blown when it registered that they had been living next to Jimi Hendrix's brother and father. I convinced them to let me bring the record over to our apartment to show my dad. No matter what I told him, he wasn't going to accept that it was indeed Buster unless he saw and heard it for himself.

Dad's mouth hung open as he stood examining the album's cover art: the distorted fish-eye photo of Buster and his two bandmates in the center, the bright yellow background, and the puffy purple lettering. "Oh my goodness. It *is* him. That's Buster. That's my boy." Turning the jacket over, he caught sight of another large black-and-white photo of the band on the back. Dad must have flipped it over a dozen times until he actually started to tear up. Whether it was the photo on the front or the back, there was no questioning it now: it was indeed his son, *Jimi*, staring straight back at him in all his psychedelic rock-star glory.

Seeing my brother on the cover of his very own album also had a lasting effect on me. It provided me with a boost of confidence. If Buster could go out into the world and achieve what he wanted, then I was convinced I could do the same. It was truly an inspiration to me. Maybe I had the ability to make my mark, too. When we were young boys, I always felt confident with Buster. Now, years later, he was still building my confidence, even from the other side of the world.

Dad and I blew off work for the rest of the day, and Cornflake and her boyfriend joined us, along with June, in our apartment. June made tea for everyone, and together we sat and listened to the album from beginning to end. The couple even insisted we keep the record after the last song, "Are You Experienced?," ended. Once the music stopped, Dad's whole demeanor changed in an instant. He may have been amazed that Buster had put out a record and his photo was on the album cover, but overall he still wasn't amused. To him, no matter what anyone told him or what he saw, this music thing still wasn't "real work."

"Well," he started out, rising from the couch, "who knows? There are a lot of records out there."

From that day forward, it seemed as if June suddenly became the perfect Japanese wife. The yelling was over and the fights stopped. As soon as she spotted Jimi on that album cover, everything was miraculously resolved, and calm was restored in the apartment. I didn't think much of it and left the situation alone. There was no use getting into the middle of anything that was going on in their relationship. Their bickering had been driving me out of my mind for months, and I was simply glad there was peace and quiet.

8

SEATTLE STREET HUSTLING

After our next-door neighbors gave us my brother's album *Are You Experienced*, I constantly listened to it on Dad's record player at home. The music also caught on with many of my buddies downtown, although at first most of them didn't want to come right out and admit it. Since my brother was a black artist who also appealed to many white kids, some black people considered being a fan of his a betrayal of their race. I heard this from time to time on the streets, but never paid much attention to it. That way of thinking was silly to me. I suspected that the people who complained the most about my brother's music being popular with the white kids probably had his record stashed away somewhere in a closet and still listened to it at home at night.

The songs on the album were some of the most soulful and beautiful pieces of music I'd ever heard. Although "Hey Joe," "Purple Haze," and "Foxy Lady" were the standout radio hits, I found myself drawn to the more autobiographical songs such as "Manic Depression," which related Jimi's frustration in trying to chase his musical dreams. For me, the lyrics explained how he'd been trying to touch and feel his music from the day he took apart Dad's radio back when we were boys. "The Wind Cries Mary" also spoke to me because although the lyrics weren't exact—"The Wind Cries Lucille" probably wouldn't have had the same cool ring to it—I had the feeling Jimi was conveying some of the intense feelings he had kept bottled up inside about Dad and our mama; emotions he never came right out and expressed while we were growing up. "3rd Stone from the Sun" was more out-there science fiction, similar to the stories he used to tell me as we lay on the front lawn looking up at the stars at night. My brother was still exploring, just as he had always done. In the song "Are You Experienced?" he even came right out and asked his fans and listeners how far they were willing to go to reach the outer limits of their minds' consciousness and subconsciousness. Listening to the album was like having the important conversation we were never able to have when we were young.

It was also interesting how people took Jimi's lyrics to have very definite meanings. Almost from the start, "Purple Haze" was rumored to be about a certain type of weed or LSD, but it made no sense to me. In my mind, the song had little, if anything, to do with drugs. My take on the song was that Jimi was writing about his relationship with God and his general feelings on religion. "Kiss the Sky" was a reference to praying and connecting with the spiritual realm. Mother Mary was that girl who put a spell on him. She was showing Jimi the way as he struggled to make his own path. Jimi's lyrics were wonderful, and the beauty of them was that you could bend them and mold them to mean whatever you wanted them to.

Dad and I caught glimpses of my brother in a few music magazines and got periodic updates about his growing fame. Because of my brother's rising star, the Hendrix name received plenty of attention throughout Seattle. People wanted to hire Dad's landscaping business to work at their homes. Because of the increasing demand, Dad and I didn't have to take the jobs cleaning out garages and attics anymore. We moved onward and upward to strictly lawn care and landscaping. Upper-middle-class Jewish families in the suburbs wanted the Hendrixes to come to their houses. Dad fielded so many requests for work that we were forced to farm them out to other crews or reject them outright for lack of time in the schedule.

The newfound notoriety also carried over for me into the streets, where I became a local celebrity. The big downtown players were not only interested in hanging out with me, they also wanted to do business together. Everyone wanted to talk to me and see if I could pass a message on to my brother, especially my brother's old musician buddies from high school, who wanted a chance to get back together and jam.

"When is he coming back into town?" they'd ask every time we crossed paths.

"I don't know, man," I told them. It was true. Everything seemed to be coming together for my brother so fast that I didn't know what he was up to.

Although I was pulling in decent money from our landscaping, it was nothing compared to what I was able to get out on the street. Besides, there wasn't much action in spending the days cutting grass and trimming bushes in the hot summer sun.

Back in the mid-to-late 1960s, Seattle was virgin territory. During my time hanging out in the pool halls, I followed the natural progression from selling joints and sacks of weed, to hooking people up with crisscross speed pills. Eventually, I also found my way into robbing and stealing after I hooked up with three street guys, Ross, Charlie, and Johnny, all originally from upstate Washington, and a Japanese guy named Dan. Every one of them was a professional thief. It was odd because Dan was already a millionaire and owned a successful pineapple plantation in Hawaii. At first, it was difficult to understand why he would need the money. But then I realized his involvement had nothing to do with making cash. The guy was addicted to the gangster lifestyle and the excitement of taking down scores. It was puzzling because the only reason I was going along and pulling jobs was for the money.

In the beginning, the guys let me tag along and showed me the ropes to becoming a burglar and a jewel thief. Their favorite spots to rob were smaller-size restaurants on Sundays and Mondays after all of the weekend receipts were locked away. The restaurants usually used small safes, which were the easiest models to crack. The guys didn't bring along many tools; usually the only thing they needed was a crowbar, which they called a jiffy bar. When I asked Dan why they didn't bring along more equipment, he simply glanced at me and laughed. He told me not to worry because that was all we were going to need.

I wasn't so sure until I saw the guys go to work on that first safe. At the corner on most of the smaller models, where the metal was welded together at the hinges, was a specific pressure point. When you hit that exact spot just right, the metal split in the corner. Then you took the jiffy bar and started prying that eighth of an inch of metal away from the door until the whole front cover was separated. They used to call this "peeling an orange." Once that was done, only a layer of cement held the lock gears in place. We'd take the jiffy bar and chip all of it away until nothing was left but the bare gears. From there, you could simply turn them with your hand and open the safe. If we couldn't crack the thing at the location, the four or five of us picked it up and simply put it in the back of Dan's truck, so we could work on it later at someone's garage.

We typically shied away from the larger, more intricate safes because the few attempts we did make to crack them didn't work out well. The guys and I once worked on a safe for five or six hours, until around four in the morning, and when we finally opened that sucker up, *nothing* was in it. From that point on, we decided not to waste our time on those types of jobs. We'd rather pull off three smaller scores, such as family restaurants, rather than a larger one such as a department store or an electronics store.

Our biggest score was probably around $35,000, which we split among us. We were so happy with our take that we actually hung out in the restaurant after we cracked the safe and cooked ourselves food. We may even have fixed a few celebratory cocktails from the bar, all the while cackling like a bunch of madmen.

Half of the interest in stealing from banks and other companies was certainly the money, but the other half was something I refer to as the jazz: the adrenaline rush from outwitting authorities and making off with the loot. Many times I found myself laughing out loud as we made our getaway after a job. I was caught up in the thrill of danger. Anyone with that type of addiction will tell you that once you get locked into a crime spree, the hustler's natural tendency is to push his luck all the way until he ends up in jail or dead.

One beat cop patrolled most of the area we hung out around, and we wasted no time in befriending him. It was the easiest way to make sure we knew what kind of a schedule he was on and what his next destination was. The patrol cop wasn't a problem at all, and my buddies and I joked about how easy we had things downtown. At first, there wasn't anything for us to worry about anywhere in the city, but that changed slightly as soon as Detectives Walter and Hightower emerged on the scene. Although they both knew we were up to no good, they could never seem to catch us doing anything against the law. They were more of a regular nuisance than a true threat.

They weren't going to get much assistance from the local businesses in trying to pinch us either. Barely any of the downtown buildings were equipped with alarm systems, and few security guards were on duty. The guards that did work downtown were usually friendly with one of our crew anyway. If you could bust into a business undetected and crack the safe, you were in and out without any problem. No one or nothing was going to stop you.

After our crew pulled off a series of sizable jobs, cleaning out a few local Jewish stores like Weisfield's and Ben Bridges, we got to know all the major players and real gangsters who operated downtown. It paid to know people because after we pulled a job, guys downtown bought the merchandise for cash on the spot. We'd deliver a bunch of suitcases full of stuff and in return sometimes receive as much as $15,000 or $20,000 to split among us.

Sure enough, Detectives Walter and Hightower always tracked us down in the days following a score. The officers were like two little dogs constantly nipping at our heels wherever we went.

"You boys think you're smart, don't you?" Detective Hightower asked us one day. "Your luck is going to run out. And when it does, my partner and I are going to be the ones to get you."

All of their big talk aside, nobody was afraid of the detectives. They had to be willing to move when our crew moved, and that was most likely going to be in the early-morning hours. For all of their big talk and threats, they weren't devoted enough to put in that type of effort to get something on us. We were too cocky to think, even for a moment, that anyone could ever stop us. Even when we slipped and got careless, no one was around to see what we were doing. We were far beyond brazen, and it got to the point where we'd see something one of us liked in a store window and in an instant the lockpicks came out. We were through the door in five seconds and out of the store in fifteen with our arms full.

Every time my pockets were flush with cash, I went over to an expensive gentlemen's clothing store named Lord's to set myself up.

I was in there so often that I became pretty tight with the sales staff. My days of wearing raggedy secondhand clothing were over. Now I treated myself to silk suits, expensive casual wear, and alligator-skin dress shoes. The ladies in town took notice. I was more popular than ever and always had a fine woman on my arm whenever I went out to the clubs.

My number one hangout spots were the Green Felt and the 211 Club. I quickly learned that many hustlers and pool players were much better than me. I'd been shooting stick most of my life, and these guys would come in, even spot me a few balls, and still wipe me out. So, instead of trying to scrape out a few games and win bets here and there, I decided to take myself out of contention and back a couple of the better hustlers in the city. After I hooked up with two amazing pool players, one named Iceberg Slim and another named Shorty, we started making good money. It seemed we never lost. And when pool games weren't being played, a high-stakes dice game was always going on in the corner of the club.

In addition to what I was pulling off the streets, my brother also gave Dad and me money. He even wired Dad enough to buy a nice house in Seward Park. Although it was a huge step up from the apartment, and I had my own bedroom instead of having to crash on the couch night after night, I still wasn't around much. However, the new house meant a lot to Dad because it was the first time we were able to move out of the Central District and into an affluent neighborhood.

As 1967 came to a close, posters and billboards were erected throughout the city announcing "Jimi" was finally returning to Seattle to play a gig. The news was all over the radio and in the papers. My brother's explosive performance earlier in the summer at 1967's Monterey Pop Festival had already sent shock waves through the music world, and his album *Are You Experienced* was at the top of the pop charts. I couldn't turn on a radio without hearing such songs as "Purple Haze," "Foxy Lady," or "Hey Joe." It was official: my brother was one of the biggest rock stars on the planet. The musical success he'd always longed for had finally arrived, and I was thrilled to be able to soon share it with him. Dad and I couldn't wait for the three of us to be reunited.

A sizable crowd was gathered on the morning of February 12, 1968, when we arrived at the terminal at Sea-Tac Airport to pick up my brother.

"I wonder what all these people are doing here?" Dad naïvely asked.

"Come on, Dad," I said. "They're here to see Jimi."

My heart jumped the moment I spotted my brother casually step off his plane. Jimi was the last passenger to deplane. Later, he'd tell me that his philosophy was always to remain in his seat until the crew opened the cabin doors and most of the passengers had filed out.

"There's no reason to stand all hunched over for ten minutes if nobody's allowed to get off the plane anyway," he explained.

Dad and I had been waiting a long time for Buster to come home to visit. We hadn't seen him in almost seven years, since he'd been released from the army, continued down South to chase after his dream of becoming a professional musician, and eventually jetted off to London. Now there he was, surrounded by persistent photographers, eager news reporters, and crazed fans. We weren't used to being asked questions and having our pictures taken, but we did our best to deal with the chaos surrounding us.

As far as I was concerned, we were going to the airport to pick up my brother, but to everyone else gathered, it was a chance to catch a glimpse of a rock star; actually *the* rock star of the time.

My brother's hip black leather jacket, matching flared velvet pants, hat, and colorful scarf were impressive. The last time I'd seen him in person he was a clean-cut army soldier, but those days were long gone. I made sure to wear my best street hustler's outfit to the airport that day, my skinny glasses, blazer, and sharp hat, but I still didn't come close to my brother's unique style. We stood just outside the terminal area sizing each other up.

"Hey, Buster!" I shouted, widening my arms. "How're you doing?"

My brother flashed a wide smile and gave me a hug. "Man, you look sharp, Leon," he told me. I also looked completely different from the last time Buster had seen me when he was on leave from the army. Back then I was still a fresh-faced schoolkid. I don't think he was prepared for the sight of my hustler clothes.

"You look sharp, too," I said. After taking another glance at my brother and then at myself, I realized I needed to upgrade my wardrobe. My mind was set on copping a cool new look like his.

People gathered and flashbulbs continued to go off as my brother shook Dad's hand and got a strong hug from Aunt Ernestine, who had made the trip with Uncle Ben.

Jimi rode with us from the airport back to the house in Seward Park. For some reason, Dad couldn't wait to tell him what I'd been up to since Jimi had been gone.

"Leon's got a string of girlfriends all over town," Dad announced, glancing into the rearview mirror at Jimi as he rode next to me in the backseat.

"Oh, come on. Give me a break," I remarked, rolling my eyes.

"He's out all over town getting in trouble with the law and up to no good," Dad kept going. "Hell, I only see him maybe once or twice a month. The rest of the time he's out on the streets."

Whatever reaction Dad hoped to receive from Jimi never came. My brother could not have cared less about what kind of trouble I was getting into. What did Dad think Jimi was doing while living in the fast lane out on the road? As Dad continued to jabber away about me up front, my brother tuned him out and began reciting lyrics to me.

"This is just the beginning, or it could be the end," he told me with a smile.

Even though a few years had passed, it was easy for the two of us to pick right up where we left off. Jimi was happy to be home, and neither of us could get over how it had been so long since we'd seen each other. Still, to me, he was the same old Buster. He was too humble for all the money, fame, and success to have had much of an effect on his personality. Unfortunately, Jimi and I didn't have much time to ourselves because when we arrived back at Dad's house, it was full of friends and family. Everyone knew Jimi was finally in town. Aunt Ernestine and Uncle Ben were there, as well as June's daughters, Janie, Donna, Marsha, Linda, and our cousin Jackie. A few of the neighbors also dropped by to see what all the commotion was about. Dad was excited to finally parade Jimi around the nice, new place he'd moved into, but there wasn't much time to relax. There were too many people to meet and greet. He was being pulled off in different directions, and things got even more hectic when his old buddies showed up. Before long we broke out Dad's bottle of Seagram's Seven and started drinking.

Later in the afternoon, one of Jimi's crew guys dropped off a few of his guitars. My brother called me into the back bedroom, where he spread them out on the bed. One case was already opened, displaying a beautiful, new white Fender Stratocaster guitar.

"I'm going to give you a present. I want you to have a guitar," he told me, reaching down toward the bed. Only, he didn't grab the new white Stratocaster; he pulled a different, scuffed-up black case over toward us and opened it. I walked around the bed and saw a sunburst Fender Stratocaster inside. I was thankful for the gift, but I had my heart set on the polished white one.

"Thanks, Buster. But, um, what about the white guitar right there?" I asked with a smile.

Jimi laughed. "No way. You don't even know how to play, man. You can start off on this one here and work your way up. It's a real nice '64 Fender."

After Jimi gathered his things together, one of his managers, a guy named Michael Jeffrey, pulled up out front. Mike comanaged Jimi along with Chas Chandler and controlled everything my brother did. To me, Mike looked like an undercover cop with his short, buzzed hair, clean-shaven face, sharp suit, and sunglasses. He certainly acted the part of the overzealous handler. From the moment I met him he was cold and distant. He refused to talk to me or anyone else in our family and for the most part spoke only directly to Jimi. The few times Mike did address me, he was all business and pushy. He certainly wasn't interested in exchanging pleasantries with any of us. Mike tried to separate Jimi and me from the start. I got the feeling he wasn't in favor of Jimi's returning to Seattle because he didn't want interference from our family. In his mind, we were in the way of whatever he was trying to accomplish. He was used to ordering my brother around out on the road, but back home Jimi wanted to spend time with family and probably for the first time refused to go along with whatever Mike said.

"We'll have you go down to the sound check in this limo and then have Leon and your family take another limo down to the show later," Mike told Jimi.

"What do you mean?" my brother asked. "What's wrong with Leon taking this limo?"

"But, Jimi, I think it would be better if we rode together to talk some business."

"We can do that later, Mike. Come on, Leon. We're going to the venue."

When I hopped into the back of the car with Jimi, it pretty much ended the conversation. Dad and the rest of the family weren't interested in going down to the venue early, so they would take the limo later on to meet us before the gig.

Jimi's crew was still putting the stage together when we arrived and made our way backstage at the Center Arena. People were already filing into the dressing room and picking at a full spread of sandwiches, soft drinks, and alcohol. Although I never saw him fix a drink, Jimi always made sure a bottle of Johnnie Walker Red was backstage. He soon introduced me to his two bandmates, his bass player, Noel Redding, and drummer, Mitch Mitchell. Their English accents were so thick and pronounced that I could barely understand what they were saying, but they still seemed like cool cats, especially Noel. From the start, he was personable and, for the most part, the only member of Jimi's crew who talked to me. Noel came across as a down-to-earth guy and didn't have any attitude. Mitch Mitchell and most of the other roadies were fairly standoffish and didn't have much interest in making small talk. Noel and Mitch got on much differently with my brother than his old buddies in town. When I called my brother Buster, Mitch and Noel looked confused. They didn't know anything about someone named Buster. To us, my brother had always been Buster, and now everyone around him called him nothing but Jimi. When we were around his crew and management, I started calling my brother Jimi as well so I didn't confuse everyone. It got to be too annoying having to explain who Buster was every time I used the name. Most of the time, *Jimi* was much easier.

My brother strolled around the backstage area for a while, then grabbed a few of his guitars to string up and tune. He always rested his head on the top of his guitar's body when he did this so he could not only hear the plucked note but also feel the vibration. Watching him reminded me of the way he used to lean his head against the post of our old brass bed after stringing rubber bands and wires to it when we were kids.

I sat with him as he warmed up until they called him out onto the stage for his sound check. I walked around the venue while they checked the drums, which seemed to take forever. Every time they had the levels set, they'd change them again. Some fifty or so crew members were running around the stage like ants, feverishly working. Guys were marking the stage with tape, listening to the PA system through headphones, and rigging the lights. This complicated production was a long, *very long*, way from the late-time slot at the Black and Tan on a Saturday night. When Jimi plugged in, he played a couple of licks on his guitar and that was it. He was ready to go.

Around 4:00 P.M., we took the limo back to Dad's house, and June cooked sweet-and-sour chicken and fried rice for everyone. We didn't hang out there long though and relaxed down in the basement smoking a joint until the limo came back to pick us up around 8:00 P.M. Once we returned to the venue and were led backstage, Jimi took me aside. We stepped to the corner of a room, where he discreetly reached into his vest pocket and pulled out a few tabs of LSD.

"Here, hold this until after the show for me. Don't take it now. Wait and we'll do it together later."

"Sure, Buster. No problem."

Perhaps it wasn't the best decision, but I lied about waiting until afterward. The excitement and anticipation of the sold-out gig was too much for me to handle. As I stared down at the crumpled tab of blotter acid in my palm, something deep inside told me the wild ride was only beginning. Since I'd never done LSD before, I was very attuned and aware of the gradual oncoming effects. My trip may have started out mild and mellow, but a half hour later it came on like a freight train. Just when I wanted to fix myself a drink and chill out, Dad showed up backstage.

As soon as he spotted me, he scowled and made a bee line to me. "What are you doing back here, Leon? You should be out front with everyone else."

"I'm with Buster, Dad. We're hanging out back here."

"*Hanging out?* You're all in his business and ain't doing nothing but bugging him."

"No, I'm not. Buster asked me to be here. You should go sit out there with the rest of the family and watch. This is where I want to be."

As soon as Jimi took the stage, I stood off to the side watching him perform. For maybe the first time in my life I was exactly where I wanted to be. That night I witnessed my brother play the most powerful and beautiful music. The last opportunity I'd had to watch him perform live, he was still doing covers as part of the Rocking Kings and Thomas and the Tomcats. What he was creating now was something completely different. I witnessed firsthand what the rest of the world was losing its mind over. I looked on from the side of the stage as my brother worked the crowd to a frenzy. He strutted around like a peacock and attacked his guitar—playing with his teeth, behind his back, between his legs, and over his head. Maybe more than any other person in the building, I knew Jimi had been preparing his entire life to be up there in front of a packed house of screaming fans. As he had always done, he expressed his deepest emotions through his guitar and allowed his true personality to shine through. Nobody, and I mean *nobody*, could play like Jimi.

As I scanned the expressive faces of the crowd, I could easily see they were just as blown away. Down in front, June's daughters Marsha, Linda, and Donna held up a giant sign they made: WELCOME HOME JIMI! LOVE, YOUR SISTERS. The rest of the crowd was busy trying to figure out what Jimi was doing on the guitar and stared at the stage in astonishment during his long sections of improvisation. My brother's music wasn't jazz. It wasn't straight rock and roll. And it sure as hell wasn't simple rhythm and blues or plain old soul. Jimi was perfectly blending many genres of music onstage into one perfect form and a completely new category of some kind. In brief moments within his songs, you could detect pieces of all of his musical influences. The songs incorporated a little touch of everything.

As I continued to watch intently from my spot, I experienced a strong sensation of floating. The LSD was kicking into another gear. I took a long, deep breath and tried to relax, but when I looked down at my feet, I suddenly realized I was *hovering* above the stage. In one gradual and fluid motion, I rose higher and higher until I finally reached the rafters. After I came to a stop, Jimi was already floating beside me. Together, we looked down and watched ourselves from above. But how could that be? He was down on the stage performing with his band. Wasn't he? That's what I knew to be true, but now my head was on fire and I wasn't so sure. From up high, I also stared wide-eyed at myself standing just offstage watching the show. How could I possibly be in two places at once? That was my first experience of astral projecting and leaving my physical body. When I glanced over at my brother, both of us busted up laughing. I was excited, anxious, and scared to death all at the same time. Part of me wanted to float higher; the other part wanted to retreat to the safety of the stage as soon as possible.

During a break between songs, the fear finally took over and panic rippled through me like an electric current. We were way too high in the air. If we fell to the stage below, we'd both be dead. At the moment when the increasing dread was going to cause me to freak out, a switch seemed to flip and I found myself back in my physical body on the side of the stage. When I realized I was no longer floating, I looked back up into the rafters to see if Jimi was still there. But he was gone, and only wires and cables were hanging up above.

Many people might say, *Come on, man, you were just loaded.* That certainly was the case, but it was still my experience as well as my reality at the time. Looking back, of course I attributed the sensations to the acid because it was the first time I ever had an out-of-body experience. But it felt real.

As I stood tripping on LSD and watching my brother electrify the capacity crowd for the rest of the show, it all suddenly made sense—the sights, the sounds, and the heightened sensations of being at the show. I was directly in the middle of the Jimi Hendrix Experience. Needless to say, the show completely blew my mind. The performance was a display of pure freedom. My brother had taken everything to a new level and place where music had never been before. Everyone wanted to know where an artist so original and innovative had come from.

I overheard all types of wild questions coming from people in the crowd that night. Everyone attempted to process and justify what he or she witnessed onstage.

Was Jimi on drugs all of the time?

Was Jimi drunk?

Was Jimi crazy?

After the show, the tour manager, Gerry Stickells, immediately met with the promoter and received a briefcase full of money, which was Jimi's fee for the night's show. I had no idea how much was in the case. Everything was cash back then and it was collected right on the spot, minutes after the end of the show.

Jimi and I jumped in his limo and checked into an enormous two-bedroom suite at the swank Olympic Hotel. During the ride, he only needed to take one look at my face to know I'd gone ahead and taken the LSD without him. He wasn't angry and just looked across the limo and gave me a smile. When we walked into his suite, Herb Price, a guy Jimi kept around as a personal assistant, was organizing his outfits and unpacking his things. On the road, my brother traveled with multiple suitcases full of accessories and custom-made stage clothes. He couldn't possibly keep everything organized without Herb.

The party was already in full swing when our dad, June, and Janie strolled through the front door to the suite. I don't think my brother even invited Dad, but somehow he found his way to the hotel.

Around midnight, my brother told me to order room service for everyone. When I suggested getting filet mignon, Dad had a fit. "Come on now, Leon. Your brother can't afford that. There must be a vending machine around somewhere we get some snacks from instead."

"Dad, look where you are," I said, gesturing to the giant two-bedroom suite. "It's no problem. Buster told me to order for everyone so that's what I'm doing."

"Naw, naw, naw," Dad said. "You ain't doing that."

Jimi overheard us going back and forth and made his way across the room. "Dad, let Leon handle it. Go sit down on the couch and watch television or something."

Thankfully, Dad backed off once Jimi put his foot down. No matter where Dad went or what he witnessed, he found it impossible to believe that his son had money. Even after Jimi bought him a house and a brand-new truck, Dad still wasn't so sure. Jimi and his band played a sold-out show only a few hours before, and still Dad wasn't sure if Jimi was successful. The long years of struggling had taken their toll on Dad, and he resisted the idea that Jimi didn't need to scrape by anymore. Now that God had finally blessed Jimi with an amazing life and answered his prayers, Dad was almost in fear of the situation.

After all of my time living in hotels downtown, I was no stranger to ordering room service. As planned, I ordered filet mignon for everyone, along with crème brûlée and a few bottles of top-shelf champagne. As I mentioned each item to the woman on the phone, Dad still heckled me from the couch. I finally put the receiver down by my side and asked, "Have you lost your mind? Be quiet!"

After all his talk, we didn't hear another peep out of him once our dinners arrived and Dad cut into his delicious filet mignon.

As the party wore on, Jimi worked his magic on a couple girls, but I also noticed he was getting on particularly well with June's daughter Marsha, who was very attractive. On the couch, Dad, June, and Janie sat like a set of statues, essentially staring at everyone with nothing to say. This type of scene wasn't exactly a great fit for them, and they weren't sure how to relate to the rest of the people in the room. Jimi would never pipe up and say anything to them. If I left it up to him, he'd probably let them sit there all night. But when I looked over at the clock and noticed it was closing in on one in the morning, I decided it was time to make a move.

"Dad, can I talk to you for a minute?" I pulled him aside. "Listen, most of the people have left and Buster and me are going to hang out. Besides, little Janie needs to go to bed. It's late."

Thankfully, Dad got the hint and knew exactly what I was talking about. "Come on, June," he announced. "It's time we got going now."

After Dad and June left with Janie, Marsha stayed to hang out. It was easy to see that Marsha was attracted to Jimi from the moment they met. Soon, Jimi disappeared with her into one of the bedrooms, while I and one of the other girls who stayed around took the other.

The next morning, I woke up alone in the suite at the hotel. I later found out that my brother and Marsha had headed back to Dad's house in the early hours of the morning because Jimi had a local appearance to make. At 7:00 A.M., a local Seattle journalist named Pat MacDonald showed up at Dad's front door to pick up my brother and drive him over to his scheduled appearance at Garfield High School. I'm sure the guy was a little more than concerned when he saw Jimi hadn't showered and was wearing the same clothes from the previous night. Not to mention my brother was also fighting a hangover from hell. I missed out on the whole Garfield appearance, and when I met back up with Jimi later in the afternoon, he wasn't all that happy about how the scene had turned out. He told me it was a disaster.

"Man, going over there without my guitar was like a nightmare," he said, collapsing onto the couch next to me in Dad's basement. "The whole school was at the assembly and asking me all sorts of pointless questions. I couldn't wait to leave."

My brother wasn't a natural public speaker and always needed his guitar in front of an audience. That was his thing. A speaking engagement was way out of his comfort zone. I felt bad for him because it surely wasn't the triumphant return to his old high school he envisioned.

After Jimi crashed out down in the basement for a few hours, Mike Jeffrey came by the house and declared it was time for Jimi to go. He had a flight to catch out of Sea-Tac for his next gig in Denver, Colorado, at Regis College. Before he left, he gave me a copy of his latest album, *Axis: Bold as Love*, which he said contained a song called "Castles Made of Sand."

"That's a song about us growing up," Jimi told me.

Together, we all drove in Dad's car and saw him off at the airport. My brother's homecoming was a whirlwind lasting only a little more than twenty-four hours, but we certainly made the most of it. I hated to see him fly off so quickly, but I understood he was busy.

After arriving back at the house, I listened to "Castles Made of Sand." Just as Jimi said, the song's lyrics told some of the story of our childhood. The first verse was all about Mama leaving Dad for the final time after the car crash in his convertible. Jimi's words brought back a vivid memory of that day. I was surprised to find myself the main character in the second verse, which spoke of the "little Indian brave" who was snatched up in a "surprise attack" before he turned ten years old. That was exactly when Dad was forced to place me in foster care at the Wheelers. The most powerful section of the song was the third and last verse, which recounted our mama passing on and how we had seen her that final time in the hospital. She was the young woman who was "crippled for life" in the wheelchair. The song ended brilliantly with the young woman jumping on a "golden winged ship" and flying off into the distance forever. Jimi put it perfectly because that's exactly how I wanted to envision Mama up there in heaven.

SEPTEMBER 6, 1968

Not long after my brother left to continue touring, he wired me $5,000 and sent Dad enough money to go out and buy himself a brand-new '68 Chevrolet Malibu and '68 GMC three-quarter-ton, V-8 pickup truck. Dad was as happy as I'd ever seen him driving each gorgeous new car off the sales lot.

Dad and I didn't hear from Jimi much after his homecoming concert. It was close to impossible for him to stay in touch, given the schedule he was keeping out on the road and in the recording studio. But every once in a while he'd call the house to check in. Since something was always going down on the Seattle streets to get hooked into, sometimes I was around for his calls and sometimes I wasn't.

The stakes were getting higher for me out on the streets. Our crew usually tried to hang back and lie low for two or three months in between scores, but it wasn't easy to ignore my addiction to the action. As soon as someone plotted our next move, we typically went back into action. Although we always insisted it was important to stick with the smaller jobs, one of us came up with the idea to hit a large company called Wyeth Laboratories, which manufactured the diet pills we called crisscross speed. The rumor swirling around downtown was that the company kept somewhere around 1 million pills in the building. Crisscross pills were the best speed you could get and were all the rage at the time. Although I could take a bunch and stay awake for days hustling and gambling, it was an absolute world of pain when I came down. My joints and muscles ached like hell. It wasn't a pretty scene.

After casing the Wyeth lab for around a week, our crew went in exactly as planned. We hit the back room and began rifling through boxes and boxes of different drugs.

"What's the number again?" I asked Dan, scanning through the shelves.

"Nine eight three six two . . . I think," he told me.

"You *think*?"

"It's either 98362 or 98367. Why don't they just say 'amphetamine' on them or something!" he yelled.

Not only did all of the boxes look the same, but the pills were also carbon copies of each other. Plus, we were trying to identify these tiny things in the dark. However, I had no intention of giving up. A million or so pills were supposed to be on the racks somewhere, and at around a quarter apiece on the street, that meant we could be looking at a nice payday. No way were we leaving that kind of money behind. I kept scanning the different boxes with my flashlight until luckily I found exactly what we were looking for. There were shelves and shelves of them. We had finally hit the mother lode. The guys and I scrambled to pull the boxes from the storage shelves and stack them on the floor.

"Oh, man! We've got trouble!" one of the boys yelled back from the front room. "The cops just drove by in their car!"

Everyone sprinted for the back door. I didn't even hesitate to smash a window with the jiffy bar and dive through out into the alley. We made it back to our car, but before we reached the main road, the cops boxed us in with their squad cars. Luckily, we tossed the jiffy bar and lockpicks out the window before they stopped us.

"They ain't got nothing on us," Dan said, trying to stay calm. "Just stick to your story. It wasn't us. We were just driving around and hanging out."

The plan might have worked out, but one of the cops spotted the shards of glass in the sweater I was wearing. The expensive cardigan had gotten chewed up from my leap through the window at the lab. We were all cuffed and stuffed into the back of the squad cars.

We later found out that we hadn't properly disabled the security alarm when we broke in. It was a silent signal, so we never knew the difference . . . until the cops unexpectedly showed up.

Because we were already tight with most of the big players downtown, we had access to a team of top-notch lawyers. We thought they could make anything happen if we paid them enough money. The guys and I were out of jail within two hours and back on the street. While we were out on bail, we held a meeting with our lawyer to plot our next move.

"Listen, Leon, they caught you with all of that glass in your shirt, so you are absolutely burnt," the lawyer told me. "You're going to go down for this either way, so it's better to take the fall for everyone. Without you, they have no case against the other guys."

I didn't like the way any of it was sounding. The lawyers had already tried coming up with different scenarios to save our asses and made repeated attempts to deflect the blame. They argued it could have been the maintenance people that broke into the laboratory or possibly someone else in town that was trying to set us up. But none of it was sticking. Throwing me to the sharks was a last-ditch effort. I didn't know what to do. No matter what the lawyers said, no way was I going to shoulder all of the blame and confess to a crime like that. When the other guys saw I wasn't going to be a patsy for them, the realization hit that we were all screwed.

"There's no other option," one of the lawyers told us at dinner one night. "If Leon isn't taking the rap, then everybody has to plead out. I'm talking about guilty pleas all around. If you do that, they will give you a reduced sentence. Hell, some of you might even get probation."

My future wasn't looking too bright. I already had a couple pinches on my police record, and who knew what kind of effect that would have when the judge went to hand down my sentence.

With my sentencing hovering over my head like a dark cloud, Dad and I learned that Jimi was coming back to town to play a second gig on September 6, 1968, this time at the Seattle Center Coliseum. On a cool and crisp early morning, we picked him up from the airport.

On the car ride back to Dad's house, my brother slipped a new record out of his bag and handed it to me, a copy of his upcoming album, *Electric Ladyland*. I quietly sat in the backseat looking at the cover photograph of a group of naked women together in front of a black background.

"What do you think?" Jimi asked.

"It's cool," I offered, handing the record back. "But it doesn't look like there are too many fine ladies in the group."

Jimi laughed.

"Most of them are pretty regular," I added. "Couldn't the record company find some better ones?"

"Man, you crack me up, Leon."

Not that it mattered what I thought of the artwork; the album went on to garner plenty of coverage from the press. A UK book and record chain even initially refused to stock the album because of the nudity on the cover.

That night at the Center Coliseum, I looked on as Jimi played a rendition of "The Star-Spangled Banner" to the capacity crowd. I'd never seen him perform the song before, and overall the reaction was mixed. As I looked out over the audience, some fans cheered wildly, while others appeared confused and in some cases even a bit frightened. I thought it was unique and powerful; I loved Jimi's interpretation.

Later after the gig, his old buddies and bandmates from back in the day were waiting to reconnect with him at Dad's house. Not long after we arrived, they swept through and basically kidnapped us. Together, we spent the rest of the night making the rounds, visiting friends and partying. We hit Jimmy's friend Pernell's house to smoke a few joints, then made the rounds through the Encore Ballroom and the Black and Tan. By the time my brother and I made our way back to Dad's house, it was around four in the morning. Even at that hour, a few neighbors were still lingering. As we came shuffling up the walkway, the front door swung open and our dad staggered out onto the porch. He'd obviously been drinking all night. Dad wasn't happy we'd skipped out with our buddies and missed most of the party. He was disappointed because he wanted to introduce Jimi to the people he invited over.

"You boys get in this house!" he yelled. "I brought all of these people over for a nice party for you, and you take off for the night!"

Dad was acting as if we were both little kids again. Neither Jimi nor I could keep a straight face. We sat down on the couch and watched as he slammed the front door shut and walked into the room.

"I didn't know you were having a party, Dad," Jimi told him.

"Even your sisters Kathy and Pam were over here looking to meet you!" Dad shouted.

"Who?" I asked. My brother and I exchanged a smile, which one made Dad angrier.

"Both of you get back there in that bedroom! You're gonna get a whoopin'!" Dad shouted.

We couldn't hold it together any longer. Jimi and I looked over at each other and broke out laughing. The days of Dad's putting his hands on us were long gone. When we got up and walked past him, he didn't make another move. After we went downstairs and fell onto the couches, we still heard him growling at us from upstairs. I'm not sure what Dad was thinking, if he was thinking at all. One of the biggest rock stars on the planet sure as hell wasn't going to be getting a whoopin'. Jimi and I rounded out the night by smoking a joint. We spent another hour or so continuing to joke at Dad's expense. We traded our best imitations of him until we finally crashed out.

A few hours later, Mike Jeffrey had to bang on the door forever to wake us up. As I struggled to pull myself together and find my clothes, Jimi called out to me from the bedroom. When I walked in, he threw a blue, crushed-velvet suit on the bed and told me to try it on. *Now we're talking*, I thought. Since my brother and I were exactly the same size, the clothes fit perfectly. After I slipped on the pants and frilly shirt, my brother reached into his pocket and pulled out a couple of silver rings, which I also put on. When my outfit was complete, I stepped back and admired myself in the full-length mirror on the wall. It was impossible to wipe the smile from my face. I looked like a rock star.

When we met Mike out in front of the house, he told Jimi the limo was ready to drive him to his gig up in Vancouver. He was set to play the Pacific Coliseum with Vanilla Fudge, later that night.

"I'm not going in the limo," Jimi told Mike. "I'm driving with my dad and brother up to the gig in Vancouver. We're going to make it a family trip."

By the look on his face, I could tell Mike wasn't too happy with Jimi's idea. "But, Jimi, listen, I think it would be better if—"

Our mama with little Johnny not long after he was born, in early 1943 *(Courtesy of Rockin Artwork LLC)*

Me on Mama's lap and Buster with Dad—1948
(Courtesy of Rockin Artwork LLC)

Me at two years old and Buster at seven
(Courtesy of Rockin Artwork LLC)

My brother posing in his new red jacket
he bought to play in the Rocking Kings
(Courtesy of Rockin Artwork LLC)

Opposite: Playing
The Woodstock
Festival—August
18, 1969 *(Credit:
Leonard Eisenberg/
Courtesy of Rockin
Artwork LLC)*

Miami Pop Festival—May 19, 1968 *(Ken Davidoff/Courtesy of Rockin Artwork LLC)*

Miami Pop Festival—day—May 19, 1968 *(Ken Davidoff/Courtesy of Rockin Artwork LLC)*

Boston Garden—
November 16, 1968
(*Credit: Leonard Eisenberg/
Courtesy of Rockin Artwork
LLC*)

My brother performing in
Framingham, Massachusetts—
August 26, 1968 (*Credit: Leonard
Eisenberg/Courtesy of Rockin Artwork
LLC*)

Our mama's final resting place—Seattle, Washington (*Courtesy of Rockin Artwork LLC*)

Left to right, bottom row: Chandre Green (extended family), Jonelle Hendrix (daughter), LeAnne Hendrix (daughter), *middle:* Christine Hendrix (wife and mother), *top row:* Jason Hendrix (son), little Jimi Hendrix (son— born on the same day as his uncle Jimi), Alex Hendrix (son), *on his lap:* Tyrell Green, son of Chandre), Freddy Narancic (nephew) (*Credit: Personal archives of Leon Hendrix*)

Dad and I at his house in 2000 *(Jasmin Rogg/ Personal Archives of Leon Hendrix)*

Performing with my band in Italy—2010 *(Credit: Cristina Arrigoni)*

"I'm not taking the limo, Mike," my brother repeated. "I'm going to Vancouver with my family, and we're going to meet up with our relatives there after the show. The last time I came through town, I didn't have any time with my family. So, I'm riding north with them."

It was ridiculous for Mike to think my brother was going to sequester himself in a limo when his family was there to spend time with him. The only person that situation made sense to was Mike. He didn't want any part of Jimi's coming back to Seattle to play in the first place, and the family trip up to the next gig definitely got his blood boiling. He sure as hell was mad about Jimi's deciding to ride with us, but still, Mike realized he was fighting a losing battle and eventually relented. Nothing he did was going to change my brother's mind.

Before long, Dad pulled the Chevy Malibu Jimi had bought for him out of the garage. When Dad swung the door open and sprang out of the driver's side, I could see that something was bothering him. He took a few steps up the sidewalk and pulled me aside.

"What the hell are you wearing, Leon?" he asked, looking me up and down. "Where'd you get that crazy getup?"

"Buster gave me a few things."

"Well, you look stupid."

"What do you mean? I'm wearing the same stuff as Jimi. And Jimi doesn't look stupid, does he?"

Dad simply shook his head in disgust and climbed back into the car. Besides, I wasn't going to stand there out on the street and go at it with him. I looked cool and that was all that mattered. Jimi and I jumped in and we set out on the road headed north to Canada. We spread out in the backseat with Janie sitting in between us.

No matter how present it was in the back of my mind, I still didn't come clean to my brother about my trouble with the law. It felt as though if we didn't talk about what had happened, then it wasn't real. I'm sure my brother was hearing bits and pieces about how I'd been arrested, but he never came right out and asked me anything about it. Besides, he was much too caught up in the pace of his own life. I was simply thrilled to be able to tag along for a while and share in his wild success with him.

The drive north to Vancouver was a solid four hours or so in the car. As Buster and I whaled away in the backseat, cracking each other up with stories about back in the day, Dad and June sat up front almost completely silent. Dad didn't have much to say to Jimi when he came back home to visit. Most of their exchanges were small talk about nothing in particular. Dad was still the same old guy as when Buster had left town, and my brother couldn't have been more different. Dad must have asked my brother about the weather in England a half dozen times.

"What's it like with all that rain over there, son?"

"About the same as the weather in Seattle because both places are at the same latitude."

"Huh? Lati-what?"

"There's more rain in Seattle, but more fog in London, Dad."

"Oh, is that right?"

The conversations were a real snooze. Not long after we made our way out of Seattle, Jimi and I fell asleep in the backseat. About halfway through our trip, we pulled over and stopped at a Denny's restaurant in Mount Vernon, Washington, to get a late lunch. Our mixed-bag crew attracted some attention. From the moment we stepped into the restaurant, it felt as if all eyes were on us. We were introducing an interesting cast of characters to their local eatery: a short black man, a Japanese woman, a six-year-old Japanese girl, me in my hip new threads, and of course the "great Jimi Hendrix." The place was filled with nothing but white people. They didn't know how to react, so everyone just left us alone . . . including the wait-

staff. After we sat at a booth in the corner, they kept us sitting forever. Not a single waitress came by our table to check to see if we
wanted anything. I was fuming. Dad, June, and Buster would never
pipe up and say anything, so as usual it was going to fall on my shoulders. But before I made a move to start cussing people out, a pretty
young girl not more than eight years old appeared at our table.

"Hey, mister, are you Jimi Hendrix?" she asked my brother.

"Yes, I am," he told her.

She held up a piece of notepaper. "Can I have your autograph?"

"Of course you can."

Once my brother signed the little girl's piece of paper, the flood-
gates opened and most of the younger kids in the restaurant began
making their way over. Some of the waitresses even came over, too,
looking for Jimi to sign something for them. Because of all the
attention, the manager emerged from the back and offered us an
apology. As soon as he left, a waitress finally decided it was okay to
take our order.

"I am very sorry about all this," she said, keeping her voice low so
only our table heard. "The manager enforces a policy that we don't
serve blacks in the restaurant, but he said this was the first time we
could do it."

Whatever the reason, I'm just glad we ended up getting our food
because I was starving. A few more minutes of being ignored and
the scene was going to get ugly.

When we arrived in Vancouver, we went straight to our aunt
Pearl's house, even though Jimi's management had already booked
my brother a hotel room. He was more interested in spending the
afternoon with our cousins Diane and Bobby, Grandma Nora, and
Aunt Pearl, as it had been years since the last time he'd seen them.

That night, Jimi put on another amazing performance in front of
a packed house at the Pacific Coliseum, but I don't think some of

our family knew what they were getting themselves into. They had never been to a big rock-and-roll concert before. To make matters worse, the management sat all of them in the front row and made the mistake of positioning Grandma Nora in front of the biggest speaker of them all. Maybe they thought she was so old that she couldn't hear, but that wasn't the case. The sheer volume of the show surprised Grandma Nora and nearly blew her out of her seat. I looked down from up on the side of the stage to see her covering her ears with both hands. Thankfully, Dad recognized what was going and got her moved to a different seat in the back of the venue so she could enjoy Jimi's show. As an added bonus, my brother even dedicated "Foxy Lady" to her toward the end of his set.

I only caught half of Jimi's performance because I was busy hanging out with many of my buddies who made the drive up from Seattle to check out the show. I split time between standing on the side of the stage, hanging out back in the dressing room, and walking around in the crowd. It was a nonstop party.

By the time we made it back to Aunt Pearl's house after the show, it must have been around midnight. Our family feasted on an amazing turkey dinner she put together for us. It was important to her to cook a Thanksgiving meal for Jimi because she knew he'd probably be on the road somewhere when the holidays rolled around and wouldn't have family to spend them with. We talked about the old days when we used to spend summers in the area, and it was a great reunion. Jimi was happy to be around family and wanted to do something to help out Aunt Pearl and Grandma Nora. He was also generous enough to give me some more money. Just before he went to bed for the night, Jimi pulled me into one of the bedrooms to show me a suitcase full of cash he had gotten from Mike Jeffrey after the gig. There must have been around $20,000 or so in stacks of $5 bills. After separating out four equal amounts, he gave Aunt Pearl and Grandma Nora each an equal share. They were both incredibly thankful that Jimi helped them out with their expenses. Life wasn't easy for them up in Canada, so Jimi's kind gesture made a big difference in their lives. It was the least my brother could do to repay both of them for all of the times they'd helped take care of us when we were young.

When he returned to the bedroom, he grabbed a leather shoulder bag off the floor. After stuffing a stack of bills into it, Jimi handed the bag to me. "Here, Leon, I want you to get a plane ticket and meet me in Los Angeles in a few days. I've got a gig coming up at the Hollywood Bowl next Saturday, so you can come out just before that."

As I sat on the edge of the bed listening to what he was telling me, I looked down at the cash inside the bag. There must have been somewhere around $5,000. It was probably the third time Jimi had given me money, and I was thankful. He was more than generous and always helped out Dad and me when we needed it most. So, whatever he wanted me to do, I was going to come through for him. No way was I going to let him down.

"No problem at all, Buster. I'll be there."

The next morning, we woke up early, and after a tearful goodbye with Aunt Pearl and Grandma Nora, Dad, June, Janie, Jimi, and I rounded up our stuff and set out on the road south to Seattle. Time was of the essence because Jimi was scheduled to perform in Spokane, Washington, later that night at the Coliseum. He had a flight to catch.

At the airport, I waited with Jimi until his plane was ready. When it taxied toward us, I noticed it was nothing but a small prop plane that didn't look too sturdy. I would definitely have had second thoughts about flying in it, but Jimi wasn't the least bit concerned. He'd already spent too much time in the army jumping out of all types of aircraft.

Over the next few days, I told anyone who would listen about my plans to meet up with Jimi in California. I was flying high and couldn't wait to get to Los Angeles and check out the hip scene everybody was talking about in the streets. As usual, Dad tried to put a damper on my plans. When I broke the news to him, he wasn't too impressed and tried to convince me that Jimi didn't want me to come to California to meet up with him.

"He asked me to go and meet up with him," I explained.

"You're only going to be bugging him. He's trying to work and you're going to mess him up," Dad told me.

"I am not! He wants me there to help him with things," I snapped back.

"I'm just saying that he really doesn't want you there with him."

"What are you talking about? Do you remember all of those times Buster called us up while he was on the road playing in bands and told us good times were going to be coming? Well, those good times are finally here. I'm tired of you having a problem with it all of the time."

Dad stormed off mumbling to himself about something, which was fine with me because I wasn't listening to anything else he had to say. My mind was made up and the plan was in place. But I stopped packing and threw my suitcase back in the bedroom closet. Why bring all of my old threads when I could buy newer, hipper clothes when I landed in California? I had five grand in the bag to throw around.

The next morning, I took a cab down to Sea-Tac Airport and bought a one-way ticket on Alaska Airlines to Los Angeles International Airport for $48. Although I was out on bail and my next court date loomed in the near future, I couldn't pass up my brother's offer. No way was I going to let myself miss out on the opportunity of a lifetime.

CALIFORNIA DREAMING

"We will soon be preparing to land at Los Angeles International Airport. Please be sure to gather your belongings," the stewardess informed us over the plane's speakers. Her announcement quickly reminded me that in my rush to leave Seattle, I didn't bother to pack any bags. I simply caught a cab to the airport and boarded the plane. No that it really mattered; I still had a decent-size wad of cash in my jacket pocket to buy clothes once I hit town. Hopefully Jimi would let me dive back into his wardrobe and pick out a few cool outfits.

After touching down in Los Angeles, I quickly hopped a taxi to the Beverly Hills Hotel, where Gerry Stickells had said Jimi would be. My brother was nowhere to be found, so I wandered around the hotel's lobby, trying to figure out what to do. The people working at the front desk weren't much help. They insisted they couldn't tell me if Jimi had already checked in or when he was set to arrive. It looked as if I was on my own for the time being.

Without much else to accomplish at the hotel, the first order of business was to hit the town. There was no point sitting on my hands in the lobby waiting for Jimi to finally walk through the front door. And when he did finally show up, I didn't want him seeing me in the same old threads. I had to get my hands on some cool new outfits if I was going to be hanging around the Hollywood scene. After taking a taxi to check out the sophisticated shops on Rodeo Drive, I realized they weren't going to do the trick. Every piece of clothing carried a price tag anywhere from $500 to $1,000. I saw no reason to dish out my cash for that type of rip-off. I was way out of my element and didn't have much of an idea where to begin. I decided to catch another cab and have the driver take me to Hollywood to check out the clothing shops along Melrose Avenue. After spending much of the afternoon wandering around different boutiques with the rest of the tourists, I finally pulled the trigger on a fine pair of alligator boots, a few shirts, and a pair of leather pants. Before heading back to Beverly Hills, the driver dropped me by the Hollywood Wax Museum, and later I grabbed a meal at the famous Musso & Frank Grill.

When I arrived back at the hotel, there was still no sign of my brother. However, a different woman was working at the front desk.

"Are you aware that your brother has a limousine out front?" she asked. "I believe it is at your full disposal."

It was difficult not to laugh. There I was jumping into cab after cab all day while a limo was sitting directly out in front of the hotel waiting to take me anywhere in the city. Throughout my life, I'd never expected to be given anything, so it was going to take a little while to get used to this new type of privileged lifestyle.

"How are you today, sir?" the driver out front asked, opening the rear door for me. "Where would you like to go?"

"To tell you the truth, I have no idea," I said, easing down onto the plush leather of the backseat. "Just drive around, I guess. Hell, take me anywhere."

From the hotel, we set out on another tour of Los Angeles. We made our way down Sunset Boulevard through Beverly Hills, past the mansions of Bel Air, and finally back toward the Sunset Strip, traveling east. The time spent being chauffeured around the city flew by, and by the time I finally looked at the clock up front, it was already 8:00 p.m. There wasn't much left for me to do out on the town.

"Where to now, sir?" the driver asked.

Since the daylight was running out and there was still no sign of Jimi, it was important to find some place to crash. "Take me to a cheap hotel downtown," I answered.

It seemed like my only option. However, as we made our way farther east on Wilshire Boulevard, the ritzy streets of Beverly Hills quickly disappeared and the refined landscape was replaced by run-down neighborhoods and dilapidated buildings. Since I'd fixed myself a few glasses of rum in the back and was feeling a buzz, I didn't mind so much. The driver probably knew what he was doing, so there was no reason for me to get on his case. When we finally came to a stop downtown at an old, raggedy hotel off Figueroa, the driver got out and opened my door. Back home in Seattle, I'd spent more than enough time in sketchy motels, but the place he brought me to was on a whole different level. Despite having second thoughts about my bright decision to flee the luxurious surroundings of Beverly Hills, I sent the driver on his way and told him to pick me up the following morning at 9:00 A.M. That night, I slept with one eye open in the most cockroach-infested motel room ever.

As planned, the limo came to grab me the next morning, and we returned to the Beverly Hills Hotel. Luckily, this time I found Mike Jeffrey in one of the conference rooms where the road crew was having a production meeting, and he gave me Jimi's room number. I couldn't have been more relieved because there was no way I was going to survive another night in that slum of a motel downtown.

When Jimi swung open the door to his suite, his face lit up. "Where have you been? I was looking for you."

"I grabbed a room downtown last night."

"What are you talking about? I booked you a *suite* here in the hotel." He laughed.

"Well, you weren't around and I wasn't sure what to do. The people at the front desk weren't talking either."

"Didn't I tell you we were going to be out of town last night? We played in Oakland and got into LA this morning."

Stepping into the room, I spotted his assistant Herb unpacking suitcases and arranging clothes in the closet. Two fine girls were also sitting on the couch, whom Jimi introduced as Devon Wilson and Carmen Borrero. They were both as beautiful as any girls I had ever seen. My brother definitely knew how to travel in style. Carmen was a pretty Puerto Rican girl who looked more like a model than Devon and was also slightly more refined. Devon was a streetwise black girl who seemed to be out of it and half-loaded most of the time. The four of us didn't hang out in the suite for long because Jimi had plans to meet up with some people at the Rainbow Room on Sunset for a little while before going on to do a sound check over at the Hollywood Bowl.

Before we set out for Hollywood, I quickly made my way back down to the lobby, checked into my suite, and changed into the clothes I'd bought in the shops on Melrose. When I showed up out front in my new alligator boots and leather bell-bottom pants, the awkward expression on Jimi's face let me know that he wasn't digging my outfit. After giving me a once-over and a smile, he kept walking out to the limo. I felt a little out of place, but tried not to let it bother me. My new getup wasn't exactly part of my regular look out on the streets of Seattle, but I figured it was Beverly Hills and Hollywood, the home of glitz and glamour. Everybody had a flashy style. In a way I was trying to blend in and stand out at the same time, if it was possible.

As we set out in the limo that afternoon, pouring drinks from the minibar in the back and passing around a joint, it felt as if Jimi and I were setting out on adventures the way we did when we were little boys. The two of us couldn't have been happier to be reunited. Everything was so difficult early in our lives, and now, years later, life couldn't have been better. All of my brother's wildest dreams had come true, and I was fortunate enough to be right by his side and share the experience.

The Sunset Strip was completely transformed since the last time I had seen it the previous afternoon. It was *alive*. As we drove north up La Cienega Boulevard and turned onto Sunset, long-haired hippies were walking the streets everywhere with flowers in their hair, wearing wild outfits. Once we hit the crowded Rainbow Room, everything was chaos. The place was full to capacity with a who's who of show business. Everybody was somebody. At least, that's what Jimi was telling me. Being fresh off the city streets, I wasn't hip to any of the popular superstars. My time during the last few years had been spent listening to the likes of the Supremes, Wilson Pickett, and classic Motown music. I was busy looking around for people like those and didn't know any better.

As soon as we posted up at a table and ordered some drinks, waves of gorgeous girls soon began approaching in hopes of meeting Jimi. One after another, they came to the table with a gushing, nervous enthusiasm. Jimi was respectful and pleasant, but didn't have any interest in taking things any further since he was already with Devon and Carmen for that night. Jimi was content to sit back sipping his Johnnie Walker on the rocks and listening to the music. I, on the other hand, worked my way around the club. There was no point in staying in our reserved booth and having everyone stare at me like an exhibit at the zoo. Fine women everywhere were staring at me just because I was with Jimi. As they slipped me their phone numbers on little pieces of paper and cocktail napkins, I stuffed them into my pockets. After a few laps around the bar, my pockets were full.

When I returned to the table, I could see Jimi was getting antsy. "Listen, I've got to head over to the Bowl for sound check," he said, rising from the table. "Meet me later backstage before the show, okay?"

"Sure thing."

"You gonna be okay here?"

I paused and surveyed the room, the beautiful women. "Yeah, I think I can manage," I said with a smile.

After Jimi departed with Devon and Carmen, I hung out for another hour or so, then called the hotel to have the limo drive over to pick me up.

Not until reaching the rear gate to the venue did it dawn on me that I'd never grabbed a VIP pass for the Hollywood Bowl from Jimi. My limo driver offered to pull over and sort everything out with security, but I was a little loaded after hanging out at the Rainbow Room and was too impatient to wait in the back of the car. "Don't worry," I told him, popping the rear door open. "Just drop me off and I'll find my way." After knifing my way through the crowd, I walked over to the security guard standing in front of the gate entrance. At first, I tried to casually pass through the velvet ropes as if I didn't notice him standing there.

But he was already hip to that trick. He raised a giant forearm into my chest and stopped me in my tracks. "Hey, where do you think you are going?"

"Don't worry, it's cool," I said with a smile. "I'm Leon Hendrix. I'm Jimi's brother, dude."

"I ain't got time for this shit, kid. Do you think I'm stupid or something?"

"I'm telling you the truth, though," I insisted.

"Whatever." He shook his head. "I've already turned away at least *five* of Jimi's brothers and sisters, ten of his managers, a couple of his lawyers, and probably a half dozen of his wives and girlfriends. Every other girl that walks up here says she's having Jimi's baby and needs to see him. So, no matter what your deal is, I'm going to need you to stand back behind the rope. I can't let you in."

I obviously needed another plan. When I stepped aside, a guy with a big Afro walked up next to me and started drumming against a nearby picket fence with drumsticks. As I stared absently at him while trying to figure out how to get myself into the gig, a long, black limousine rolled past us and stopped at the gate. Two security guards slid the tall fencing aside so the limo could fit through the rear entrance of the Hollywood Bowl. Suddenly, the car jerked to a stop and the rear door swung open. Jimi stepped out and pointed a finger in my direction. I waved back at him from behind the velvet ropes at the gate.

"Hey! That's my little brother right there!" he yelled. Then he pointed to the guy standing near me with the big Afro and the drumsticks. "And that's my friend Buddy Miles! Let both those guys through the gate!"

As Buddy started walking through the gate, I jogged over to the limo and hopped in the back with Jimi, Devon, and Carmen. After making our way to the rear entrance, we were ushered through a maze of corridors until we finally reached a small dressing room backstage. As I walked into the room, I noticed the interesting buffet laid out on the table against the wall. Bags of cocaine and weed were mixed right in between the sandwich platters, bags of potato chips, and fruit bowl. Even though Jimi never requested that drugs be available to him backstage before a show, they always seemed to be present. In providing those types of things, people were usually paying tribute to him. It may have been an essential part of the rock culture at the time, but my brother didn't typically indulge before his shows. He didn't need to. All he needed was his guitar and an amplifier to get off on his music. Jimi didn't want anything getting in the way of the connection between him, his playing, and his fans. He didn't want interference from anything or anyone before he stepped onto the stage. Don't get me wrong, after the show was a different story. He did a little of everything here and there, but typically it wasn't at the expense of his playing.

My plane may have touched down in Los Angeles the previous morning, but I still felt that I was floating high above the ground. The whole scene at the Bowl felt surreal. It was tough to shake the sensation and get my head straight. Jimi made it known to all of his people as well as the venue's security that I was his brother, so I had free rein there. People simply stepped back and let me wander around, no questions asked.

Devon, Carmen, and I hung out together while Jimi and his band talked things over before they took the stage. The girls got VIP tickets to go down and sit in front of the stage, just past the fountain, and I took up a spot on the side of the stage to watch the show. But because of the way the Hollywood Bowl was set up, it was tough to see anything from my position. So I went down to the VIP section and watched from in front of the stage. As soon as Jimi broke into his first tune, fans started running and jumping in the fountain, especially when he tore into "Foxy Lady." The water was splashing up everywhere—all over the people sitting in the VIP section and onto the stage. The fire marshals couldn't do much but look at each other confusedly. Nobody was supposed to be in the fountain, but the only solution was to cut the power to the stage and shut the show down. Eventually, the splashing in the fountain got so wild that half-way through the introduction to "Little Wing," Jimi stopped play-ing for a moment and looked out over the audience. Noel grabbed the microphone and asked the crowd to be careful about electrocut-ing Jimi. After the sold-out crowd of some eighteen thousand began cheering, the band started the song up again.

After the show, Jimi, Devon, Carmen, and I were rushed out the back exit and stuffed in his limo. I completely forgot about my limo, but thankfully when the driver didn't hear anything from me, he returned to the hotel. The four of us cruised back to the Rainbow Room for a little while, but when the place started getting too crowded, we decided to make our way up the block to the Whiskey a Go Go, where Carmen used to work as a cocktail waitress before she met my brother. The walk west on Sunset was the two longest blocks I've ever traveled in my life. It must have taken us a half hour with all of the swarming fans clamoring for autographs. Once we reached the entrance of the Whiskey, the security ushered us right in past the line out front. It wasn't hard to find a place to sit—a reserved booth in the corner had a sign with JIMI HENDRIX written on it.

Jimi put his hand on my shoulder and pulled me closer as we made our way through the room. "Hey, there's Janis Joplin over there." He gestured toward a table in the corner.

"Cool," I answered, although what was actually going through my mind was *Who is Janis Joplin?* To me, Jimi was simply pointing out some girl. Hell, the place was full of them. Big deal. My brother continued identifying every famous rock-and-roll musician there throughout our night at the Whiskey. Every time I wasn't familiar with somebody Jimi motioned to, or with that person's music, he simply shook his head in disappointment. He was genuinely frustrated by my lack of knowledge of rock-and-roll stars. But I was too preoccupied with the growing ring of fine girls around Jimi and me, giving us the eye. As soon as one group moved on, another stepped right up.

"Listen, Leon, you need to try to keep some of these girls away from me," Jimi finally said in my ear over the loud music.

"Well, how can I? There's too many of them."

I did my best to shield Jimi from the overly excited girls, but the task was nearly impossible. We were under siege. And the girls weren't your everyday plain-Jane types off the street; they were the most beautiful models and actresses in the world. Even the girlfriends of other famous rock stars were doing everything they could to get Jimi's attention. In all my time in Los Angeles, I never met a girl that *didn't* want to get with Jimi.

Just because Carmen and Devon were my brother's constant companions, it didn't mean he wasn't allowed to disappear with other girls. When he didn't have time for them or lost interest, I was the next-best option. There was no possibility of Jimi settling down with one woman. Even if that were his intention, it would have been impossible because of the constant touring and traveling. Carmen and Devon knew the score and, to my knowledge, didn't have a problem with the situation. It was all free hippie love. A few times Devon even brought around other girls that she thought Jimi would dig.

Although Jimi told me he was ready to leave the club for the night, I wasn't interested in going anywhere else, not with that many beautiful women around. After Jimi exited the club, I hooked up with a fine girl, and together we took the party back to her luxurious apartment on Sunset Boulevard. She was probably only interested in being with me because of who my brother was, but I didn't care. Getting laid was getting laid. There was nothing to complain about.

Although it was an amazing night, I woke up the following morning with a hangover from hell and discovered not a penny was left in my wallet. While parading around like a big shot at the Whiskey the night before, I spent the rest of the cash Jimi had given me in Vancouver. I must have bought half the girls in the bar a drink.

"Make sure you let Jimi know you got the best pussy you ever had last night," the young lady I hooked up with told me from bed. "Tell him how good I was so he knows about me."

"You know what? I'd better just make sure one more time," I said, jumping back into bed with her.

With no cash to grab a cab, I dragged myself the two miles back to my suite at the Beverly Hills Hotel and passed out. But no more than a few hours later, the phone in my room jolted me awake. Gerry Stickells was on the line explaining that Jimi had already departed for his gig that night at the Memorial Auditorium in Sacramento. However, Gerry said I could still catch a ride with the rest of the band and the crew on the tour bus, which was leaving from out front in fifteen minutes.

"Yeah, sure," I mumbled into the phone. "I'll be out there in a few minutes." I then rolled out of bed and fixed myself a Jack Daniel's from the minibar to ease the pain.

The bus was like a deluxe hotel suite on wheels, and I wasted no time in spreading out on one of the plush couches. The crew and I didn't talk much because I passed out for most of the trip to Northern California. When I finally broke out of my slumber, we were already pulling into the parking lot of the Memorial Auditorium. Not long after we arrived, I connected with Jimi and he told me he wanted to drive out to see our cousin Gracie, Aunt Pat, and Uncle

Buddy, who lived about twenty miles away in Stockton, California. I was all for it because I hadn't seen any of them in a long time. As Jimi and I set out in his limo, his crew went to work loading all of his equipment into the venue.

Later that night for the final show of the tour, Vanilla Fudge, Fat Mattress, and Eire Apparent opened for Jimi at the Memorial Auditorium. As usual, I spent most of my time backstage hanging out or just offstage watching until the show was over. Together, Jimi and I took the limo back to Aunt's Pat's in Stockton and spent the night there. As he had done with the rest of our family, Jimi gave our cousin Gracie and Aunt Pat some money before we said our good-byes and set out onto the road headed south toward Los Angeles. On the way back, we stopped off to have lunch in Big Sur and later spent an hour or so in Santa Barbara checking out the town.

My life back in Seattle seemed to fall away during my time in California. My impending court proceedings never crossed my mind, and therefore I never felt the need to bring it up with Jimi. The only thing I was interested in was keeping the party going day and night. Fortunately, we were going nonstop and I had little time to dwell on my situation anyway.

After returning to Beverly Hills, I was woken up in my hotel suite by the telephone's loudly ringing. "Hello," I quietly said into the phone.

"Mr. Hendrix, this is the front desk with your wake-up call," a woman said.

"Okay," I told her, then hung up. Wake-up call? Did I request a wake-up call? It must have been Jimi playing with me. Sure enough, the phone rang again a few minutes later, and my brother was laughing on the other end. He always loved to clown around. My brother then gave me an address to take down. He said he wanted me to come over to a gorgeous house he had recently started renting on Benedict Canyon Drive in Beverly Hills.

After getting myself together, I made my way over to the posh part of town. The mansion had more than enough space for everyone in the band and the stage crew. When I walked in the front door, I saw a giant pipe organ in the living room with pipes that went up to and out through the roof. A drum set was set up, as well as a few of my brother's amplifiers and guitars. Noel and Mitch were there hanging out as well as Buddy Miles.

For the most part, I hadn't seen much of them since I'd arrived in Los Angeles. Mitch and Noel typically didn't join us whenever we hit the Hollywood scene. They mostly kept to themselves or hung out with the roadies, who were also mostly from England. It wasn't as if they didn't want to hang out with my brother. For starters, Jimi wasn't the easiest guy to track down, even for the guys in his own band. Second, he was more interested in surrounding himself with girls than spending time with his buddies. It was true for both of us. From early on, we gravitated toward women and sought their affection. They were always there to take care of us, to nurture us.

After scoping out the house, I made the mistake of walking in on Jimi in bed with two fine blond girls.

"Hell, Leon, I'll talk to you later! I'm busy!" Jimi snapped.

"Sorry, Jimmy," I said.

After sheepishly exiting the bedroom, I shuffled into the living room, where the band's equipment was set up. After picking up one of Jimi's guitars, which was still turned on and humming through one of the amplifiers, I started going at the thing like a madman— strangling the strings on the neck and wildly strumming. When I walked up in front of the monitors that were set up, the feedback was absolutely deafening. The sound coming out of the speakers sounded like a hurricane of noise and feedback. It was as if the guitar were possessed. Then underneath the racket I was creating, I heard something and stopped playing.

"Damn, Leon! Put my guitar down!" Jimi yelled from the other room.

"Whoops," I shouted back. "Sorry, Jimi."

In my mind I may have been creating a flurry of unique sounds, but my brother had a different take on it. Other people in the house suddenly came walking out of the other rooms and flashing me confused expressions.

When I made my way out back to the pool, at least twenty girls must have been parading around in bathing suits. The backyard was like a waiting room full of beautiful women just hanging out and prepping themselves for their turn with the great Jimi Hendrix. They were there with one purpose in mind—to get with him. It took some getting used to, standing on a pool patio that hung off a cliff. When I looked down over the railing, it must have been fifty feet down to the ground below. No matter how many times I walked around out there, the sensation never felt right.

It wasn't difficult to detect the great deal of tension in the house. I noticed that Noel, Mitch, and some of the English road crew mainly kept to themselves in one wing of the house, while Jimi, Buddy Miles, me, and other crew members remained in the opposite wing. I tried to make conversation with Noel or Mitch every once in a while, but whenever I knocked on the doors to their rooms, they seemed to be watching cartoons, of all things, and weren't too interested in talking. Their behavior made more sense after Jimi explained that they were growing bitter about the money arrangement. On more than one occasion, I overheard Noel and Mitch complaining to Gerry, who didn't hesitate to remind them that Jimi was the one making the millions of dollars and they were still "hired guns," as he put it. Neither of them had much to say after that.

Buddy Miles was also disgruntled at the situation and let his frustration boil over now and then, especially when we found ourselves alone out by the pool at the house or in a club. Because I wasn't associated with Jimi's management and was outside their circle of influence, Buddy felt more comfortable confiding in me.

"How come Jimi isn't trying to put our band together?" he asked me on more than a few occasions. "Enough with all of this other stuff. He says he wants to move on and have us do our thing, so what's taking him so long?"

Many people thought I possessed some type of influence over Jimi, but that was never the case. Sure, we were brothers and loved and trusted each other, but I would never exert pressure on him to do anything he didn't want to. My brother was his own free spirit and wasn't going to spring into action because of anything I ever said. Besides, he was already being pushed and pulled in enough directions by his management. The last thing he needed was for me to start putting in my two cents every time an opportunity presented itself. And no way was I going to start serving as a lobbyist for other people's agendas. Jimi was going to do what he wanted.

I'm sure that moving into a posh home in Beverly Hills sounded like a great concept to Jimi in the beginning. He probably assumed it would be a perfect place to retreat to at the end of the day to relax. But the Benedict Canyon Drive house quickly became a central party location. Once word spread that Jimi was residing there, shady characters descended upon the place, slipping in and out at all hours. Most nights, Jimi and I'd return after a night down on the Strip to house full of strangers.

As he had done back in Seattle, my brother eventually opened up his closet, partly because he was tired of seeing me wearing the same old threads around town. The clothes I'd bought were sharp in a street sense, but never measured up to what others in the scene were wearing. Since we were the same size, everything fit perfectly and looked as if it were custom-made for me. Jimi owned more shirts than most stores.

"Where did you get all of these clothes?" I asked.

"Most of the blouses come from my girlfriends, or Devon and Carmen pick them up in the women's departments at the stores," he told me.

His closets were full of mostly colorful and vibrant women's garments. There was absolutely nothing "street pimp" about walking around in a woman's silk, floral-print blouse, but there I was trying one on and checking myself in the full-length mirror of the bedroom. If Jimi could make the clothes look hip, then maybe they'd work for me as well.

A couple nights later, we were hanging out at the Beverly Hills Hotel until we decided to head down to the Whiskey to check out the scene. I hopped in the limo with Jimi and Carmen, and together we headed to Hollywood. But word of Jimi's arrival in town had already hit, and everyone was waiting to get a glimpse of him. The sidewalk in front of the club was complete chaos—a wild crowd of hippies. The valets had already stopped taking cars. Luckily, a short guy emerged from the congested entrance and knifed his way through the bodies. After spotting us, he walked over to where our limo was parked.

"All right, we're going to my house!" he announced.

After he jogged away from the limo, my brother turned to me. "That's a friend of mine, Eric Burdon from the Animals. And I guess I won't even ask you if you know who they are," he told me with a smile.

Almost at once, it seemed as if the entire population in front of the Whiskey cleared out and followed Eric to his place high in the Hollywood Hills. When we arrived, the narrow roads were clogged with limos and cars for blocks. The entire neighborhood was complete gridlock. When a limo dropped people off, it had to go all the way around the backside of the hill to make its way back to wait down the street.

I walked in the front door with Jimi and Carmen to see a dozen or so Playboy playmates dressed in their signature bunny outfits. Plenty of cocaine was also going around. Everybody broke out little bindles and spread the powder out on any flat surface available. Since I didn't know anyone at the party, doing coke was an easy way to blend in with the crowd. I had never done the stuff before, but that didn't stop me from jumping right into the mix. As soon as that first line of white powder was cut up in front of me, it was full speed ahead. Besides, Jimi and Carmen headed down to hang out with people around the pool, and I wasn't going to just hang around with them and cramp their style all night.

Believe me, I was putting the vibe out there and laying the thick pickup lines on the ladies. It was tough to choose because there were so many of them. I didn't want just one of the girls to come back to my hotel with me; I wanted *all* of them to come back with me.

When I finally pulled myself away from doing lines long enough to meet up with Jimi out by the pool, he told me he was splitting. The plan was to meet up the next day and hang out over at the Benedict Canyon place. After the brief pause in my debauchery, I returned to the house and found my way back to the cocaine. Since I didn't know many people at the party, the rest of my night was spent snorting lines. By the end of the evening, which was probably more like the early morning, I was ridiculously loaded. After calling my driver, I waited in front on the house, swaying back and forth in place. When I walked into the lobby of the hotel around three o'clock in the morning, girls were *still waiting* to meet Jimi. I wasted no time in grabbing one of them and inviting her up to my suite.

With the thriving hippie scene on the Sunset Strip, I soon found out that the drug dealers were almost as persistent as the girls. They wanted our attention just like anyone else. Jimi and I had access to whatever substance we wanted. People would simply walk up and hand us little bindles of drugs. Once I made my identity as Jimi's brother known in clubs such as the Whiskey and the Rainbow Room, all the dealers routinely converged on me. Not only did they want to know what I needed, but they were also more than willing to pass on free samples of whatever goodies they were holding at the moment. I got more loaded than I had ever been in my life. Being under the influence of booze or drugs day and night only added to the surreal nature of my trip to Los Angeles.

After years of touring the world, my brother was finally given the opportunity to relax and enjoy himself in Los Angeles. With only a few shows scheduled for later in the month, Jimi had a few weeks of clear sailing. We fell into a routine of hanging out in the Hollywood clubs until the early hours of the morning and sleeping late into the afternoon. He was a superstar even among superstars, and we were ushered around the city like royalty. Every major entertainment-industry player was looking to meet my brother. Nightly, we hit up private parties in the Hollywood Hills and hung out with A-list celebrities. During the hazy, booze- and drug-fueled nights, Jimi regularly introduced me to hip-looking people, and most of them talked with English accents. The encounters came at a frantic pace in loud clubs or at crowded house parties. Later, Jimi would explain the guys were members of famous bands such as the Beatles, the Rolling Stones, Steppenwolf, the Doors, and the Who. Looking back, it is odd to think I met Ringo Starr and Paul McCartney, Jim Morrison, Jerry Garcia, Johnny and Edgar Winter, John Kay, and Mick Jagger while having absolutely no idea who any of them were, but it's true. That was Hollywood during that period.

STILL DREAMING

A little more than two weeks into my stay in Los Angeles, I suddenly found it impossible to get in contact with Jimi. Although I did eventually learn he'd checked out of his suite at the hotel, nobody would tell me his whereabouts when I called the Benedict Canyon house. When I finally got in touch with Mike, he mentioned Jimi was down in San Diego for a couple days, so there wasn't much more to say. It wasn't as if I ever had a reason to worry about getting bored in Hollywood. With no word from my brother, I spent the following nights at the Whiskey holding court at his reserved table.

A couple of days turned into almost a week before Jimi finally rang my suite to find out how I had been doing. He stopped me when I asked him about his recent trip to San Diego.

"San Diego?" he repeated. "Who told you I was down there?"

"Mike did."

"Man, I was playing a gig in Hawaii. I told him to let you know."

Apparently I had gotten under Mike's skin, to the point that he intentionally deceived me to keep me separated from Jimi. He was starting to play dirty, and I obviously needed to start keeping an even better eye on him. I was already constantly on Mike's case about the way he and Gerry were treating Jimi. From the first time meeting the two of them back in Seattle during Jimi's first homecoming gig, I was a thorn in their sides. Our relationship took on a similar tone in Los Angeles. Maybe I was only a twenty-year-old kid in their eyes, but I was also a savvy hustler. If I sensed some shady dealings, I wasn't keeping quiet about them. This drove Gerry and Mike crazy. They were used to running every facet of the show and having control of Jimi's every movement. Now that my brother had brought me into the equation, that wasn't the case anymore.

Jimi once said to me, "Always remember, Leon, if you don't get in the mix, you can't make any music." Now, I wasn't indeed "in the mix" and was making a ridiculously sour note with his management. They maintained a stranglehold on his finances, and it was close to impossible to get any cash out of them. Jimi was the most popular musician in the world, and they kept him on an allowance of *fifty bucks* a day. Most of the time my brother was generous enough to split half of that money with me. It wasn't difficult to see something wasn't right. But Jimi never wanted to get in the middle of it. My brother didn't have a confrontational personality; he just wanted to work on his music. The material side of things and the finances didn't interest him. I, on the other hand, smelled something going on and bitched and moaned to management at every opportunity. In response they routinely insisted money was tight. I believe Mike's favorite phrase was "everything is accounted for." But that was all a lie.

"Man, I just saw you go into the box office after the show and collect *eighty thousand dollars*," I once told Mike. "If my brother wants some of his hard-earned money, give it to him."

Man, were they pissed. But I didn't care. And neither did Jimi. He hugged me when I later told him what had happened. Although plenty of people were in his entourage, such as his two fellow band members, the road crew, and management, none of them were his blood. I felt it was the perfect opportunity for me to stick up for him. Jimi was always there to protect me while we were growing up, so it was nice to know that I could return the favor in Los Angeles. Management might have been picking up all of our expenses, but Jimi was paying the ultimate price. My brother may have had access to cars, hotel suites, planes, and rental houses, but none of it was his. At the end of the day, every bit of it came out of Jimi's pocket.

The party continued, and during the second week of October, Jimi was scheduled to play a string of dates at the Winterland in San Francisco. On the morning of October 10, we jumped into the limo and drove the six and a half hours to Northern California. After checking in at the hotel, Jimi and I took a walk over to Haight-Ashbury to check out the scene. Once the hippies caught sight of my brother walking down the street, they typically freaked out. He blew their minds even more when he stopped to play with a few street musicians. When he asked the guy if he could borrow his guitar for a song, I thought the guy was going to faint right there on the spot.

Coke may have been my new drug of choice, but LSD wasn't far behind. Since I was dropping acid regularly, long periods of time, sometimes days, were extremely hazy. It wasn't difficult to drift in and out of Jimi's orbit and sometimes disappear for a few days every once in a while to explore the scene. That's exactly what happened up in San Francisco. I got loaded on LSD at Golden Gate Park one afternoon and split from Jimi as he was going to meet up with Buddy Miles somewhere in the city. Not long after, I met a group of cute hippie girls who said they were going to see the Grateful Dead play at a club called the Matrix later that night, so it seemed like a perfectly groovy idea to jump onto their bus with them. I was going where the natural currents were set on taking me. Besides, Jimi was more than busy and off dealing with his own situation. That night, the girls and I didn't even make it into the Grateful Dead show at the club. We stayed on the bus in the parking lot partying into the early hours of the morning.

The three days I spent in San Francisco were a blur—a complete haze of weed, LSD, and sex with my new hippie girlfriends. I used up so much time getting loaded and traveling around the city on the hippie bus that I didn't catch even one of Jimi's shows at the Winterland. When it came time to leave town, I didn't join Jimi in the limo for the ride back to Los Angeles. I decided to have the hippies drive me south on their bus because I never wanted the party to end.

Back in Los Angeles, Jimi began heading into TTG Studios every night to record material for a new album. The studio was located at 1441 N. McCadden Place not far from Sunset and Highland in Hollywood. I was sort of surprised at how tiny it was the first time I walked in through the front door. The bare-bones facility had a narrow control room and not much space to maneuver in—not that the cramped layout prevented Jimi from bringing the party into the sessions with him. After the San Francisco trip, Devin and Carmen went their separate ways, so there were even more girls around. Initially, Jimi didn't have a problem with them, but they eventually proved to be a major distraction when he was trying to concentrate on his work. The girls simply wanted to be a part of the scene and go down to the Whiskey to party. For the most part, they didn't have any interest in the art Jimi was struggling to create.

As Jimi kept to his nightly schedule of hitting TTG Studios to work on material, I did my thing all over town in the clubs. In the beginning, I simply jumped into the limo and set out into Hollywood on my own, but as time wore on, I saw the same faces in the same places. Everyone usually met up at the Rainbow Room because it was the joint to be seen in. Most of the conversation revolved around the search for drugs, and you never had to look all that hard. If somebody had some LSD, we did LSD. If they had coke, we did a few lines. If they had weed, we smoked.

As always, there may have been wall-to-wall musicians, actors, models, and industry cats, but I still wasn't concerned with who they were. My existence was about the party. Everyone was getting loaded at the clubs. People put out cocaine on the table as if it were an appetizer similar to dip and chips. It was all part of the scene, and people always had a bindle or two of powder on them. Being handed a rolled-up bill to snort drugs was as common as a handshake. Every time I walked through a door, it seemed somebody was there to offer me a few lines. Glacierlike chunks were all over the place with piles on every table—and not simply little bumps. I'm talking about long, thick rails of the stuff that went on forever. One time I mentioned, "Man, this thing looks like it goes all the way to Alaska!" From that point on, we started calling the giant rails of coke "Alaska lines."

Not only was I a hit with the girls on the scene, but also with the overambitious agents and managers that lurked around every corner of the Rainbow Room and the Whiskey. I had no reason to feel out of my element because I had a lot of street sense and knew how to navigate rooms full of players and imposing figures. Plus, I had no problem handling myself around the women. It is hard not to feel like a big shot when you've got a fine girl on each arm. Everyone insisted on getting a few minutes of my time because they were desperate for some way to get in contact with my brother. They wanted to get a piece of the magic he was creating with his music. They usually pitched me an idea for a gig they wanted Jimi to do or a tour they were interested in recruiting him to perform on. Although I was cordial and heard them out, I was never comfortable approaching my brother with any offers or possible business deals. That was never my area of expertise, and I didn't see that changing in the near future. At the end of the night, I'd sometimes walk away with as many as fifty business cards, which were immediately tossed into the garbage upon arriving back at my suite at the hotel or at the Benedict Canyon house.

I got the feeling that many of the rock stars on the scene were jealous of my brother. He was considered the number one cat. Although many of the other rockers also dressed flamboyantly and possessed genuine swagger, Jimi overshadowed them whenever they were out at the same spot together. Those who had issues looked uncomfortable and uneasy as soon as Jimi entered the room. I especially detected some tension with Arthur Lee, the lead singer of the band Love, and his entourage. Arthur considered himself the original crossover black artist with a white band and was probably put off that Jimi came onto the scene and took over everything. Jimi and Arthur had met back in the early Hollywood days when Jimi was playing for Little Richard's band, but they didn't seem to be all that tight when Jimi introduced me to him. Meanwhile, my brother could not have cared less. He did his own thing and wasn't in competition with anyone else.

When we retreated back to the Benedict Canyon house night after night, there were always pretty girls to greet us. But luckily during the day, we also had some breaks in the action. Jimi and I spent many afternoons relaxing out by the pool. I remember these moments most about my time in Los Angeles because there weren't any distractions to deal with. It was simply my brother and me hanging out alone. It was easy for me to see that the lifestyle was taking a toll on him. I thought back to the excited phone calls I used to receive from him back in 1966 after he arrived in New York City and how he was truly happy in those days. Now that he was more famous than he'd ever expected to be, that joy was almost gone.

Jimi told me about all the trouble he was encountering in building Electric Lady Studios in New York City. He said that the project was a nightmare to put together. They found out the building sat on top of an underground river and was constantly flooding. Jimi also said he was forced to take out a loan to keep the project moving forward, which seemed ridiculous. Management insisted that all of his money was tied up and there was no other choice. As always, the financial arrangements didn't make much sense. It would be tough for anyone to explain why one of the most successful rock stars on the planet needed to take out a loan for anything. But as usual, when I pressed Jimi about the details, he didn't want to talk about it. The whole situation obviously made him miserable, so there was no point in pressing.

One afternoon, we lit up our first joint of the day and finally had the chance to talk about his playing.

"How do you make all of those noises out of there?" I asked. "How do you get all that wild sound?"

"The pedals—the wah-wah and the fuzz tone. The Marshall amps I'm using have a huge sound, and the Fender Strat is a great guitar," Jimi told me, leaning back and spreading out on his chair. "You know, Leon, after all of those years of being in those bands and people telling me what to play and having to play exact arrangements, those are second nature. My stuff exists outside of those lines. I'm free. As long as the bass player stays in the root, I can do what I want. If it starts feeding back, then fine. The strings and notes and tones are fighting against each other, but the guitar is still tuned to E, so it's going to at least be in that area. I could be playing a lead way up high, but that low E string could still be feeding back. So there are two tones going on. It's like you're playing two guitars at the same time. You have to let it go, but still control it. The guitar is pretty open. You can't really hit a bad note unless you don't know how to bend it and shape it into all the other melodies and tones going on. It's all about recovery. It's the most important part of soloing and improvising. You know what I'm talking about?"

I did. When Jimi explained things, they always made perfect sense.

One of my favorite songs of Jimi's at the time was "Bold as Love," off his second album, *Axis: Bold as Love*. When I told him my feelings on the track, he went into detail about some of the thinking that went into the writing of the lyrics. Jimi was interested in the relationship between emotions, colors, and musical notes. He mentioned a concept called Energy Sound Color Dynamics—which he playfully sometimes referred to as $E = sc^2$ to borrow a little style from Einstein's $E = mc^2$ theory.

Jimi was fascinated by the connection of the seven notes in a musical scale to the seven colors of the rainbow. Not to mention the interesting fact that red, yellow, and blue—the first, third, and fifth colors of the rainbow—are primary colors, while root, third, and fifth—the first, third, and fifth notes of a major scale—make up a major chord. If there was such a thing as "hearing in color" or "playing in color," that was exactly what my brother was intent on accomplishing (or it may even be said that he had already accomplished it by then). Regardless, he was interested in practicing it. Jimi felt that if he couldn't physically hold on to the music, he could at least describe it in color and somehow make it three-dimensional. He took his fascination with radio frequencies back when we were little boys to the next level. Not only was there sound and color to mold and shape in his songwriting, but there was also the energy—the soul, spirit, and emotion. The three elements together were something as powerful as anything. Jimi attempted to link everything together in one form, which was his music. My brother was always educating me in different ways. I felt as if he knew the answers, and that knowledge was total freedom to me.

"I'm glad you could come out here, Leon," Jimi said, leaning back and lighting a cigarette.

"I know. This is great, Buster." I rose from my chair and stared out over the railing at the canyon below.

The days my brother and I spent hanging out together in Los Angeles were amazing. We sat around for hours on end by the pool at the house and talked about everything that had happened in our lives. We weren't little boys any longer, but it still felt that way.

There was a long pause as Jimi went into his jacket pocket for a cigarette and lit it. He eased back down in his chair. "So, what do you want to do?" he asked.

I sat quietly and thought about what Jimi was asking. The one thing that was certain in my mind was that I didn't want the party to ever end. I was completely content with simply being the younger brother of the most famous rock star on the planet. Girls, parties, drugs, reserved tables in VIP sections—the situation was treating me well. But what I didn't realize at the time was that my brother was getting at something different that afternoon out by the pool. I didn't realize that the question he was asking and the question I was hearing were two different things. He wanted me to consider the long-term arrangement and what I wanted to do in the future. He had tours to set off on and music to record. I couldn't hang around on the fringe forever not doing much except partying.

"Do you want to play an instrument, work in a studio, or maybe learn to be an sound engineer?" he asked.

"I want to work with you, Buster."

He moved his chair a little closer to mine and leaned toward me.

"Here is the deal. I'm under contract for a few more months and then I'm getting a new deal. We have some more shows to do, and then I'm going to New York to start my own record label."

"That's sounds like a great plan. I want to go, too. Or I'll meet up with you in New York. I've never been there before, but I want to check it out."

"It's all going to change, Leon. I'm going to do some different stuff and go in a new direction. I want to write symphonies with string sections, you know, violins and horns. I want to compose. I'm going off to do a few shows in Hawaii, and then you and me are going to meet up in New York and start doing our thing."

Sitting there with my brother out by the pool in the wonderful California sunshine, I still couldn't bring myself to tell him I had to go back to Seattle for my sentencing. The future looked too bright for us and I didn't want to ruin the vision we were creating together. I was still caught up in the dream.

Jimi also expressed his frustration over the direction of his career. In his mind, Mike and Gerry were only concerned with keeping the Hendrix money machine moving forward. They worked him to the bone and had my brother going nonstop. He was clearly burned-out.

"You know something, Leon, I'm firing these guys. And they know they're getting fired. So that's why they're fucking with me so much right now. It's the same thing over and over again. I'm so tired of playing "Foxy Lady" and "Purple Haze," man."

Jimi just wanted to create, but his management was burning him out. He wanted to go into the studio, but it seemed something always came up to prevent him from putting together a schedule that he was comfortable with.

He had one more show that month up in Bakersfield on October 26 at the Civic Auditorium, but I have little if any recollection of it.

I only remember that the venue looked more like a good place to have a bull-riding competition than a rock concert. Jimi and I rode the hour and a half north in the limo, he played the gig, then we jumped back into the limo and returned to Los Angeles.

It had been a little over a month since I arrived in Los Angeles, and I was starting to hit a wall. The pace of the party lifestyle wore me out. It didn't help that I had overdosed on every vice Tinseltown had to offer: sex, drugs, and rock and roll; *especially* sex. My body gave out and it became nearly impossible to have sex. I never thought there would be a day where I found it impossible to get excited for girls anymore.

When I mentioned my problem to Jimi, he smiled. "You just need to cool it with the ladies for a little while. Don't worry. You'll be okay in a few weeks."

I clearly needed to take a break from the entire scene. Besides, it was becoming harder to ignore the reality of my situation back home. I had to leave and face the consequences waiting for me. As Jimi headed out to do his gigs in Kansas City, Minneapolis, and St. Louis, we said our good-byes at the house. I took a cab to the airport and jumped on a flight back home to Seattle.

IN AND OUT OF THE ARMY

After arriving in Seattle, it took me a while to decompress from my time living like a rock star in Los Angeles. It wasn't easy adjusting to reality after living the dream with Jimi. I finally got some much-needed sleep and must have spent two full days in bed. After I recuperated, my new reality slowly set in. Although I had yessed Jimi to death back in Los Angeles about hooking up soon in New York City and setting back out on the road together, that plan wasn't happening.

As I was preparing for my next court appearance, a letter came for me back at my dad's place: a draft notice from the army. My number had come up and there wasn't any getting around it. When I brought the letter down to my lawyer's office, he was overjoyed.

"You know something," he said, smiling wide, "you are one lucky kid. Do you have any idea what you have right here? It is a get-out-of-jail-free card."

My lawyer persuaded the judge to defer my sentence so that I could enter the military and serve my country, just as Jimi had done years earlier. The good news: I wasn't going to jail after all. The bad news: they were shipping my ass off to Vietnam. I didn't know much about the war at that point, but it looked as if I was about to soon get a firsthand education.

On the morning of December 5, 1968, Dad drove me down to the same building we'd dropped my brother off at seven years earlier. Dad even had the same stern expression on his face as we pulled up the front drive.

"I was in the army, your brother was in the army, and now you're going in the army, son," he told me. "Make the best of it."

My days of wearing flamboyant blouses and alligator-skin shoes were over. The reserved table at the Whiskey was long gone. Not a fine girl was to be seen.

The army sent me off to Fort Lewis, where they shaved my head, issued me military fatigues, and gave me a simple bunk. There was absolutely no messing around the first day I entered the service. The army brass knew chances were almost a hundred percent we'd be going over to Vietnam, so it was all business as soon as the new recruits hit the base.

"If one of you goes over to Vietnam and gets killed because you couldn't kill, then that's your own damned fault, Bubba!" the staff sergeant yelled the first day after we fell into line. It was a statement to remember. I realized how important it was to mentally and physically prepare to go into battle and take somebody's life. I never considered myself a violent or even a physical person; I had to dig deep and discover an inner strength not only to make it through the rigorous training, but also the war.

Oddly enough, advanced infantry training, or AIT, turned out to be a welcome challenge for me. Although it was a crazy adventure, I was down to follow it however far it was going to take me. Once I adapted to the new and demanding schedule, I had no problem waking up at four in the morning and rising to the daily challenges. From the start, I excelled and was one of the first in our squad to be able to take apart an M16 in the dark and put it back together without much difficulty. The instructors started off by running us through land-mine training and teaching us how to construct bombs. They also had us walk through a house full of tear gas without wearing a mask. So we'd feel the full effects of the gas, they forced us to sing songs such as "Jingle Bells" the entire time we were inside. If you held your breath and ran through, your eyes were the only thing that burned, but if you were singing and breathing in and out, your lungs were on fire and burning in a way you'd never before felt.

Early on, I discovered a natural ability to lead in a group. The higher-ups noticed as well and made me a squad leader. My responsibility was to make sure the men under me learned everything they needed to know and passed the necessary tests. For one of the first times in my life, I'd been awarded a leadership position and I embraced it. If being a squad leader when we shipped out to Vietnam was going to give me a better chance of survival, then I was all for it.

Around eight weeks into the service and not long after completing AIT, I got a chance to go back home on leave for a week. Even though I had been away at Fort Lewis for two months, I readily eased back into the scene downtown. The army may have thought they were in control of my life, but I had no intention of letting my hustling lifestyle go. The weeklong break renewed my taste for the action.

Shortly after returning to Fort Lewis, I discovered that if I slipped into my civilian clothes and acted cool and unassuming, I had no problem walking right around the base's front gate up to the taxi stand without any hassle from the guards. I started taking taxis from Fort Lewis to downtown almost nightly for $20 each way. Sneaking back onto the base later in the evening, I usually brought a couple sacks of weed with me. Three fingers' worth of weed ran about $10, and I sold joints to my platoon for $2.50 a piece. I turned a decent profit. Plenty of cash was to be made on the base, and before long my entire platoon was getting loaded. We'd routinely go out for drills and everybody would be high.

All of the guys I was tight with in the squad knew Jimi was my brother, but the officers didn't have much of an idea until the word got out that Jimi regularly played a version of "The Star-Spangled Banner" at his live shows. That certainly got their attention, and the higher-ups didn't like it one bit. To them, it was a major distraction having a local celebrity under their command. They especially liked to assert their authority over me in front of the entire platoon out in the field and constantly singled me out from the rest of the group. The officers tried to make an example of me. They felt a constant need to break me down. I understood that the armed forces stressed victory through unity, but I wasn't doing anything to exert my individuality and separate from the rest of the platoon.

"You call that music, Hendrix?" one of the sergeants shouted at me in the middle of drills early one morning. "Well, you know what I call it? I call it desecrating our national anthem. It's a mockery! Do you think someone should be able to do that and get away with it? No way, Bubba!"

But nothing the officers said affected my popularity around the base. If anything, by repeatedly singling me out from the rest of the group, even more soldiers recognized my name and discovered my identity. But still, the officers never missed an opportunity to chew me out in front of an audience.

Even one of the one-star generals on the base got into the middle of things. One day at an assembly, he produced a photograph of Jimi with a rifle in one hand and an American flag in the other.

"This is not an army-issue weapon, men!" he shouted, pointing to the gun in the photo he was holding. He paced angrily back and forth in front of our platoon. Then he stopped and pointed to where I was sitting a few rows back. "And Leon Hendrix is not a general in this army! Make sure each and every one of you never forget that fact! We've got only *one* general at this base, and his name sure as hell ain't Hendrix! Jimi Hendrix disrespects the American flag and has desecrated our great national anthem by playing it the way he does!"

Although to me this was comical, nobody was laughing. The army couldn't seem to understand that the soldiers absolutely loved Jimi. A large part of a generation was going to war on his music. His songs were an essential part of the sound track of Vietnam. Nothing any of the higher-ups said or did was going to change anyone's mind. The soldiers weren't going to have a different outlook on Jimi's music or his message because of what someone else was trying to tell them.

After the general's rant, my stripes were immediately taken away and I was assigned to three full weeks of grueling KP. The term might technically have been defined as "kitchen police," but I was certainly in no position of authority. My job was to prepare vegetables for cooking and then to mop floors. I must have peeled at least ten thousand potatoes. When I was done, the pile was almost up to my shoulders. The labor was absolutely grueling. They'd sometimes drag me out of my bunk at three in the morning to go peel potatoes for hours on end. Everyone knew that they were making an example of me. Still, all the KP in the world wasn't going to make a dent in my popularity with the rest of my unit. By that time, I don't think there was a soldier on the base who wasn't aware of my identity. Even though I wasn't doing anything wrong (that the officers knew about anyway), other than simply being myself, the officers continued to fume over the situation.

One officer even explained things further: "The bottom line is that you are causing too much of a disturbance, Hendrix. You're disrupting the whole unit and we just can't have that. We're going to send you to the stockade for a while to cool your jets."

That is exactly what they ended up doing. They were determined to break me down by any means necessary. They kept insisting that I was "interfering with military progress," whatever that meant. So, for two months they banished me to the stockade, also known as the army prison. When they finally released me and allowed me to mix with the other soldiers again, my stripes were returned to my uniform. But they wanted me off their base as soon as possible. That meant my next stop was going to be Vietnam.

We were moved into a hangar at McChord Air Force Base so they could determine my exact position when we shipped out. Was I going to shoot cannons? Drive a tank? Maybe handle communications? While the army decided our fate, we were issued our equipment. When they instructed us to take three hand grenades apiece; I took *six*. When they told us to load up with two hundred rounds of ammunition, I grabbed *four hundred*. If I was going into battle, I was going to be fully strapped. As I walked away with double grenades, double ammunition, an M16 rifle, a ten-inch knife, and a .45-caliber handgun, I was as ready as possible for the journey ahead.

Then our squad waited in the hangar at McChord. Then waited some more. We bunked out on cots in that sweltering hangar for almost two months and still received no orders to move out. The waiting was excruciating, and all I wanted was to get to Vietnam and do what we were supposed to do. Our platoon was ready to fight. We'd been prepared for a long time. But week after week, the same news came from the higher-ups: we weren't set for deployment overseas. Then one afternoon we all were ordered to line up for a big assembly. All of the colonels and majors were present as well as around ten thousand soldiers out in the field. It looked as if our numbers had been called to go off and assume the role of "ground pounders." This was it: Vietnam, here I come.

"Men," the general announced up at the podium, "we've been ordered to stand down for the time being and return to regular operations at our bases."

A hush quickly fell over every one of the soldiers out in the field. We stood trading confused looks until the reality of the moment hit. Then, we all began yelling at the top of our lungs and tossing our helmets in the air. Some soldiers even collapsed to the ground and began thanking Jesus for their good fortune. We'd been saved for the time being and were being sent back to Fort Lewis.

The army didn't know what to do with us because the base was overcrowded. The time I'd spent in the stockade during my stay at Fort Lewis didn't count toward my overall tour of duty, so I still had plenty more time to serve.

When I got word that my brother was scheduled to once again return to Seattle to play the Coliseum on May 23, 1969, I immediately put in for a leave in order to attend the show. The military brass also knew Jimi was again coming back home to play and made it abundantly clear that they had no intention of granting me permission to leave the base. When my request was promptly rejected, I reached my peak of frustration and let my dissatisfaction be known at every chance. The military's answer: a never-ending cycle of KP and groundskeeping duty. They were intent on forcing me, by any means necessary, to fall in line like a good soldier. But that wasn't ever going to work. The more opposition I ran up against, the stronger my will to overcome became. I wasn't going to let them beat me.

No matter how hard I pled my case, they wouldn't budge on their decision. If anything, my insistence to be allowed a proper leave only further angered them. One lieutenant even ordered me out in back of a tent one night and started slapping me around.

"I want you out of our army, Hendrix!" he yelled. "You think you're some sort of big shot? Well, you ain't no big shot!"

After that night, I wasn't going to allow myself to endure the military's physical and mental abuse any longer. Maybe even more important in my mind, I wasn't going to miss one of my brother's visits home. Nothing the army said or did was going to stop me from reuniting with Jimi when he came to town. So, after weighing the options, I came to a hasty decision: if the army wasn't going to grant me a leave, then I had no alternative but to go absent without leave, or AWOL.

A couple of days before Jimi was set to arrive, I changed out of my fatigues and into my civilian clothes. After packing my belongings in a duffel bag, as on so many previous nights I walked directly out through the front gate to the taxi stand. A car quickly pulled up in front of me. After getting into the back of the cab, I hoisted my bag onto the seat. Staring out the window, I watched as an army transport thundered past and stopped at the front gate of the base. I looked at all of the soldiers jogging in formation across the field in the rain. Their rhythmic chanting was barely audible, but I knew all too well what they were saying. I took in a deep breath, then let out a long exhale.

"What can I do you for, buddy?" the cabdriver asked from up front, glancing at me in the rearview mirror.

"Take me to Seattle," I told him. "I'm going to 7954 Seward Park Avenue."

As my cab traveled north on Interstate 5, it felt as if a giant weight had been suddenly lifted off my shoulders. Not that I didn't have doubts about the repercussions of my actions, but it wasn't all that uncommon for soldiers to go AWOL. I routinely heard stories about guys leaving the base for short periods here and there. What was the worst that could happen—maybe a couple of weeks in the stockade?

I could certainly handle that type of punishment. I'd done it before and could certainly do it again. It wasn't as if I were going to be put up in front of a firing squad or anything. Looking back, maybe my line of thinking wasn't much, but it was enough to justify my actions at the time.

My dad was surprised to see me show up on his doorstep. "What are you doing here, son?"

"I'm on leave, Dad. It's all good."

Dad didn't have any reason not to believe what I was telling him, so he was happy to have me home. Over the next few days, I let my hair go and started to grow a mustache. I thought I had it all figured out and the army would never catch on. Hell, after a while maybe they'd forget about me altogether. Anything was possible.

A day later, Jimi flew into town, and just as we had done during his prior visits to Seattle, we met him at the airport and helped him navigate his way through the assembled group of inquisitive reporters and excited fans. Dad, June, Janie, and I picked him up at Sea-Tac Airport and brought him back to the house to hang out and unwind before his show later that evening at the Coliseum. I could tell by Jimi's demeanor that his drug bust in Toronto three weeks earlier was still bugging him, but I didn't bother him about it. Not that there wasn't plenty to say about the incident. From what I heard on the news reports, the whole arrest didn't add up. The authorities concentrated only on the heroin they allegedly found, which didn't sound right to me. If they also reported that they found LSD, weed, or maybe even a small amount of cocaine, that would have made sense. But heroin is and was the ultimate evil and certainly provided a heavier, more-attention-grabbing headline in the papers. If there was one way for the authorities to try to turn people against Jimi, it was to promote finding heroin in his belongings. The last thing I wanted to do was start asking my brother questions as soon as he stepped off the plane. It was more important for him to be able to decompress and relax with the family.

As usual, his management lurked in the background wherever we went, peering over our shoulders and watching our every movement. Gerry and Mike hadn't seen me since my time in Los Angeles some months back, but I could see they were still pissed. They were certainly no fans of mine or anybody else in our family.

Later that night at the Coliseum gig, Jimi appeared onstage in deep orange velvet pants and a gold blouse. He looked like a ball of fire onstage. Toward the end of Jimi's set, he dipped down and his pants split right up the back. In an instant, one of the roadies ran out with a Confederate flag, of all things, for Jimi to cover it up. So for the last two numbers he played with the flag around his waist to conceal the rip. I'm surprised wardrobe malfunctions didn't happen more frequently when he performed. Jimi's stage clothes were typically made from delicate and fragile fabrics such as velvet and satin. Sometimes my brother's wild movements onstage pushed the clothing to its limits. They were made to look good under the stage lights, but weren't that durable. His outfits were what I called "temporary wardrobe."

The Coliseum had a revolving stage as well as a glass dome. The rain pouring down outside and the lightning flashing every so often that night gave the show a supernatural quality. Because of an electrical or a mechanical problem, the rotating stage broke, and the band was left facing in one direction. Almost at once, the crowd attempted to shift from one side of the venue to the other to get a better view. But the place was so packed that there was nowhere to move to.

After the show, Gerry drove us over to the suite they'd booked for Jimi at the Sherwood Inn in Seattle's U District. As the conversation turned toward the future, Jimi told me that he was flying off to do a show in Hawaii, but after that he was traveling back to New York

City to continue recording. I could sense he was finally ready to move in a new direction with not only his music, but also his life. He was done being in the Jimi Hendrix Experience with Noel and Mitch. He was also finally fed up with the way his management was manipulating his every movement and operating his business arrangements. It was comforting to see he had ultimately come to his senses.

"All these business cats have me signing new legal documents every other day," Jimi said. And I just want to concentrate on my music. It's getting to be impossible. But I'm finally getting rid of these guys and starting my own trip—a new band, finding new management. I've got the recording studio and I'm starting a new record company."

The next morning, Dad came by the hotel and together we saw Jimi off to the airport. Dad always wanted to make sure he said good-bye to Jimi right before he stepped on the plane. We walked him to the gate and he was on his way. As Jimi left town to continue on to his gigs at the International Sports Center in San Diego, the San Jose Pop Festival in Santa Clara Country, California, and eventually the Waikiki Shell in Honolulu, Hawaii, I crashed out for a few more nights at the house with June, Janie, and Dad. Although a wonderful new world of possibilities was opening up in the future with Jimi, I failed to recognize how important it was that I return to the base and serve out my tour.

At first, I figured maybe I'd wait just a few more days to spend a little more time with my girlfriend Lydia. Then I told myself that I'd go back at the beginning of the next week. When that time came and went, I promised myself it would only be another week. Instead of returning to the army to serve out my time and focusing on a bright future that lay ahead, I fell back into every one of my old habits. After a few months of making and then breaking promises with myself, I was too scared to go back. I'd reached a point of no return. It looked as if the army was going to have to come and get me.

THE DARKEST DAYS

F ollowing Jimi's latest visit home, I tried tracking him down at
his apartment in New York City, but he was never there. Whoever answered the phone explained they didn't know where he was
or when he was due back. It could have been another case of people
around him keeping us apart, but who knows. No matter how hard I
tried, I couldn't ignore the lure of easy money. Now that cocaine
was part of my repertoire (along with weed, LSD, and alcohol) after
I dove into it headfirst in Los Angeles, I was loaded day and night.
And when I was loaded, the streets were the place to be.

During the summer of 1969, I moved from Dad's place in Seward
Park and checked into a nice hotel, the Washington Plaza. It was
much easier for me to operate out of there because I could come and
go at all hours of the day and night without being hassled by my dad.
Even though I still had a few grand left from the cash my brother
had given me, I continued looking for another scheme to turn that
into more cash. Not that I couldn't just send a message to Jimi, but
he had already given me more than enough. LSD was more popular

than ever and seemed to be the new drug of choice in Seattle. Everyone wanted to trip. My buddies and I began hitting up the local concerts at venues such as the Coliseum and making as much money as possible. The trick was to put a few drops of LSD in a squirt gun and then fill the rest up with Kool-Aid. Walking through the parking lot, I'd charge six dollars a hit or two for ten. Anytime someone wanted one, I'd squeeze the trigger and give them a shot in the mouth.

Concerts were an occasional great moneymaking opportunity, but most of my time was spent at all the regular pool halls, bars, and clubs. Because of Jimi's generosity, my pockets were deep and allowed me to graduate to some of the highest-stakes backroom craps games in Seattle. The scene required me to have a bodyguard at my side at all times. I learned one thing about gambling that my dad never did: as soon as you are up a few bucks, *leave*. It's important to get the hell out of the room before dumping the money back to someone else at the table. If on the off chance I got lucky and actually got up a few thousand in a night, I needed serious protection to make sure I made it out the door before some pissed-off gambler tried to rob my ass.

My buddies throughout the city provided me with regular updates of when the army MPs or the cops were out looking for me and asking questions. A few times, I barely avoided being caught and was forced to change clothes with a friend of mine to make my escape. I should have known better; maybe my ego was bigger than my brain. I thought I could do no wrong. But I was only fooling myself. A smart man would at least have gotten out of town for a while or done the right thing and turned himself in. I did neither.

It wasn't much of a problem to steer clear of the army MPs every time they made their patrols through town because they were easy to spot, but the Seattle cops were another story. It wasn't so easy to stay out of their way because they were everywhere, and not all of them were in uniform. Plainclothes Seattle police finally snatched me. One night after having dinner at the Kansas City Steak House downtown, I was walking down the sidewalk on Pike Street with a girlfriend when officers sprang out of the alley and cuffed me. The whole thing went down so fast that it was impossible to see them coming. They stuffed me into the back of a squad car, transported me to a facility downtown for the night, and then the army picked me up and brought me back to Fort Lewis the next morning.

Once I arrived at the base, they threw me in the stockade and didn't allow me out of my cell other than to report for exercise and meals. Major Jackson, an imposing old black man who looked as if he'd seen more than a few tours of duty, put me through the ringer. Still, I remained defiant and refused to allow him to get the best of me. I even officially filed as a conscientious objector on the grounds of freedom of thought and refused to perform my duty.

So, as Jimi was again twisting his rendition of "The Star-Spangled Banner" into a snarling thing of beauty at his legendary performance at the Woodstock festival in August 1969, I was in military jail. Now my life was nothing more than cold concrete and steel bars. It was all my own doing, and I had nobody to blame but myself.

After I rotted away in the stockade for a couple of months, the army realized that no matter what they did, they'd never mold me into a soldier. Major Jackson came down to my cell one night to explain their plan.

"The army is discharging you, Hendrix."

"Cool," I told him. In my mind, I'd endured everything they tried to throw my way and now I was going to finally be let out.

"No, it's not exactly 'cool,'" Major Jackson said with attitude. "We're handing you over to the Seattle police and you're going to jail."

A few days later, the army MPs took me downtown to the King County jail on Fifth Avenue and handed me off to the police. The military granted me what they termed an "under other than honorable conditions" discharge. I stayed at King County for four months of nothing but solitary confinement and cold oatmeal. From there, they transported me to Shelton penitentiary for thirty days of what they called "diagnostics," where I was given a physical and met with counselors to determine where they were going to ship me to next. After leaving Shelton, it was on to Monroe Reformatory on March 17, 1970. The guards led me to a single cell in the C-block section, a dark and imposing area with four tiers of inmates.

When they finally reinstated my limited privileges at Monroe and allowed me time outside, entering the yard was almost like attending a homecoming reunion. Plenty of faces were familiar from my time on the streets downtown. Word of my arrival quickly spread throughout the facility, and as in the time I spent in the army, everyone paid me a great deal of respect.

Hustling on the streets was similar to hustling in prison, only cigarettes were the preferred currency. Bartering and wheeling and dealing were a way of life. If you didn't know how to do that, you didn't get anything. Inmates traded tobacco for anything—food, weed, or other drugs. My old girlfriend Lydia snuck weed into Monroe for me. She'd slip it over to me in the visitors' room, where I'd put it in a styrofoam cup. When I was getting ready to leave and go back to my cell, I'd place the cup on the floor and look over at one of my buddies, who worked as a janitor. After I left, he passed by with the broom and put it in his pocket. Later, we'd split the bag down the middle.

We did anything we possibly could to pass the time. Getting loaded was a perfect way to do that. I even discovered a way to make alcohol from one of the other inmates. I'd get two slices of wheat bread and a glass of cheap fruit juice, put them together in a glass in my cell, let it ferment for around two weeks, and in the end I had my glass of prison booze. It may have been rancid and nasty, but it still gave a good clean buzz.

After I was incarcerated, Jimi got word to me through our dad that he wanted to visit Monroe and put on a free concert for the inmates. He figured a show might help me in the eyes of the justice system and influence them to reduce my sentence. But ultimately Jimi's management shot the idea down. My brother had already been through his ordeal in Canada when they supposedly found drugs in his luggage. Jimi dodged a bullet with the police in that instance, and his management didn't want him getting involved in my situation any further. I never spoke with Jimi directly on the phone, and most of our communication was through Dad.

When my brother did return to Seattle for the fourth time to play Sicks' Stadium on July 26, 1970, management didn't want him coming to visit me at Monroe. They were dead set on protecting Jimi from any further bad press. So, he blew into town, played his gig, and I never got the chance to see him. Even though he never made the trip to visit me in jail, my brother was still with me almost every day. His music dominated all of the radio stations at the time, and I especially remember "Crosstown Traffic" and "If 6 Was 9" being in constant rotation.

I was never angry with my brother for not calling or coming to visit me in jail because I knew what he was dealing with day to day. From my time on the road, I'd seen what went on behind the scenes and had been exposed to the never-ending pressure his management put on him. Besides, it wouldn't be long before I was out and back on the scene with him. My spirits were actually pretty high because I watched as prisoners with much more time were paroled daily. My sentence wasn't anything I couldn't handle on my own. Disappointment didn't faze me because I had grown accustomed to it in my life.

Maybe even too accustomed. But I had put myself in the position I was in and had to work my way through it until it was over.

I got periodic updates from Dad during our weekly phone calls about what Jimi was doing and how his career was going. When Dad mentioned that Jimi was finally putting together the group he'd always dreamed of playing with, the Band of Gypsys with Buddy Miles and Billy Cox, I was happy for him. And I knew Buddy must also have been overjoyed to finally officially be in a band together with Jimi. He'd wanted that for a long time, and he stuck it out and made it happen. Jimi had been struggling to reclaim control of his music and career for a long time, and it seemed that he was finally able to do that with his new group.

On the morning of September 18, 1970, I woke up in my cell and got ready to begin my morning shift working in the kitchen. A few inmates had their radios on and were listening to the news stations.

"Hey, man, Jimi Hendrix died of a drug overdose!" somebody suddenly yelled from the first tier of cells down below.

"Don't say that, man!" another voice shouted.

"I'm telling you, Jimi Hendrix is dead! They just reported it on the radio!"

"Shut up! You know his little brother is right up there, man."

Every once in a while a rumor circulated that Jimmy had died, so I didn't put much thought to it. But then came the distorted message booming out over the prison PA system.

"Inmate Leon Morris Hendrix—number 156724. Report to the chaplain's office."

After the announcement, my heart sank. Almost all of the other inmates in my wing were awake by then, but a hush immediately fell over the cellblock. It was as quiet as I had ever heard it. As I made the long walk down the corridor to the office, the other inmates looked on in silence through the bars of their cells. After being led through the gate, the guards ushered me into the chaplain's office. When he handed me the telephone, my dad was on the line.

"What's going on, Dad?" I asked.

"I hate to tell you this, but Jimi's gone, son. They told me he died last night," he said quietly through his tears. "But don't worry. It's going to be alright."

"Okay. I understand," I told him.

I desperately wanted to believe him, but I wasn't so sure. On the way back to my cell, I numbly shuffled down the corridor. I kept my emotions under control because if I acted out in any way, started screaming or banging my fists against the wall, they'd send me to the hole for who knew how long. Not that I could really move anyway. A heavy numbness washed over me. It was the most horrible moment of my life. They put me on a seventy-two-hour lockdown, and I wasn't allowed to leave my cell. It was standard operating procedure anytime an inmate got bad news. They didn't want the intensity of his emotions to cause a problem among the other inmates.

I drew in my sketchbooks and wrote some poetry for the rest of the morning. Every once in a while another inmate walked by on the catwalk outside and threw a few cigarettes or a small, crumpled paper filled with some weed through the bars of my cell.

I was looking for anything to help me with my heartache, so I rolled up a small joint and smoked it in one or two quick hits. In the reformatory we called it "hit it and quit it," because if the guards caught you in the act, there would not only be disciplinary action, but added time to your sentence. I didn't have any interest in being sent to the hole or staying at Monroe any longer than law required me to.

Sitting on the edge of my raggedy mattress, I stared at the wall for hours on end. As I replayed the years my brother and I had spent together, the good times and the bad, it was impossible for me to wrap my mind around his being dead. I'd never see Buster smiling over at me again. Those days were gone forever.

I noticed that one by one the other inmates had turned off their radios. It might have been one of the only times there was complete silence in my cellblock since I'd arrived at Monroe. It meant a lot to me that the other guys would look out for me like that. It was a show of respect. Five rows of cells full of inmates were silent for most of the afternoon. You never heard of that ever going on at Monroe. It was probably the first time in the history of the place.

I didn't know what to do. I couldn't stop crying in my cell, and no matter how much I complained, they wouldn't let me out. Through the bars of my cell, I stared across at the window positioned high up on the opposite wall as the sun slowly set. It was going to be impossible for me to get any sleep at all that night.

The next morning, I channeled my heartache into writing and putting together a poem called "Star Child of the Universe." The words popped into my head and I jotted them down as fast as they came. I was in mourning and wanted to say my final good-bye to Jimi in my own special way. My brother always seemed to be touched, chosen by a greater power. From the beginning, he was destined to be a star. He had *it*—that something special that separated him from everyone else. Jimi was ahead of his time while he was alive, and I knew that he would grow even larger in the afterlife. The last lines of my poem said it all . . .

> *He knew peace and love he'd find somewhere,*
> *So he wrote the music to guide us there.*
> *I know you are grooving, way out somewhere,*
> *And when I'm experienced, I'll join you there.*

I'd battled my way through countless hard times during my life, but for the first time I felt there was no hope. When they finally let me out of my cell to go to chow three days later, the other inmates showed me great respect. My brother was a hero to a generation of young people, and many of them were locked up alongside me. That night at dinner, I was offered more ice cream and cake than I could ever eat. The generosity was a nice gesture. I sensed many of the other inmates were going through an important time of mourning, too.

I wasn't sure what I was going to do if they didn't allow me a leave from Monroe to attend the funeral. All I could do was wait and hope for the best. It was beneficial to me that Jimi's body didn't arrive from England until almost a month later. To my lawyer's credit, he used that time to have my leave properly authorized. I called him and my dad from jail a few days before I was to leave and asked them to set me up with a nice suit for the service. On October 1, 1970, the day of Jimi's funeral, my fine silk suit arrived and I went down to the property room and got dressed.

One of their conditions for letting me out of Monroe for the day to attend the funeral was that my dad had to hire three U.S. marshals to escort me. After I dressed up in my nice suit, it was once again completely silent as I made my way down the corridor. Many of the inmates simply stuck their fists up in the air as a show of respect for me on that important day. Even as I exited the reformatory and stepped down into the backseat of the patrol car in the parking lot, I could see guys out in the yard lined up against the fence looking on.

During the hour's drive to the south side of Seattle, I still had a hard time wrapping my head around the fact I was going to Buster's funeral. It was tough to say a single word for the entire trip. Once we pulled into the parking lot at Dunlap Baptist Church on Rainier Avenue, the marshals were nice enough to cut me a break.

"Listen," one of them told me, helping me out of the backseat of the patrol car. "I'm going to take the cuffs off for the ceremony."

"Thank you, sir," I told him. "I appreciate that."

He took a small set of keys out of his inside jacket pocket and began unlocking the cuffs. "But listen to me," he said, staring me directly in the eyes. "We're going to be one step behind you at all times. Don't make me sorry I did this and try to go anywhere."

From the moment they took the cuffs off, my dad and aunts were there to welcome and embrace me. It was a surreal experience walking around the church filled with hundreds of people for the ceremony. It was a tremendous outpouring of emotion. Every time I saw one of my relatives, my heart broke even more. It was a deep sadness I had never before felt. Dad and I walked down the aisle together and took our seats in the first row with June, Janie, Grandma, and Grandpa. None of us could stop crying. The whole church was in tears. Noel Redding and Mitch Mitchell were there, as well as Buddy Miles, Johnny Winter, and Miles Davis. Even the mayor of Seattle, Wes Uhlman, made an appearance. When I pivoted and glanced a few rows back, about fifty young women dressed in black were mourning Jimi's death. You would think they were all ex-wives or girlfriends, which, knowing my brother, they could certainly have been. But I recognized only a couple of them.

The ceremony was led by the Reverend Harold Blackburn, who was accompanied by a soloist who sang a few traditional hymns. Off to the right side of the pulpit stood a gorgeous six-foot guitar made out of white and purple blossoms. One of Mama's best friends, Mrs. Freddie Mae Gautier, got up and addressed the two hundred or so people in the room. After saying a few kind words, she read from a poem Jimi wrote just a few months before his death, called "Angels," and then recited my poem, "Star Child of the Universe." As soon as she finished, people erupted with amens and hallelujahs.

My legs were like rubber as I walked up to Jimi's gray and silver-metal-trimmed casket to say my final good-bye. They'd dressed him in green brocaded silk, and he looked calm and peaceful, almost as if he were sleeping or maybe just closing his eyes thinking about his next musical project. I liked to believe he was, anyway. After saying a quick prayer, I folded the paper with my poem on it and placed it next to him in the casket.

After the ceremony, Dad and I rode together in silence from the church to the Renton cemetery, which wasn't too far away. News of Jimi's funeral was all over the radio, and people stood waving at us from the front lawns of their homes as we passed by in our limousine. As soon as we pulled into the cemetery and I caught a glimpse of the surroundings, I wasn't impressed with the place. It was a shabby, old lot and the main office looked like a run-down hunting shack. I didn't feel at ease knowing that after all of the spectacular things my brother had done during his life, this was going to be his final resting place.

"Why'd you bury Buster in a place like this?" I quietly asked Dad.

"Because your mama is buried here," he answered.

"She is?"

"Yeah. She's somewhere in this cemetery, but I don't know where. We haven't found her yet. But this is where I decided our family plot is going to be, son."

I didn't push it any further. It wasn't the time or the place to get into a heated discussion, so I let it go.

A few of Jimi's childhood buddies—Eddy Rye, Donnie Howell, and Billy Burns—served as pallbearers, along with James Thomas, the leader of my brother's earlier band, and Herb Price, his valet. Together, they carefully rested the casket next to the grave that had been dug. As they then lowered it into the ground, some people tossed guitar picks and folded letters down onto it, while others threw joints. All of my family surrounded my dad and me, and we tightly hung on to each other. I never wanted to let any of them go.

My gangster buddies from downtown thought the funeral was the perfect opportunity for me to make my great escape from jail. A plan was already worked out and a car was waiting on the far side of the cemetery. But my heart and mind were in another place. My brother was gone, and I was focused on serving out my time in the penitentiary and trying to get through it as best as I could. Making a run for it and skipping out on the marshals was only going to make matters worse. Even I could see that. My buddies weren't happy to hear I wasn't going to be taking them up on their escape plans, but still brought me a couple cartons of Pall Malls to take with me back to jail—only the cartons weren't full of tobacco. They'd removed it, repacked the cigarettes with weed, and meticulously gone through each individual pack and rewrapped the carton in plastic. It was impossible to tell it was tampered with.

I glanced across the lawn to where the three U.S. marshals were standing with their hands clasped in front of them. When one of the men waved me over, I looked away and avoided making eye contact. The whole day went by too fast, and I wished it would last just a few hours longer. But it was time to go back to the last place on earth I wanted to be at that moment: jail. I ignored the marshals until one of them briskly walked over and put a hand on my shoulder.

"Come on, Leon," he quietly said. "It's time."

It felt as if all of the air were being sucked out of my body. "Okay, okay, hold up," I told him. "Please let me at least say good-bye to my dad."

The marshal was nearing the end of his patience, but he still let me slide. "All right, well, do it then," he snapped.

I stepped over to my dad and we put our arms around each other.

I wanted nothing more than to stay and be with my family during such a horrible time, but that day would come as soon as I served out my time and straightened out my life.

The guards at Monroe didn't pay my cartons of Pall Malls any attention when they checked me back into my cell. So, thanks to my gangster buddies, my whole wing in the jail was loaded on weed for *months*. The guards couldn't figure out how all of their prisoners were getting so lit up. No matter how many people they tried to shake down, nobody talked. The party didn't come to an end until one of the guards spotted me smoking a joint out in the yard one afternoon. I rushed back to my cell right away and flushed the rest of the weed down the toilet. When the boys marched down to my cell later that night to give me what they called "a breakdown" and turn my cell over, nothing was to be found. They tossed around everything and even overturned the bed, but not a single joint was left.

Charles Pascal, a lawyer Dad had hired to help him with my brother's business dealings, came up to visit me and give me an update on how everything was proceeding. With my parole hearing approaching, the most important thing Charles did was to get me a job at the company Dad created with Freddie Mae Gautier in my brother's name: the Jimi Hendrix Foundation. That I had a paying job, a permanent address (Dad's house), and a structure waiting for me on the outside helped me score some major points with the parole board.

Thankfully, at my parole hearing the board approved my request for release. It would be thirty days later before they actually let me out. I wasn't going to let anything come between me and walking out the doors of Monroe Reformatory.

"Man, lock me in my cell for a month," I told the guards. "I don't want any trouble. I don't need to go to the mess halls, and I don't need to hang out with anyone. Just let me sit my time out in my cell until my release date."

They laughed in response, but I was completely serious. Nothing was more important to me than quietly serving out my time and finally being allowed to reunite with my family.

FREEDOM AND THE AFTERMATH

In January of 1971, I stepped out through the giant set of iron gates of Monroe Reformatory wearing the same suit I'd worn only three months earlier to Jimi's funeral. Finally, I was able to draw in my first breath of fresh air as a free man. My stay at Monroe may have been just short of ten months, but it felt much longer. I moved back into the house with Dad, June, and Janie, but living with them wasn't where I wanted to be. Unfortunately, it was necessary for me to abide by the guidelines the parole board had set and maintain a residence at a regular address. At home, Dad was constantly on me about maintaining a full-time job and walking the straight and narrow. My position at the Jimi Hendrix Foundation wasn't anything to take seriously. Dad gave me the official title of vice president (of what, I have no idea), which existed only on paper. Although I had my own office, nothing was in it but a table and a single chair. We wanted to make sure my situation looked stable to the parole board so they wouldn't get any ideas about revoking my parole and changing my status.

I had no need to show up to work because I wasn't responsible for anything. To make Dad happy, I slipped into a job working in the laundry room at the University of Washington, but it didn't last long. It was no surprise to anyone that washing clothes and ironing sheets didn't hold my interest. There was easy money to be made hustling, and it was nearly impossible for me to settle for a regular job paying the minimum wage. You would think I might have learned my lesson after rotting away in Monroe for all that time, but I was still too young to get the message.

From the moment Jimi's body was lowered six feet into the ground on that dreary afternoon at the cemetery, the legal frenzy started. Even though everything Jimi owned was passed on to Dad after Jimi's death, Dad soon found out there wasn't much to step forward to claim. Mike Jeffrey tried to tell him that most everything in Jimi's estate was "tied up" in various investments, mostly in real estate and stocks, in different locations all over the world. My translation of Mike's excuse: *I've been siphoning suitcases of money from Jimi's estate for the last few years and stashing everything away in secret international bank accounts. Good luck in trying to find the cash.* Of all the suitcases I witnessed Jeffrey pulling out of the box offices after Jimi's gigs, I wondered how many of them never found their way into my brother's accounts. As if that notion wasn't bad enough, after Jimi's death Jeffrey also insisted that only around $25,000 in cash was left in Jimi's bank accounts.

Dad saw that some underhanded business dealings had taken place on Jeffrey's part. From the first day I met Jeffrey, I thought something about him was shady. Now that Jimi was gone, we hoped all of Jeffrey's secrets were going to be exposed. Dad hired a lawyer named Ken Hagood to find out where the bulk of Jimi's money had gone. This complicated search and negotiation with Jeffrey dragged on for months, with those months of waiting soon becoming years.

There looked to be no end in sight to the legal proceedings. Dad and I had to carry on with life constantly wondering when it was all going to be over and done with.

When all of Jimi's personal belongings were delivered to the house one afternoon, Dad and I didn't know where to start. There was barely enough room to store most of the boxes, and we ended up keeping most of them in the living room at first. Although Dad told me to take whatever I wanted, it was tough to sort through it all. There were endless stacks of recording masters, notebooks, and clothing. We eventually moved most of it to underneath an old Ping-Pong table in the garage.

Only a couple years removed from the official Summer of Love, the once-thriving hippie culture was all but dead and gone. After Janis Joplin, Jim Morrison, and Jimi passed away, it seemed that the young generation moved on with their lives at once. People suddenly had wives, children, and bills to pay. You couldn't simply be a hippie and hang out all day getting loaded and having sex anymore. Those days were over, and the hippies were now a part of the working class looking for jobs and a new direction in their lives.

In my case, I made the mistake of not choosing a new direction, and I reverted to spending all my time in an old, familiar environment downtown. Not many people can say that hustling was their way to make a living, but it worked for me . . . most of the time. Eventually, I was even able to buy myself a brand-new Cadillac. Although I might have been thrilled with my new ride, Dad wasn't happy the first time he set eyes on it.

"You sure as hell didn't get that car from working with your hands, boy," he told me, shaking his head in disgust. Dad knew all too well what I was doing with my time.

Not only did I have the car, but I also made sure my clothes were just right—the whole outfit to match, from the alligator boots to the silk shirts and velvet pants. As long as I was out running my game, I had no time to sit and dwell on Jimi's tragic death. But it was impossible to run forever, no matter how much action there was on the streets.

Once I was out of Monroe for a few months, my emotions about losing my brother finally started to surface. During a break in the action, the weight of everything that had happened finally came crashing down on me. In some ways, Dad was going through a similar experience. The only two times I ever saw him cry were when he heard the news that our mama, his Lucille, had died and the day my brother was finally laid to rest. Since my dad never liked to show his emotions, he didn't have much of a response to losing Jimi after that day in the cemetery, but I still sensed he was hurting just as much as me. Clearly we were both finally feeling the pain.

I have no idea what happened to my brother that fateful night in the London hotel room. Nobody knew what happened and probably no one ever will. Mike Jeffrey knew he was done and on the way out. But was he really done? Maybe he wasn't going to go down without taking my brother out first and claiming even more money from a life insurance policy. From the moment I met him, I always considered Mike a liar and an all-around shady character. I don't know if he would have gone that far, but he definitely seemed to be trying to work Jimi to death. In the end, who is really to say?

From what I have personally been told over the years by people who were at the party in London that evening, many of them got sick and left to go see a doctor. But Jimi didn't and went back to his hotel room. He had a few sleeping pills in his system, some wine, and a fish sandwich, but that was about it. There are too many loose ends to sort through. Each story I heard somehow contradicted the one before it. The truth will never be known, and all that remains is rumor and speculation. Nobody, including me, has proof to back up any theory about why Jimi died.

June regularly visited Jimi's gravesite, but Dad and I weren't interested in making the trip. Neither of us needed to see a gravestone to help us remember my big brother. To us, it was nothing but a large rock in the grass. In my mind, my brother's spirit had left this earth the moment his heart stopped on that tragic night in the London hotel room. Still, each year on Memorial Day, Dad figured he should at least go down to make an appearance and typically asked me to join him. But I had no interest. I'd rather just sit home, put on some of Jimi's music, and rewind through the years of good memories. When his guitar screamed through my stereo speakers, it was as if he were right there in the room with me.

While Jimi was alive, I was more into the whole groove and vibe of his music, but after he passed on, I recognized the power of his lyrics as well. That was the case for many of his fans, too. People were so mesmerized by the power of his guitar playing and the spectacle of his stage show, they sometimes didn't pay the proper attention to his poetry.

My buddies and I listened to Jimi's records for hours. I am understandably drawn to what I consider Jimi's more autobiographical and heartfelt songs, such as "Castles Made of Sand," "Wind Cries Mary," "Manic Depression," and "Little Wing." I particularly identified with "Little Wing" because in my mind my brother was paying tribute to all of the wonderful loving women who took care of us over the years. He wrote it for his girlfriends, our aunties, and especially for our mama, who looked over us from high above in the afterlife. His more fantastic and far-off songs such as "Burning of the Midnight Lamp" also appealed to me because they are similar to the stories he used to tell me when we were boys.

The Band of Gypsys material appealed to me maybe the most because it was incredibly soulful. The band was exactly what he'd always wanted to put together to convey his vision without others getting in the way. The material on the band's live album sounded as if my brother was at the height of his creative freedom. While Billy Cox and Buddy Miles held down the bottom-end groove, Jimi set off in any direction his guitar took him. He was able to get away from being a pop star and concentrate again on maintaining his integrity as a true artist. The album's first track, "Power of Soul," was a standout. In the long, free-flowing jam "Machine Gun," I could feel my brother's fear and paranoia. The tune was like the sound track of a battlefield, complete with Jimi's feedback resembling gunfire and explosions. The lyrics were about somebody trying to shoot and kill him. Many people who were close to him were out to get him, and he certainly felt it every day. Listening to the song frightened me in a way because of how everything played out. It was almost as if he sensed the end coming. The band was a major step in the right direction after moving on from the Experience, but I also knew it would not have been the last step on his musical journey. He always insisted he wanted to compose symphonies and conduct orchestras as well.

Another of my favorite songs was "Angel," off my brother's posthumous studio album *The Cry of Love*, which was released in February 1971. The track seemed like a continuation of the ground he covered in "Little Wing." Again, he sings about a supportive, protective, and loving woman who watches him from up above and even visits him to finally save him from the rest of the world.

Overall, my brother's music took on a whole different tone for me after he passed away. I often came away with the feeling that my brother was greatly unhappy. I didn't identify that while he was alive, but now that he was gone, it seemed obvious. He may have been looking for a way out of his business affairs and management, but it certainly wasn't by taking his own life.

Most of our friends and family members were inconsolable after Jimi died, but as time wore on, I unexpectedly found an inner strength deep inside me. Buster's spirit was always with me. I could feel his presence wherever I went, and that feeling helped me overcome the sadness of not having him around anymore.

Not to say life was exactly easy. Everyone wanted only to talk about my brother. It didn't bother me at all while he was alive, but after he passed away, it became a chore most of the time.

All over town, it was the same: "Hey, man, aren't you Jimi Hendrix's brother?"

"No, that's not me, buddy. You must have me confused with someone else."

I wanted to go about my life and be able to walk down the sidewalk or have a drink in a bar without being hounded by curious people. I didn't want to get into deep discussions with strangers every five minutes. It was way too draining. Every time I got involved in a conversation about Jimi, it brought the whole nightmare back to the surface. Besides, it seemed as if no matter what I said concerning my brother, there was no winning with people. Even when I did come clean and admit that Jimi was my brother, some people didn't believe me. "Oh, quit lying," they'd snap.

People were and are after the Hendrix name. Around every corner, it seemed they were trying to take advantage of Dad and me. Businessmen from all over the world wanted us to sign off on a multitude of deals and product endorsements. People wanted to purchase the rights to our life stories or produce documentaries and feature films. They always made sure to inform us that we were going to make money on "the back end." But I knew better. On the streets, we called it "the ass end," and no good ever came from settling for it.

The outpouring of respect and gratitude for Jimi was constant after he passed away. The next year, when my dad called and told me Bob Dylan had contacted him, saying he was playing a show and wanted to send a car for us, I thought it was a kind gesture. But I had no idea that he'd be sending a limousine to my dad's house to pick us up. And on top of that, Bob was sitting in the back of that limo when we climbed in.

Bob was a reserved, soft-spoken artist, but also incredibly friendly to Dad and me. He didn't dress or act like most of the rock stars I had come across during my time with Jimi. Bob kept everything low profile. He wore a hat, dark sunglasses, and didn't say much. So when he did finally open his mouth, everyone made sure to listen. On the way to his gig at the Paramount Theatre, he even asked if we'd be interested in joining him to go bowling later on. When he mentioned that he'd met me at the Pantages Theatre a few years earlier in Hollywood with Jimi, I didn't know how to respond. Honestly, I was pretty loaded and barely recalled the encounter.

"I was a big fan of your brother, Leon," Bob also told me. It was one of the few things he said in conversation that night, but I will remember it forever. It meant a great deal to hear him praise my brother because Bob was one of the biggest rock legends of all time.

Unfortunately, we never did get a chance to go bowling with Bob later that night.

I kept going with my hustling lifestyle, and by 1972 the money was pouring in. For a short period, it seemed as if everything I touched turned to gold, whether it was moving pills around on the street, playing pool, or throwing dice. Everybody started calling me Lucky Leon. My good fortune also allowed me to move into my own suite at the Washington Plaza for a while. But deep down, I knew it couldn't last forever. There was no way to keep up such a hectic pace and also keep my sanity. I needed to have eyes in the back of my head at all hours to make sure nobody tried to rob me or maybe do something even worse. When most of my friends started going to jail, it wasn't tough to see that the party was over.

I bounced around for a while trying to find a legitimate way to make ends meet. Since I already knew everything about Seattle nightlife, I formed Hendrix Productions and booked bands at clubs for a time, but didn't stick with it. The only other alternative was to go back to working with my dad at his landscaping business, which I also did. His business was booming, and the lawns he once cut for $8 or $9 were now being priced out at around $50. We rode around to his work sites all day checking up on workers and chatting with clients.

The settling of Jimi's estate took an even more complicated turn on March 5, 1973, when Dad and I got word that Mike Jeffrey had died in a plane crash. What followed was a sensational story about how his aircraft collided midair with another either over France or Spain. It was difficult to be convinced the official account was true because Jeffrey's body was never recovered. The situation got even more interesting when reports surfaced on the news and in the papers about Jeffrey's past service in the British government's MI5 unit and his possible ties to the CIA. Noel Redding mentioned in more than one interview that he wouldn't put it past Jeffrey to stage his own death and escape with some of Jimi's millions to a remote island. This turn of events resembled something out of a James Bond story.

Once Jeffrey was removed (or removed himself) from the equation, our auntie Freddie Mae Gautier referred Dad to a well-known entertainment lawyer named Leo Branton, who had represented many celebrity clients, such as Nat King Cole and Dorothy Dandridge. In the beginning, Dad considered Branton a stand-up guy, not only be-cause of the celebrities he'd worked with, but also because of his involvement in the civil rights movement in the early 1960s. As Branton took control of securing Jimi's estate and legacy, he also reached out to a producer named Alan Douglas, who had worked with jazz greats Duke Ellington and Miles Davis, to oversee Jimi's music. Dad basically gave both of the men complete control of Jimi's estate and went about his life. He figured that with Leo and Alan in place, he was free to go back to concentrating on his landscaping business.

While booking bands in the city, I met a beautiful young girl with red hair and green eyes named Christine Ann, whom I in-stantly fell in love with. We soon moved into an apartment together, and a year later we were married on February 3, 1974. Dad was over-joyed for me and eventually helped us come up with a down pay-ment on a house out near Lake Washington. Not long after settling into our new home, Christine and I were blessed with the birth of a little girl we named Leontyne, or Tina for short. Things were look-ing up and life was good.

Although Dad was overjoyed to help my family and me get off to a good start, June began caring a great deal about how he spent his money. After Dad put the $25,000 deposit down on my house, she called me. "Your dad can't afford a house for you!" she yelled over the phone. "Stop taking advantage of him!"

It was laughable. I wanted to yell, "It is his money to spend! What do you care?" I never bothered my dad for things; he offered them to me. Dad gave me money when I needed it and provided for his grandchildren. He was happy to do for me what he couldn't do when I was younger.

It was important to keep a close eye on people whenever they came over to the new house because they were always trying to find something of Jimi's to steal. Even a few good friends of mine went to ridiculous lengths to coax something out of me.

"You got any of your brother's old socks?" a friend of mine actually asked one day. *Socks.* The guy was always bugging me for anything that was even close to memorabilia, so I figured it was time to put one over on him.

"Sure, man," I told him, gesturing over to a pair of my dirty socks on the floor next to the clothes hamper. "Right over there in the corner. Those used to be one of Jimi's favorite pair."

I probably wouldn't have believed it if I hadn't seen it with my own two eyes. Without another word, my friend raced into the kitchen to grab a plastic bag, then came back in and carefully scooped up the socks as if they were gold. I sat on my couch just staring at his dumb grin as he raised the bag up in front of his face to get a closer look.

"I'm never going to open this bag again!" he told me.

"No problem," I said. "I'm feeling generous today, so I'm going to let you have those free of charge. They're all yours, buddy." Hell, the guy probably has that plastic bag of socks still sitting on his mantel to this very day.

Even if I leveled with him and confessed that the socks were not my brother's, he probably wouldn't have believed me and would have taken them anyway. People wanted to believe that certain items were Jimi's and didn't want the truth to get in the way of their fantasy. Everyone was desperate to find some sort of connection with him. I call it the Hendrix voodoo. Once people catch it, nothing can stop them.

As the late 1970s rolled around, Christine and I had two more children, another daughter, named LeAnne, and a son we named Alex. For the first time in my life, I was doing my best to keep everything in line. I even secured a part-time job as a private courier that paid me full-time money. Day after day, I spent my time delivering sensitive documents to banks all over the city. They even provided me with the keys to most of the major branches to pick up packages after hours. After all those teenaged years of doing everything I could to break into banks, I now found myself being able to waltz right through the front door. It was comical. If only my old buddies could have seen me. And if you are wondering why a courier company hired me to do such work with a rap sheet like mine? Let's just say my police records were misplaced downtown by a family friend.

For the most part, the Hendrixes were one big happy family. We spent every holiday and birthday together. Dad absolutely adored Christine for giving him such beautiful grandbabies. His face lit up every time he came into our house and the kids surrounded him. Dad loved to spoil them with gifts and made sure they were always taken care of. Anytime my wife or I needed a helping hand when bills were tight, he was there to support us.

Dad continued to run his landscaping business as it grew from year to year. Although I was busy with my courier job during the week, he picked me up in the mornings on weekends, and we visited his various job sites throughout the city. No matter how many times I went through the details of the financial situation with my dad, he couldn't understand that he never needed to work again. He alone controlled all of Jimi's music and money, but he still never came to terms with that. In his mind, he viewed the whole experience as a passing trend. He saw himself as nothing more than an employee of Jimi's estate and placed his trust in lawyers and accountants. Even after everything, it was almost as if he refused to believe what Jimi had accomplished. The biggest problem was that Dad believed whatever the lawyers told him. He signed anything they wanted him to sign and approved anything they wanted him to approve.

Not more than a few years after handing over control of Jimi's estate to Leo Branton and Alan Douglas, Dad finally confessed he was only receiving around $50,000 a year. When I heard the news, my jaw nearly hit the floor. Whatever they told him the estate was pulling in each year off Jimi's music, Dad believed. Besides, that kind of money was more than he'd ever made in his life. In his mind, he was already rich, so there was no reason to get into it over the business arrangement.

"What are you talking about?" I asked him. "Jimi's albums are still on the charts and they're pulling in millions. His photos are all over the magazines."

"Branton knows what he's doing, so I'm not going to go causing trouble with him," Dad told me. "I don't want to hear it anymore from you. I got Branton yelling in one ear about something, and you and June yelling in the other."

Our family dynamic started to change not long after my son Jason was born in 1980. My relationship with June had slowly begun deteriorating from the day I started my own family, and it steadily worsened. At first it was difficult to understand where she was coming from because early on she was always kindhearted. I often called her mom after she and my dad moved in together. But she wasn't thrilled about the time and money Dad was spending on his grandbabies. I distinctly remember calling my dad's house one day and June answering the phone with more than enough attitude.

"You not my son!" she yelled at me in her Japanese accent. "Jimi my son, not you!"

I also came over to the house one evening and discovered that June had gone to the beauty parlor and dyed her hair from its usual black to *dark purple*. Over time she acted weirder and weirder. She also regularly wore some of my brother's bright and colorful blouses around the house. I don't know exactly what was going on with her, and I can only think that she had come down with a case of the Hendrix voodoo. June constantly kept herself on edge by focusing on my brother's fame and worrying about her family's finances. She then directed all of her frustration at my family and me. Eventually, all of our photos were suspiciously missing from Dad's house. There wasn't a single picture to prove my family existed. A friend of mine called it "Japanese death," where someone is slowly erased from everyday life until the person is eventually forgotten altogether. When I confronted Dad about the situation, he had a hard time coming up with a good answer for June's behavior. He found himself caught in the middle between us and didn't want anything to do with it.

"June and Janie just don't like you anymore," Dad told me.

"Why?" I asked.

"I have no idea. I don't know."

June acted like a child and threw tantrums anytime dad spent time playing with his grandbabies. She'd get on Dad's case about his giving me money and start shouting at him, telling him that I wasn't his biological son.

June's resentment was gradually reflected in her daughter Janie's attitude as well. Earlier on, the two of us had been close, and when she was just a child, I took care of her almost every day. After all, I stayed in the Seward Park house for quite a while before moving out to an apartment to live with Christine Ann. Many mornings, I walked Janie to school and babysat her when June and Dad weren't around. But once I was out of the house and started my own family, Janie's feelings changed toward me. To this day, I don't know the reason for it.

I went on with my life while June went to work on my dad, telling him I was no good. On holidays, the house was full of Japanese people . . . and then there was my dad. When my family and I showed up, it disrupted the scene, so over time I gave up and stopped going to the house altogether. If Dad wanted to see his grandbabies, he stopped by our home. June refused to speak to me on the phone and gave my dad a hard time for having any contact with me. It developed into a ridiculous situation. Janie also started ignoring me and didn't want anything to do with my family. I couldn't understand what was going on because in my mind I didn't do anything to deserve such treatment. I let it go because there was no reason to make an issue of it all. Besides, I had my kids to look after.

In time, Dad also grew tired of June's behavior and the two of them finally separated. He bought her a house down by Lake Washington and continued to occupy his time with his landscaping business. However, Dad was getting old and couldn't get around like he used to. Despite being in his early sixties, he still loved his booze and cigarettes.

A major turning point came when Dad suddenly had a heart attack in late 1983. Suddenly, lawyers and moneymen from all over showed up at the hospital and at the house carrying briefcases of documents. It was almost as if everyone were playing musical chairs and the music abruptly stopped. Each of them was scrambling to position himself in case Dad passed away.

In an odd sequence of events, Dad was admitted for his bypass surgery to the same hospital where Christine had gone into labor with our fifth child. I split time between the two hospital rooms until the doctors finally notified me that the baby was on the way. We became the proud parents of another baby boy. As I paced around in the hallway after my son's birth, it dawned on me that the date was November 27, Jimi's birthday. From that moment, it was obvious what we were going to name our new son: Jimi Hendrix Jr. It felt as if my brother were smiling down on my family from up above on that evening.

After Dad's procedure in the hospital, doctors repeated it was important that he quit smoking cigarettes and drinking alcohol during his recovery. After all of the years of severe abuse, his body couldn't take it any longer. Dad wasn't happy about their recommendations. He was stubborn and didn't appreciate anyone, even surgeons and doctors, telling him how to live his life. Dad certainly didn't change his lifestyle right away. It took a few years before he got his drinking under control, and he always struggled to cut out his smoking. He offered to let me take over his landscaping business, but I'd gotten back into my art part-time and was starting to produce black velvet paintings for a few companies. A local businessman also had begun paying me a few grand a month to produce four or five drawings that he would then mass-produce and sell by mail order.

Just as everything seemed like it was settling down in my life, things took a turn for the worse. Although I hadn't done cocaine in years, it came back around and crept into the picture. In 1985, I was involved in a horrible car accident and injured my head and my back. I received a few hundred thousand dollars in a settlement, which took years to finally collect. After that, I was on heavy medication to numb my intense back pain. Not only was I popping pain pills and antidepressants, but I was also still doing coke on top of everything else. At first, a gram would last me a couple weeks, just a little blast to keep me alert and awake when I was working on my drawings late at night. But my use ramped up over time, and the little I was doing wasn't enough.

My situation only got worse when crack cocaine entered the picture. The first time I tried the drug was one of the worst days of my life. What was supposed to be a brief feeling of ecstasy turned into ten years of my life. Although I was still working full-time and functioning, I'd fallen into the worst type of addiction.

I tried to push forward and do some good in the community. On March 8, 1988, Dad and I officially founded the James Marshall Hendrix Foundation, a nonprofit charity, in honor of my brother's generous spirit. He always made sure to give us so much while he was alive, and we wanted to ensure that his legacy of giving back lived on in the future. The foundation's mission was to inspire and support creativity and understanding in the community, especially with young children. The main focus was to raise money to establish art and music programs to promote understanding, diversity, and, most important of all, peace. It felt good to be able to have our family give something back to the city we had lived in all of our lives.

Not long after starting the foundation, I tracked down my cousin Bobby to see if he was interested in coming to work for the family charity. He was doing well at his executive job at Costco and figured he might be able to help Dad and me out with the day-to-day running of the office. But when he traveled down from Vancouver to meet with me, things didn't go as smoothly as I would have liked. When I asked Bobby to come on board as the foundation's treasurer, he wasn't interested. He explained that things were going well for him at Costco, and he didn't want to do anything to put his advancement within the company in jeopardy. Bobby actually had the nerve to tell me that he didn't want to be associated with Jimi's bad reputation from dying from a drug overdose. I figured that at least I had given it a try, and that was the end of it.

Even though I was attempting to do some good for the world around me, my situation at home didn't improve. It was nearly impossible to fix anything with drugs being in the picture. With all of the bad habits, my wife and I weren't good for each other. By the time our sixth child, Jonelle, came along, Christine and I found we were going in separate directions and our relationship was beyond repair. We rarely saw each other and took care of our kids in shifts at the house. She'd disappear for a while and then come back, and I'd go out and do my thing on the streets. I'm not proud of how everything played out, but I was completely under the control of drugs and only concerned with searching for my next high.

ROCK-AND-ROLL SWINDLE

For more than two decades, Dad was thrilled to be collecting his $50,000 a year from Jimi's estate, and when Leo Branton bumped that figure up to $100,000 and presented him with lump-sum payments from time to time, Dad was even happier. Because my dad was less than engaged, Branton did not have anyone looking over his shoulder. There was never a reason in Dad's mind, no matter how frequently I complained, to second-guess the details of the intricate financial situation. Anytime I gave him a difficult time about it, he either ignored me altogether or responded with the same line:

"It's better to deal with the devil you know than the devil you don't."

It was nice to know that the money was there if my kids needed it. They were my dad's pride and joy and he would do anything for them. Once in a while, Dad would convince Leo to cut me a check to help support my family.

While Dad and I were in Hollywood during late November of 1991 for the unveiling of Jimi's star on the legendary Walk of Fame,

Leo pulled me aside and explained we needed to discuss something important.

"I wanted to let you know that your dad has authorized me to put an agreement together for you," he informed me. "Just be patient and I will have something more concrete to send in the coming few weeks."

I wasn't sure why Leo was being vague, but whatever he was referring to sounded good to me. He was going to give me money, and I had no problem with that. After the short conversation, I didn't put much more thought into it until his letter arrived in the mail a few months later. It mentioned that some years ago Dad had licensed his copyrights to Jimi's music for a period of time in exchange for an annual return. I imagined that was where the annual fifty grand and one hundred grand were coming from for the last twenty years. The letter also said that the original copyright period was set to expire in the near future. Branton then outlined Dad's intention to license what Leo called the "reversionary copyrights" once again, but this time Leo needed not only my signature to make this happen, but also Janie's. This reflected that if anything happened to Dad, the two of us would be next in line to inherit. By signing off on the transaction, we'd both get a whopping $1 million to waive our contingent reversionary rights to Jimi's music.

Despite my suspicions of Branton over the years, I went ahead and signed on the dotted line. My drug addiction was more important to me than anything else, and scrutinizing business deals was of little interest. Despite being a seasoned street hustler, I probably made a major misstep, but my mind wasn't at all clear then. Most of the legal jargon in the paperwork made little sense to me. However, a *million dollars*? That spoke loud and clear. At the time, I wanted to set up trust funds for my children and work on planning for their futures. Hiring a lawyer to review the documents never even crossed my mind. I had mouths to feed and a family to support, so I was overjoyed with the offer.

The moment Branton called to notify me that my first $100,000 payment was ready, I was thrilled.

"I'll messenger the check to you as soon as possible," he said.

"Naw, naw, naw," I replied. "No need to do that. I'm making a special trip to pick it up myself."

Sure enough, I jumped a plane down to Los Angeles the next morning and was waiting at the front door for him when his offices opened. As I look back, receiving the money was probably the worst thing that could have happened to me then because my addiction to crack was completely out of control. Upon returning to Seattle, I bought even more dope and started selling larger amounts.

To my surprise, I soon found out that one of the stipulations for receiving my money from Branton was agreeing to enter a treatment center for my addiction. It was something I never planned on, but I went through the motions anyway just to satisfy everyone else. The drug treatment center I checked into in Oregon was more like an expensive country club than a medical facility. I ordered my breakfast from a private chef and had my own room. It was impossible to take anything my counselors said seriously because it felt more like a vacation than treatment. I counted the hours until my thirty-day stint was over. Although they wanted to send me to another facility in Minnesota, there was no chance of that. After jumping on a flight back to Seattle, I took a limousine straight from Sea-Tac Airport to my local dope house to score. In my warped mental state, everything was wonderful in my life.

Although I was technically going ahead with the plan Branton laid out, Janie had other ideas and immediately hired her own lawyer. She was much too suspicious to go along with the proposed arrangement. Janie told me that after some digging, her attorney found what he believed were discrepancies in the numbers Leo Branton had presented to us over the years about what Jimi's music was worth. Rumors were going around that Leo was allegedly planning on licensing the publishing rights to MCA Music Entertainment Group for around $40 million. Thankfully, Dad could no longer ignore the situation.

Branton's reign was finally coming to an end. With Janie's help, Dad was determined to sever all ties and hired an attorney in the beginning of 1993 to send Leo a letter revoking his power of attorney. Shortly thereafter, my father filed a lawsuit against Branton and others, alleging everything from fraud and legal malpractice to securities law violations and negligent misrepresentation. As Leo released records and other information in the lawsuit, we learned more about the inner workings of Jimi's estate. Eventually, my father alleged that the defendants had set up many offshore companies and purchased property in Hawaii using Dad's assets but putting the title in Branton's name. It appeared that everything was not "on the up-and-up as Dad had believed for the past few decades. Leo Branton's wife, Geraldine, and son, Chip, were also named in the filed complaint, as well as Alan Douglas.

The local press eventually picked up on the story, and the *Seattle Post-Intelligencer* soon ran the headline "Hendrix Lawsuit—Father of Rock Star Sues for Copyright Ownership." When the Seattle billionaire Microsoft's Paul Allen caught wind of the situation, he even offered to lend Dad more than $4 million for his legal fees in trying to get Jimi's rights back from Branton. The case was not only the talk of the city, but also the entire international recording industry.

Dad didn't know much, if anything, about the legal system, courts, and judges. The situation was a lot for him to handle, and the depositions took their toll on him over the next year. Dad was already in his midseventies, and his memory was never sharp to begin with. He tried to answer all of the lawyers' questions as best he could, but many times they weren't too happy with what he was able to remember.

Janie, on the other hand, welcomed the spotlight of the court proceedings. In her mind, she was now running the show for the entire Hendrix family. She started embellishing, if not rewriting, the truth. A sharp pain erupted in my stomach every time she referred to Jimi as "her brother." Most people didn't have knowledge of our family dynamic, so everyone took whatever she said to be true. At times she even insisted that she was Jimi's *biological* sister. Fiction was starting to take over the facts. At every opportunity, she made sure to mention how close she and Jimi were while he was alive, and how much he loved and adored her. The truth was, my brother only met her three or four brief times when she was six and seven years old. Other people may have been buying what she was pushing, but to me the whole thing was getting to be silly.

The Branton case dragged on for a couple of years, well into the summer of 1995, but never went to trial. In the end, Dad's team of lawyers, through a settlement judgment with Branton and Alan Douglas, reclaimed the publishing rights to Jimi's music. I was overjoyed for Dad and our family because it was only right for the Hendrixes to have complete control over Jimi's legacy. Dad was also able to pay off the over $4 million Paul Allen lent him to fight his case in the courts.

I give a lot of credit to Janie for setting her mind to something and seeing it through until the very end. She went on with lawyers to help create a company, Experience Hendrix, LLC, for Dad in July of 1995. Dad served as chairman and licensed the rights to Jimi's music to MCA for somewhere around $40 million. It was a big achievement for the family as a whole, but the process may have inspired Janie to become even more active in the business over the ensuing years. In retrospect, I should have paid more attention to the constant business dealings, but I was too busy with my own life.

Even after settling the court case with Branton and Douglas and establishing his company, Dad still maintained his landscaping business, occasionally making the rounds to his various job sites all over Seattle, barking orders at his workers and chatting with his clients. Throughout his life, his work was always what kept him going, and he was never going to completely give it up no matter what kind of incredible dollar amounts he heard lawyers throwing around every once in a while at company meetings. While he tended to his business, he left Janie to oversee the rest of the Hendrix estate's affairs. I had an opportunity to step in and take an active role with the company, but I wasn't interested. I was never an executive type and probably never will be.

My drug use had been completely out of control for some time, but by 1996 everything was reaching a critical level. My crack habit was debilitating and I smoked the drug every single day. Despite being in a haze, I was still able to sell coke and make upward of ten grand a week. The constant flow of money even allowed me to buy a luxurious penthouse condo on Capitol Hill in Seattle to use as my dealing headquarters. It may have been a beautiful location on the outside, but inside was another story. The scene was ugly. Random customers came and went at all hours, looking for their next fix. I often didn't leave the apartment for days and remained locked inside with girlfriends. Most of them would do anything to get their drugs, and eventually a colorful cast of girls was around, such as Michelles #1, #2, and #3, as well as the Russian girls: Sasha, Tasha, and Yasha. It was a twenty-four-hour-a-day, seven-day-a-week circus atmosphere.

My customers traded anything they could get their hands on for drugs, and my luxurious apartment eventually looked more like a pawnshop. I had drawers full of jewelry, clothing, and electronics people exchanged in order to get high. One woman even brought over a beat-up, old guitar to give me for drugs. I didn't think much of it at the time and leaned it up in the corner against the living-room wall.

One night a few months later, I was incredibly loaded and must have passed out on the couch. Suddenly there was a buzzing sound, followed by a deep bass tone. I opened my eyes to see the guitar slightly moving in the corner of the room. It's strings began humming as well, shaking off the dust and dirt that had accumulated over the months. It might have been a small earthquake, and possibly I was too wasted to realize it. Still, for some reason the guitar was the only thing moving in the room. Then, I had a vision. It was of a gray expanse where the clouds parted and I heard music fading up, beautiful vocal melodies, and otherworldly guitar tones. I heard Jimi's voice faintly in the back of my mind . . .

What do you want to do, Leon? It's been long enough and it is time for you to pick up that guitar. It is all you have left.

Breaking out of my stupor, I pushed myself up off the couch and shuffled over to the corner. After picking up the guitar, I thought back to Jimi plucking away on that old ukulele he'd found at Mrs. Maxwell's when we were young boys. I spent the rest of the night strumming. Holding the guitar in my hands, I felt something I hadn't in a long time: a sense of direction and purpose.

At first, I could barely play a chord, but I bought a guitar-theory book and hooked up with some local musicians. A few months later, we decided to start a band. Finally, after years of searching for my rightful place, I found music, or you could also say music finally found me. Either way, I am thankful it happened. I was convinced music was going to lead me out of the darkness and help me get my life together.

As soon as I discovered the guitar, it filled the void left by my drug use. For the first time in my life, I had something else to pour my emotion and energy into. Once my efforts were focused on music full-time, I never looked back because I was clearly on the right path. Others were concerned about my musical dreams. People were genuinely fearful for me. They knew how the record business chewed up musicians and spit them out. But I didn't care. I never saw being Jimi's brother as an obstacle. My hope was to express myself artistically and pay tribute to his musical spirit.

Through my music, I began meeting plenty of rock stars around the Seattle area, but some were more receptive to my music than others. Most of the other guitar players weren't too happy with my new career path. They believed I had no right picking up a guitar in the first place and were jealous that I was booking gigs all over town with my band even though I could barely play. Anytime somebody gave me a hard time about picking up a guitar, my only response was to smile back and say, "I'm sorry if you feel that way. I'm only following what's in my heart."

Despite my attempt to follow a musical path out of the darkness of my drug addiction, I was still struggling to get clean. Everyone knew it, especially my dad. He decided it was time to step in and make an attempt to save my life. He insisted it was finally time for me to go to treatment. My dad explained that he had established a trust fund for me, called the Bodacious trust, which was for 25 percent of the estate. He added even more incentive for me to get clean by offering me $10,000 a month from that fund. But still, I couldn't bring myself to stop.

It would be another year or so before I reached the end of my rope. It wasn't that I necessarily hit rock bottom, but for maybe the first time it was apparent to me that my life needed to change before it was too late. My kids understood how bad my drug use had become as well. Together, they witnessed my fall into addiction firsthand over the years. When my daughter Tina invited me over for dinner one night, I arrived to find all of my kids sitting in the living room. Jimi, Alex, Jason, Lee Ann, and even my little baby girl, Jonelle, had serious expressions on their faces. It was time for an intervention. When they put the screws to me about my out-of-control drug use, there was no point in arguing. Even my little baby girl took a turn getting up in front of me and pleading with me to clean up my life.

"Please, Daddy, please," Jonelle told me. "Everybody says you're going die if we don't help you."

The beautiful show of love and support brought tears to my eyes. I owed it to my kids to give rehab an honest effort. They didn't want to lose me and cared enough, even after all I'd put them through over the years, to offer their unconditional help and love. They had already reserved a spot for me at Impact Drug and Alcohol Treatment Center in Pasadena, California, with sunshine and palm trees.

"I don't have any clothes though. Just let me go back home for a minute and pack and then—"

"Rehab isn't a fashion show," Tina told me. "You have to go directly to the airport. No going home and getting loaded one last time."

That's as much of a fight as I put up. I went. I wasn't going to argue with them.

Fortunately, my kids couldn't follow me too far down the criminal path because for the most part I left no footprints. I was never nailed for drug dealing or anything related. Don't get me wrong, I probably didn't set a good example for them during that time, but all I can do now is hope to make up for it by setting a proper example from this point forward.

I remember one of my sons once told me, "I want to be just like you, Dad."

"Well, don't do it, son," I told him. "Hustling isn't a way to live."

After completing two months of my scheduled three-month stay at Impact Drug and Alcohol Treatment Center, I convinced the administrators to let me transfer to a place called Genesis House, a sober living facility in the Cheviot Hills area of Los Angeles. When I messed around after only a few weeks and was caught drinking, they discharged me. Although I managed to steer clear of the hard drugs, in many ways it felt like I was right back to where I started. However, I was still determined not to fall back into old habits. My future seemed incredibly dark until I was introduced to an amazing woman named Jasmin Rogg. Not long after we met, she encouraged me to regularly attend Alcoholics Anonymous meetings throughout the Los Angeles area. The meetings introduced me to ex-addicts who had truly walked in my shoes. It wasn't difficult for me to see that they understood where I had been and also where my life had the potential to go.

Jasmin and I moved in together and never looked back. For the first time in three decades, I was completely drug-free and on my way to getting my life back together. Many times in the previous decades I had thought I would never make it. My eventual breakthrough was nothing short of a miracle.

Due to the time and effort I spent on my sobriety, I paid absolutely no attention to Jimi's estate or the business dealings of Experience Hendrix. In my mind, there wasn't much of a reason to. It was important to my dad that his grandbabies and I be taken care of in the future. I fully understood that Dad was providing for my family's future, so I decided to let Janie and my cousin Bobby, who had come on as president of the company, do their thing. I guess he wasn't concerned any longer that the Hendrix legacy of sex, drugs, and rock and roll would have an effect on his position with Costco. It didn't make much sense, but I had no intention of making a big deal out of his sudden shift in attitude.

As the money rolled in to Jimi's estate, Janie took more and more of an active role in all the Hendrix business affairs. Unfortunately, many of our relatives were shut out, especially our aunt Delores and some of our cousins on my mama's side of the family. It would have been nice for them to be at least offered a job at Experience Hendrix, but nothing ever materialized. Jimi would have been disgusted by the way Janie conducted herself with our mama's side of the family. We would never have made it without the love and support of Aunt Delores and so many others. Now that the time had come for them to ask for a little assistance to simply pay their bills, they were being turned away.

Dad had claimed he was incompetent in making business decisions and signing legal documents to win the rights and estate back from Leo Branton's control, and I, for one, was wondering what exactly everyone thought was going to be different after the case was settled. Dad was still technically incompetent and wasn't fit to handle a massive undertaking such as control of Jimi's estate. I wondered whether Dad was still signing papers and legal documents he didn't understand.

Janie was even living with him at a house in Skyway, a nice suburb triangulated between Seattle, Tukwila, and Renton. There was talk of Dad's moving into a bigger house, but he wasn't keen on the idea. Besides, the million-dollar condominiums out by Lake Washington had parking complexes with low ceilings, and if Dad couldn't fit his truck into the structure, he wanted nothing to do with it. At his house in Skyway, he could leave his truck parked directly out in front just as he always had. In the back of his mind he truly thought everything could be taken away in a moment. As long as he had his truck and his tools, he would always be able to provide for himself no matter what happened.

But his health wasn't what it once was. Since his heart surgery in the eighties, dad's condition was up and down.

Janie and Bobby checked him into an expensive assisted-living center not far from downtown Seattle. When my girlfriend, Jasmin, and I visited him, Dad was sitting up and watching television. He also had a few CDs of some music I was working on sitting on the table next to the bed. As soon as he started giving orders, it was easy to see he was back to his old self again.

"Hey, boy, reach up there and change that channel on the set," he told me.

Then, he turned to Jasmin. "Sweetie, can you give my feet a good rubbing? They're sore as ever. Thank you so much."

But in the coming months, Dad's condition took a turn for the worse. He was having congestive heart failure and rejecting the new valve the doctors' inserted. They even put another pacemaker in his chest. Janie had been awarded power of attorney and didn't need to tell me anything if she didn't want to. Dad was moved back and forth between assisted living and home.

My relationship with Janie and Bobby may have not been that great to begin with, but all of the back-and-forth of placing my dad in assisted living and then pulling him out to take him back home tore us apart.

In December of 1999, Janie convinced Dad to put out an auto-biography, *My Son Jimi*, which she helped him self-publish. I found it difficult to make my way through it. Dad's memory was hazy at best, and most of his recollections were simply not the truth of how everything went down during our childhood. Alcohol has been known to do weird things to people's memories. Although there are many, and I mean *many*, all-out fabrications and half-truths, one of the more comical passages in the book has Dad recalling how he used to labor away making "good meals" for the two of us, and how we had access to cereal, milk, peanut butter and jelly, scrambled eggs and bacon, bananas, apples, oranges, watermelon, salads, hot dogs, cake, pie, cinnamon rolls, and ice cream. In reading this account, a person would think Jimi and I grew up in a grocery store. A few of my other favorite moments include Dad insisting there was never a car crash with me, Jimi, and Mama, swearing that my brother and I never met Little Richard when we were boys, and correcting my accounts that he took us to the pool hall with him from time to time when he gambled. The most ridiculous statement committed to print had to be that "Jimmy wasn't around Leon much after he was about seven."

Not long after reading through a few choice passages from the book, I called Dad up to ask him about some of the things he recounted.

"Book? I don't know nothing about no book," Dad told me on the phone.

It was difficult to do anything but smile. God, I loved my dad. No matter what happened between us over the years, he was such a good man. Despite how disappointed I was with some of the things included in his book, I wasn't going to hold him responsible. It wasn't his fault.

"Don't worry. It's okay," I told him. "No matter what they have you saying in there, I love you."

"I love you, too, son."

Janie's prints were all over the construction of the memoir. Again, she was doing her best to rewrite history. I was noticing an alarming trend in the accounts of the childhood my brother and I shared—my role was gradually being written out of the Hendrix story line. On the flip side, Janie was at every turn painting herself as the ideal member of the Hendrix family.

Over the next two years, Bobby and Janie didn't want anything to do with my family or me. It wasn't only because of my being critical of how they were treating my dad. Looking back, I can only think that it was because *I was in their way.* A few times, I went to the University of Washington hospital to see my dad only to be told I had been listed as a person *not* to be allowed entrance to the building. When I did finally manage to get in, I found Dad unable to speak anymore and clutching my music CDs. He could only nod and smile. It was tough to witness, but I tried to be strong and support him in whatever way I could. He knew I was in the hospital room with him. There was no doubt in his mind that I loved him. Janie made sure that everyone knew that I was not to be updated on Dad's health and disallowed me from having any contact with him whatsoever. I don't know whether that was because she didn't want me interfering or whether she was concerned for my dad's health.

To this day, I can't say that I am impressed by how my brother's musical legacy has been handled. Over the years, there have been countless decisions I don't think Jimi would have been at all happy with. For instance, Janie licensed his song "Are You Experienced?" to Reebok to use in one of their commercials. I'm sure that would have been a big no-no in my brother's mind.

Other musical releases haven't fared much better. Many of the recordings put out over the more recent years contain takes of songs and jams I'm sure my brother would never have approved of making available to the general public. I remember being stunned when I saw Janie gave herself a *producer* credit on a box set that was released. In the beginning I was completely behind her efforts to work on remastering Jimi's recordings and distributing them to the world. But as things progressed, it seemed as if the releases were full of outtakes and rough mixes of material he never intended to put out for the public. The posthumous albums seemed like nothing more than moneymaking ventures.

To me, the people in charge didn't have a clear vision of what they wanted to do. The repackaging of Jimi's music, the rereleasing, the remastering—everything felt overproduced and overmanaged. They saturated the market with multiple recordings of the same songs. The remasters are just tricks to keep making money off the same material. My brother released three albums while he was alive: *Are You Experienced, Axis: Bold as Love,* and *Electric Ladyland.* The albums are what he officially approved. Aside from those pieces of work, the other releases were the decisions of others. How many times can you rerelease and repackage essentially the same product? My brother would never have wanted anything to do with that. I can hear him now saying, *Why would I put out a bunch of different versions of the same thing? What is the point?*

16

LOSING DAD

On April 17, 2002, I finally received word that my dad had passed away at his house in Seattle. I was in Los Angeles with Jasmin when we heard the news in the early hours of the morning. My dad's housekeeper called to let me know what had happened. Dad may have been in poor health in the years before his death, but he still made it to the age of eighty-two. Because of his lifestyle, it was probably a surprise to many people that Dad ended up living that long.

It wasn't bad enough that my dad had just passed, but now I was obligated to travel with my children up to the funeral in Seattle and mix with people who despised me. From the moment we entered Mount Zion Baptist Church, I sensed it was going to be a bad scene. They sat my family and me way over on the side of the room while Janie and her family remained directly in the middle. The woman who got up to give the eulogy sounded more as if she was doing public relations on Janie's behalf. The woman immediately began talking about what an amazing daughter Janie was to my dad and how much trust he placed in her. It was difficult to listen to and tough to fight off the urge to stand up and shout at everyone, "This is a funeral for my dad, Al Hendrix, not some PR campaign for Janie."

The situation didn't improve after we arrived at the cemetery, Greenwood Memorial Park, which is also where Jimi was buried. Janie and Bobby took up the front row of chairs while my family had no room to sit down anywhere. As if that weren't enough, Janie's relatives were all at their seats under the tent. Meanwhile, all my dad's family and friends were huddled around on the outskirts trying to keep dry from the rain. Well, I wasn't going to let that happen. I walked up into an aisle and told people they had to move and make room for my family. Believe me, they scattered fast. They could tell by the look on my face that I meant business.

The honor guard came out to perform the flag-folding ceremony, and when the officer walked over to hand it to me, Janie popped out of her seat and grabbed it out of his hands. If the spouse is no longer alive, the flag is supposed to be given to the deceased person's son or daughter *in the order of seniority*, not to the adopted little daughter. Janie's behavior was a real slap in the face. But little did I know that it was only a slight taste of what was yet to come.

Not that we were invited, but my family didn't want anything to do with the reception Janie arranged for after the funeral. We went downtown and held our own reception. As a kind gesture, I handed a few of the invitations we'd printed up to Bobby and Janie, who immediately threw them down on the ground. Oh, well, I figured, it was their loss. Our reception was absolutely packed with friends and family I hadn't seen in a long time. It was a great send-off for my dad.

The will reading was the next morning. Let me say that I was more than upset when I was not invited to the meeting. My heart sank because it was frighteningly obvious that things were not going along as they should have. My lawyer didn't gain access to Dad's will until a few days later. After arriving at my lawyer's office, he closed the door behind us.

"They sent over your inheritance," he told me.

"What do you mean?" I asked.

"This is very hard to explain, Leon. I'm sorry."

He reached down to the floor and picked up a FedEx box that was already opened. After resting it on the desk, he pulled out a *single gold record* of Jimi's.

"Is this a joke?" I asked, standing up from my chair.

"I guess you could say that. I've reviewed the documents and there is a big problem." He paused and glanced up at me. "You've been written out of your father's will."

Needless to say, I was speechless. When I finally did get a chance to look at the document, my Bodacious trust fund for 25 percent of Jimi's estate was *completely missing*. My lawyer explained that my name had been in every one of Dad's wills until the last one, which he revised four years before in 1998. I sat in my lawyer's office for close to an hour, reading and rereading the lines about me receiving "a single gold record" . . . *of Janie's choosing*.

I pushed my chair away from the table and looked up at the ceiling, trying to make some sense of it all. Then a thought hit me. I remembered the issue of the gold record had a backstory. Back in the late 1980s, my dad's house was broken into and a few of Jimi's gold records were stolen from the walls. Over the years, Janie always maintained that I took them. The suggestion that I would actually break into my own dad's home and steal from him was ludicrous. Still, nothing I ever said seemed to change her mind.

This wasn't an inheritance; it was Janie's idea of payback.

My lawyer also alerted me to an addendum to Dad's last will that provided Janie with 48 percent of the estate, almost half of everything. The whole situation was an outrage. No way was I going to stand being cut out of my dad's will. Unfortunately, I didn't have the money to finance any type of legal action at the time. I was close to broke and out of hope when a guy named Craig Dieffenbach, a local real estate entrepreneur in Seattle, stepped up and put up his own money to finance my legal fight. With Craig's financial backing, my lawyer, Bob Curran, and I filed a lawsuit on August 16, 2002, alleging I had been denied my proper inheritance. We claimed that Janie had used what my lawyer called "undue influence" in overseeing the changing of my dad's will and trust. Dad would never have completely written me out of his will on his own. We were Hendrix blood. He loved his grandchildren and me more than anything else in the world.

As our case went forward, I found out that Janie had arranged the relocation of Dad's and Jimi's coffins in the middle of the night to a new location just down the road from where they were initially buried at Greenwood Memorial Park. The whole thing had gone down months earlier, and by the time I finally heard about the secret operation from a reporter who was interviewing me, there was nothing I could do. So much for "rest in peace," I thought. It made me sick that while Jimi and Dad were encased in a million-dollar memorial, our mama was resting somewhere without even a headstone to identify her. Janie did whatever she wanted and didn't feel the need to even check with me first.

My case dragged on into the next year as motions were repeatedly filed and depositions taken. Throughout it all, Janie and Bobby insisted they were as surprised as anyone upon being notified that Dad had excluded me from his last will. They repeatedly maintained that neither of them played any part in constructing the last will Dad signed before his death. Time after time, Janie and Bobby cited my drug use as the main reason my dad was upset enough for him to voluntarily remove me. Perhaps they were going to be able to convince a judge, but I would never believe my father would have done that.

I wasn't alone in my feeling about Janie's management of the Hendrix estate. Janie's older sister Linda and our cousin Diane also joined me and filed a separate lawsuit alleging that Janie misman-aged a trust fund Dad had set up for other family members in his will. We wanted Janie removed as trustee of Dad's living trust and both Janie and Bobby removed from their management positions in all of the family's companies. Also, we wanted the court to order them to pay us for damages. It had been more than two years since Dad had passed away and the suit alleged that the beneficiaries of the trust still hadn't received the proper return amount. Janie main-tained there were no funds to contribute to the account because of my litigation against Experience Hendrix. As usual, I was being made the scapegoat for everything.

My case didn't go in front of a judge until June 28, 2004, almost two years after its start. We also alleged that Janie and Bobby had been taking advantage of their positions of control in Experience Hendrix from day one and squandering millions of the company's dollars for their own benefit. One of the lawyers, David Osgood, representing Cousin Diane and my stepsister Linda, alleged that Janie and Bobby not only allowed themselves personal mortgages to purchase posh homes, but also paid themselves massive salaries and bonuses in the previous year. While all of this was going on, the lawyers also alleged that Experience Hendrix was not dishing out any money to the beneficiaries of one of the trusts that was set up for some of our relatives.

Witness after witness took the stand over the next couple of months; everyone from my aunt Delores, who maintained that my dad always promised her that his grandchildren and I would be taken care of, to some of Jimi's childhood friends such as Jimmy Williams, who also testified on my behalf. I think if you were measuring by popular opinion, not a person in that courtroom, other than Janie, Bobby, and their legal team, thought I should have been cut out of the will.

During the trial, I was even ordered by Judge Ramsdell to submit to a DNA test to establish if I was in fact Dad's biological son. However, Judge Ramsdell ultimately ruled that the results of the test didn't matter and kept them sealed. No matter what any blood test said, Al Hendrix was my dad. He had always been my dad and that was never going to change.

Throughout the seven-week trial, I kept myself busy with my music and tried not to let myself get too high or too low. One of the largest firms in Seattle was representing me, so I was in good hands. Although my lawyers were confident during the case, I had to stay cool and calm in my reactions. If I won, I was hoping to be awarded the trust fund Dad always wanted to leave for his grandchildren and me. If the judgment didn't go my way, I would simply have to go about my life. No matter the outcome, I wasn't going to let it make or break me.

On September 24, 2004, just over two years after I began my legal battle with Janie, Judge Ramsdell notified my lawyers that he had finally come to a decision. I entered the crowded courtroom surrounded by many friends and family who showed their support by wearing T-shirts with the phrases HIS LEGACY LIVES THROUGH HIS FAMILY AND FRIENDS and JIMI'S BLOOD RUNS THROUGH ME on them.

Everyone was hoping for the best, but unfortunately it wasn't our day.

In a thirty-five-page decision, the judge upheld the last will dad signed in 1998 and ruled that I was to receive nothing other than my single gold record. As for the claim that Janie mishandled the trust that had been set up for the other beneficiaries, the judge believed there was enough of a case and ruled not only to remove her as the head trustee, but for her also to be responsible for the beneficiaries' legal fees. It was a small win for our side and a step in the right direction.

I was mentally prepared for the verdict no matter which way it came out. I refused to let a judge's ruling ruin my life. My family was too strong to let that happen to any of us. During the trial, I was prepared for the worst. Hard times were something I had to deal with throughout my life. They were nothing new to me. I may have been broke and penniless after spending all of my money to back the lawsuit, but I wasn't going to allow myself to live and die with the outcome of the case.

After losing the case, my family and I didn't allow each other to feel down. We remained optimistic at the possibility of an appeal. I was smiling as I left the courtroom that day. Many onlookers and news reporters probably thought that I'd lost my mind. But for the first time in years, I felt an odd sense of closure after the judge's decision. Although we appealed the ruling to the state Appeals Court, which upheld it, and later the state Supreme Court, which did the same, it felt as if my team was just going through the motions. What was done was done. It was time for me to move on.

Though for some it might have seemed to be the end of the line for me, in the long run losing my case proved to be a giant blessing in disguise for my family. The final ruling allowed me to move on with my life and not have to deal with the legal issues anymore. Jasmin and I remained in Seattle for a brief time before moving back to Los Angeles and buying a house. Throughout my life, I always somehow landed on my feet, and this time would be no different. All I had was my artwork and my music to fall back on but that was fine with me. The hardships and tough times have left me resilient and positive-minded. No matter what has happened, the important thing is that today I am at peace.

EPILOGUE

As I look back, it blows my mind to consider what my brother accomplished in his short life. To millions of fans all over the world, he was the one and only Jimi Hendrix, the left-handed guitar wizard who exploded onto the scene after burning up the stage at the 1967 Monterey Pop Festival and then rocketed to superstardom. He was a larger-than-life rock icon who in three short years redefined what was possible on electric guitar and changed the world of music forever. His studio albums have gone down as classics in music history, and even today his myth and legacy grows with each new generation of fans.

No matter what anyone else says, I consider myself the keeper of the Hendrix flame and intend to help maintain Jimi's spirit and musical legacy. Of course, I don't play like my brother. *Nobody* does. But I am constantly working to develop my own style, and people tend to respond to genuine passion. It's a tremendous blessing to see fans come out to watch my band and me perform. Today, I am getting the opportunity to live a second childhood. My first one was lost to foster care and hustling on the streets. The experience is much more rewarding this time around. As I write this, I've recently returned from a string of gigs in Italy where amazing crowds came out to support me night after night at my band's performances. I am more happy and relaxed than I have ever been in my life.

It took a long time for me to remember the details concerning the difficult times in my life. For decades, I blocked out my childhood of living in foster homes and my time spent at Monroe Reformatory. But forcing myself to recall these periods provided me with a great sense of closure. I was also able to relive some of the good moments during those years. One of the most important lessons I've realized is that life is too short to hold a grudge against my family members or anyone else. People know what they have and have not done. I believe everyone answers for his or her actions in the end.

I will be the first to admit that I was not the perfect son during the years when my drug addiction was at its worst. But my family should not have been cut out of my dad's will. I'm sure that was not what my dad wanted and nothing will ever convince me otherwise. Through everything it has been important for me to keep a positive attitude. Although I'm not happy about the way my family and I have been treated over the years, the past must not ruin our future. In time, everything will work out for the best.

That being said, every man gets what he deserves, so on some level I can only accept that a higher power believed I didn't deserve any type of inheritance from my brother's estate. Some people might even say that not winning my court case against Janie even saved my life. If I would have gotten my hands on the trust fund, maybe there is no telling what I would have done. In my mind a large part of the money was already spent. I was going to first ensure that my kids were taken care of, but aside from that, my intention was to buy a giant yacht and live out the rest of my years sailing near Tahiti and other tropical locations. But in that case, I would probably never have been saved by music, stayed clean, and started playing full-time. Guitar would never have led me completely out of the darkness and helped me maintain my sanity.

It's been thirteen years since I've done drugs, and every day presents a new struggle to remain clean. If I ever broke down and took that first hit, it would be the end. It's important for me to stay away from dangerous situations at all costs. One momentary lapse in judgment would certainly turn into weeks, if not months, of chasing my next high. One slip for me and I'd be right back to where I started. For my sake and my family's sake, I can't allow that to ever happen again.

Fortunately, after a history of legal defeats, a court case has gone in my favor. In February 2011, a court ruled that my brother's "right of publicity" (i.e., the right to exploit his name and likeness) is not descendible. Thus, Janie and her company, Experience Hendrix, could not use my brother's right of publicity to prevent me from trading in images or likenesses of my brother or from using the names "Hendrix" or "Jimi Hendrix" to identify him as the person represented in those images or likenesses. It is unfortunate that everything needed to be hashed out in a court of law, but in recent years, I have reached out to Janie in the hope of working with her. Regrettably, she has not wanted to put aside our past differences and come together.

After all of the legal battles, the most recent ruling is a small consolation, but at least I now have the ability to shape a portion of my brother's branding and give my family some control of Jimi's legacy.

Today, when my little grandchildren fall and start crying or my kids run into trouble in their lives, I tell them to buckle down and not to let it bother them because, just as my dad once said, "There are many more bumps to come." To me, success is how you over-come the bad things that happen to you, learn from them, and move on. It is something that can't be measured in fancy cars and houses.

Many days I think back to all the times Jimi and I shared—the difficult early days spent running around the streets of Seattle and the glorious times cruising around Hollywood in the stretch limou-sine. The afternoon we spent cleaning out Mrs. Maxwell's garage seems as if it were yesterday. When I close my eyes, I can see Jimi plucking the single string on that old, beat-up ukulele. If I only knew where that thing ended up. Unfortunately, it could be any-where, maybe even stashed away in one of my old aunts' attics or garages. It could have been buried somewhere deep in my dad's left-over junk in his basement or possibly sold off in one of his storage lockers. It's like hunting for buried treasure.

Thankfully, I managed to hold on to the 1964 sunburst Fender Stratocaster my brother gave me back in the day. It's a guitar every-body would like to get their hands on. A businessman once even of-fered me a million dollars for it. But there is no way I would let it go for any price. It's one of my most prized possessions, and I'll do every-thing within my power to ensure that it stays within the Hendrix family for the rest of time. As long as I'm around, it will never be sold because it is literally all I have left of my personal belongings from all those years and, more important, the only remaining per-sonal item I have of my brother's.

No matter what has happened, it is hard for me to want to change a thing about my life. I've been able to travel all over the world and have lived like a rock star. On the flip side of that coin, I have been locked in a tiny cell with nothing but my thoughts and hope to keep me alive. My biggest accomplishment in life has simply been surviving—making it through the day-to-day hell of my drug ad-diction and finding a better way to live. Today, I have a beautiful family, full of wonderful grandchildren. I may not have all of the money most people believe I do, but I am still an incredibly wealthy man in love.

Having just recently turned sixty-four years old, I understand that I missed an awful lot during those dope days of wandering loaded through life without much purpose other than finding my next high. *Regret* has always seemed like a strong word to me, but if I could have done one thing differently, I would have been more present for my kids while they were growing up.

Looking back, I should have taken my brother's question a long time ago more seriously when he asked me what I wanted to do, because it was almost too late before I finally picked up the guitar. I should have been a musician a long time ago, but I was out of control and the focus wasn't there to put my life in order. Once the window of musical opportunity closed, it was a struggle to find my path. Being a drug addict and a musician never works. Many musicians eventually fall victim to drugs, and it almost always ruins their career. Well, I did just the opposite. It took going through all the years of drug abuse for me to understand that my one true passion was music. But somehow, with the help of God and the deep love and support of my family and friends, I managed. Despite my lifestyle, God did not look the other way and abandon me. For years, I repeatedly ran from him. As soon as I came to my senses and asked for his help and forgiveness, everything changed for the better in my life.

I'm truly convinced that it's also because of Buster. He's up there guiding me. Whenever I get into trouble while performing onstage, I think of him and ask for help. And I can almost hear him telling me, *Bend those notes, Leon. Stretch those strings. If you hit a flat, bend that thing until it comes into tune.*

Once people find out who I am, the most common question they ask is "What is it like to be Jimi Hendrix's brother?"

I usually just smile back at them and answer, "I don't really know. I'm not done yet."

There isn't a day that goes by that I don't think of my brother. No matter what has happened over the course of my life, I'll never forget all of the fantastic stories he told and the lessons he taught. Above all, he continues to live on in the art he created and left behind for each new generation to appreciate and enjoy. When I meet fans along the way and we share stories about him, it is as if Buster is still walking alongside me. Each day, we continue our search for adventure and excitement together. And that journey will never end.

ACKNOWLEDGMENTS

Above all, I want to thank our mama, Lucille Jeter Hendrix, for bringing Jimi and me into this world. Your life force was stronger than that of anyone else we ever knew, and both of us were blessed to have you.

I'd like to thank the following people for all that they have done for me over my life.

To my aunt Delores (Auntie) for taking care of Jimi and me when we were young, even though you took on the burden of caring for so many children. You brought me into your home and were like a second mother. You blessed our souls with love and will always have a place in our hearts.

To my aunt Ernestine Benson—you opened your heart to our family and gave us a roof over our heads during tough times. We will always cherish your kindness and remember the Muddy Waters, Bo Diddley, and Robert Johnson records you introduced us to on the old Dictaphone player at such an early age.

Acknowledgments

To Christine Ann Naransic, the mother of my six children: Leontyne, LeAnne, Alexander, Jason, Little Jimi, and Jonelle. Thank you for putting up with me over the years and bringing me the happiness of having six wonderful children. You gave me the opportunity to understand the joy of being a father. I send you my love and good blessings.

To my children—I hope you all understand how much you mean to me. Everything I do today, I am doing in your honor. May each of you continue to make an impact in this world even after I am gone. I love you all.

To Ray Rae Goldman—through the years you have been one of my best friends and hands down the greatest archivist of Jimi Hendrix. You have helped in many court cases and done an amazing job keeping in touch will all of my family and extended family. I am lucky to have such a great friend in my life.

To Bob Hendrix—even though we grew up as children during hard times, you meant the world to Jimi and myself as kids. I looked up to both of you. As kids we loved each other, not only because we were family, but also because we were friends.

To Janie Hendrix—no matter what has happened over the years, I love you as my little sister. Thank you for keeping the music alive. I wish you good blessings.

To the Wheeler family and all of their children—thank you for opening your home and being great parents. Buster and I will always hold a place in our hearts for all of you.

To my other foster parents through the years, who had a tremendous positive impact on my life—Aunt Mariah Steele, the Jackson family, the Magwood family, and the Dominic family. Without you, I would not be here today to tell my life story. Thank you for your love.

To Aunt Pat—thank you for putting up with me when my dad

dropped me off so many times at your doorstop and begged you to take care of me. You and your daughter Patty are so special. I will always care for you deeply.

To Adam Mitchell—for putting up with all of the distractions and working hard to ensure my story was finally told my way.

To Andrew Pitsicalis, my business partner and friend—it took a lot of guts to help fight for years in and out of court. You fought for me to have a voice in shaping the Hendrix legacy. When hope was lost, you sacrificed everything to make a better life for my family and me. For once I am proud to have a company for my kids and myself. Long live Rockin Artwork.

To Alan Nevins—for making this entire experience possible. This book wouldn't have happened without your guidance.

To Rob Kirkpatrick at Thomas Dunne Books—thank you for all of your hard work and dedication to this project.

To all the foxy ladies that Jimi and I had the pleasure of being acquainted with, through the good times and the bad, I apologize and thank you equally. We considered you little angels in our lives.

It took me a lifetime of searching different paths in life until I finally discovered the road that led me to "the one," Jasmin Rogg. I also dedicate my life story to you for saving my life. I love you forever.

INDEX

Index

Index

Index

Index

Index

Index

Index